THE
RESTLESS
HUNGARIAN

MODERNISM, MADNESS,
AND THE AMERICAN DREAM

TOM WEIDLINGER

SPARKPRESS

Published by SparkPress, a BookSparks imprint,
A division of SparkPoint Studio, LLC
Tempe, Arizona, USA, 85281
www.gosparkpress.com

Published 2019
Printed in the United States of America
ISBN: 978-1-943006-96-0 (pbk)
ISBN: 978-1-943006-97-7 (e-bk)

Library of Congress Control Number: 2018957895

Interior design by Tabitha Lahr

To all my Hungarian relatives, living and dead,
and to Sharon, the love of my life.

CONTENTS

1. INTRODUCTION

Growing up, I heard a lot of stories from my father. He told them with an impish smile, relishing each dénouement. He used the word *incredible* a lot, also *amazing* and *odd*. Frequently he professed himself utterly *flabbergasted* by the twists and turns of his adventures. Among the many stories he told me were those about how: He taught himself to read at the age of four. He was a communist when he was fourteen. He was arrested and sentenced to death when he was eighteen. He slept rough under bridges in Paris, while apprenticed to the famous architect Le Corbusier. He almost got my mother arrested by the Gestapo. He made and lost a fortune in Bolivia. In New York he started a world-renowned company just so he'd have enough money to pay my mother's insane asylum bills. He was a close friend of the real Dr. Strangelove. He helped protect the world from nuclear Armageddon.

I found these stories hard to believe; but when my father was in his eighties, I sat down with him and recorded him, first on audiotape and then on video. At the time I didn't know why I was doing it . . . perhaps out of some sense of filial duty or maybe just filmmaker's instinct.

As an old man with unruly hair, rose-tinted glasses, and an ironic smile, his bold tales, told in a wispy, gentle voice, seemed even more improbable. When pressed for details, dates, and context, he got very hazy. There was also the excuse that, during the Cold War, he had a top-level security clearance, so there were things he just couldn't say. As he put it jokingly, "If I told you, I would have to kill you."

―――――――――

In the past, he had been good with an audience, and was particularly scintillating when there were pretty young women in attendance. But as a father, he was not good with me. "You are naïve!" my father would say to me when I tried to defend beliefs that differed from his, such as the possibility of bringing about world peace. Brimming with mirth, he loved to share my latest childish pronouncements with the adults who came for cocktails. He would laugh and gently cuff me on the back of the head with what my sister and I called a double whammy. The gesture suggested he was trying to knock some sense into me. I felt confused; pleased on the one hand for being the focus of adult attention, but also humiliated by my naiveté, however charming it seemed to everyone.

My father, Paul Weidlinger, died in 1999. Many of the important people who came to his memorial service lauded his contributions as a captain of industry and one of the most innovative structural engineers of the twentieth century. Apprenticed to Bauhaus leader László Moholy-Nagy and to Le Corbusier in the 1930s, he came to the United States in 1943, where he collaborated on churches, museums, skyscrapers, and embassies with Walter Gropius, Marcel Breuer, Gordon Bunshaft, Eero Saarinen, and many others. He engineered the monumental sculptures of Pablo Picasso, Isamu Noguchi, and Jean Dubuffet. Weidlinger Associates, the company he founded, pioneered the use of computers in structural engineering, and came up with solutions to protect buildings against earthquakes and explosions.

A few weeks after the memorial service, a huge box arrived in the post from my stepmother. Inside were diaries, school report cards, passports, poems, love letters, bank statements, a political manifesto, several technical papers, patent applications, and prestigious awards, as well as unpublished short stories, drawings, sketches, cartoons, and many, many photographs. Except for a quick glance, I didn't open the box for several years. Then, when I did take a serious look, I was immediately overwhelmed by the sheer volume of material and by language. My father spoke seven languages and wrote in five. I could read the French and English but not the German, Hungarian, or Spanish. It was clear that it was in those documents, in the languages I could not understand, that I would most likely find the evidence to prove or disprove his fantastic tales.

The second obstacle was psychological. Its manifestation was a profound sleepiness. I would open the box, pull out a sheaf of papers, and fight to keep my eyes open. Truth be told, I half expected my father to reach out from beyond the grave and give me a double whammy for my naiveté, for my presumption that I could somehow make sense of his life on my own terms.

I went from being confused by my father's mixed messages to me when I was a young boy to hating him when I was a teenager. Among other things, I blamed him for the suicide of my sister, Michèle, when I was seventeen and she was thirty. How would I cope with reading the letters that she wrote to him in the years before she died? Truly, I wanted to know this man, but how could I do this without the facts getting skewed by my fragmented but compelling memories as his son?

Then, in 2013, through a series of circumstances that my father would call truly amazing, I found myself volunteering on a carpenter's crew restoring a Modernist house that he designed the year I was born. I had spent the first fourteen summers of my life in that house, which had since fallen derelict on national park land. As I ripped out rotten siding and pounded nails, memories of childhood came flooding back. To my surprise, not all of them were bad. Suddenly I was no longer sleepy. I could not wait to delve into the box.

Now I have gone through the box with the help of translators. On three continents I have traced my father's footsteps, interviewed his friends and associates, and sat down with relatives I never knew existed. I have visited the graves of my ancestors.

I profess I am flabbergasted. All of his stories are true. To be sure, he embellished. Yet, fundamentally, what he said happened did happen. But equally compelling is the story he never told me. We are Jews. The unpublished memoir of my father's closest childhood friend, Ilona Radó, reveals the hidden subtext of his life . . . the great suffering of our family in Hungary during the Holocaust and the rise of Stalinist communism after the war. These facts link seemingly disconnected events and explain his motivation. This is what moves me to see my father with compassion.

2. THE DISCOVERY

NEW YORK AND BUDAPEST, 1984, 2013

It was in 1984 that I learned that my father was a Jew. Thirty years would pass before I began to put the pieces of the puzzle together. I did not learn this totally unexpected fact from him, but certain developments in our relationship led up to it. I had visited him in New York over the Christmas holiday. It was a predictably uncomfortable time because, in spite of the fact I was always welcome, I never felt I belonged to the second family that he started after he and my mother divorced. One day, while looking for a postage stamp, I opened a drawer in my father's desk in the bedroom that he shared with my stepmother. I didn't find a stamp, but did find his Last Will and Testament. Of course I read it. I discovered that nowhere in this document was I mentioned. My half-brother and half-sister, eleven and fourteen years younger than me, were provided for, but it was as if I had simply never existed.

I looked around the bedroom making a conscious, mental snapshot. It was in a different apartment from the one I grew up in. The furniture was unfamiliar. There were no things to remind me of my childhood with both my biological parents. The bed was not my parents' bed, the safe harbor where I found refuge as a scared child. I was an outsider in this place of greatest intimacy. I felt hollow. Cast loose.

I said nothing then, but a few days after arriving home in Los Angeles, I wrote an angry letter. My father wrote back saying that he hoped my letter was a result of a misunderstanding. He didn't explain why I had been left out of his will (in retrospect I think it would have been hard for him to explain it to himself). Instead, he launched into a long and pleading account of his financial situation, responsibilities, and worries about growing old. I wrote back that he had missed the point. I didn't want his money; I was hurt that I had not been acknowledged as a son.

This exchange opened up a channel between us. A couple of months later, my father passed through Los Angeles on a business trip, and we spent an evening together. He had read a short story I had written about my sister, a topic we had not discussed since her death. He was genuinely moved by it. I, in turn, was moved that he was able to express this. My anger at my father started to fade. It was then I asked him if we might go together to Hungary to visit the place of his birth and what remained of his family. He said that we could.

It is significant that we had not gone to Hungary before; that I had not met my grandfather, Andor Weidlinger, or my step-grandmother, Rózsa, before they died. During the height of the Cold War, it was too dangerous for my father to travel behind the Iron Curtain. His work for the Defense Nuclear Agency and the high-level security clearances that went with it made him a vulnerable target for Soviet spies in Central Europe, but by 1984 tensions were easing. Western visitors were not as subject to surveillance in Budapest as they were in Prague, Warsaw, or East Berlin. Ordinary Hungarians could meet with them without fear of being compromised.

I didn't know what I expected to find out in Hungary about my father or myself, but I had high expectations. Maybe the shared experience would bridge the gap between us. Perhaps I would become part of the family again.

The passport control men at the Budapest airport seemed just like the ones I had encountered in other Communist Bloc countries: cold and menacing, in drab uniforms. The airport itself was a sad place. On June 21, when I arrived, the weather was cold and gray.

The airline had misplaced my luggage, but I was both too tired and too excited to care.

My father was waiting for me at the Forum Hotel Budapest, on the banks of the Danube River, with a picture-postcard view of the city's Chain Bridge and Castle Hill. I was eager to hear everything about his childhood—to see everything that was of significance. My father was eager to tell me as his memories came flooding back, triggered by the sights and sounds of his native city. He pointed through the window of the hotel's café to Margaret Island, in the middle of the Danube. There was a park there where his governess used to take him to play. He recalled that there were public benches that were free to sit on, and chairs that you had to rent. As a boy, he dreamed of being rich enough to "throw money away to sit on chairs." His family was rich enough, but his father did not approve of throwing money away.

The next day we took a taxi to the apartment of Lulu, Karoly, and Pál Valentiny. Lulu (née Weidlinger) was my father's half-sister, and Karoly her husband. Pál, their son, was named after my father. Pál is the Hungarian version of Paul, so in the family, Pál was known as Little Pál. My father was Big Pál.

Meeting these kin was weird. I expected to feel a connection, but was frustrated, since all the talk was in Hungarian. It was the first time I had ever heard my father speak Hungarian. Little Pál, who spoke a bit of English, tried to translate, but it was difficult. Who were these people? And who was that man, my father, suddenly transformed—laughing, joking, and speaking (to my ears it sounded like singing) in a strange, soft language? If only I could have understood.

I looked around for clues. I had my 35mm camera with me that I used professionally, location-scouting for films. But there was no frame, no composition that revealed anything about my father's past. The modest apartment was filled with wooden knickknacks carved by Karoly, who seemed a haughty, imposing man. Then Karoly motioned to me to stand in the doorway of the living room. I am 6' 6" and that really impressed him. He hammered a small brass tack in the doorjamb to mark my height. I imagined that, with other visitors, he would remark on the dimensions of his huge American nephew.

Then he speaks directly to me and asks Little Pál to translate. Little Pál is very reluctant, but his father insists. It's then that I realize that Karoly is suffering from dementia. He's telling a joke about shit, which is really disgusting, and Karoly is demanding that his son translate it into English. Karoly's dementia feels like a complete erasure of the past, of memory. My strong feeling of being on the brink of discovering something wonderful and amazing about my father vanishes.

The next day, we went to the apartment building where my father grew up. Once a fashionable residence, it was now quite dilapidated. The entire five-story building had been owned by my father's aunt Paula, but in 1952 all apartment buildings were nationalized as part of the communists' redistribution of wealth. Large, elegant apartments were carved up into small flats. Little Pál said he knew a family who moved into one of the flats that was part of the larger Weidlinger apartment, but to my disappointment, he did not suggest we knock on their door. I had this feeling, though I would have been hard-pressed to articulate it, that I wasn't seeing everything that was there; that I was getting a censored version of my father's past.

This feeling was reinforced when my father went to visit a child-hood friend named Ili. It was clear that she was someone who had been extremely significant in his life, but because she was ill and spoke no English, my father said it would be better if I did not go with him. I learned Ili's story only much later.

What my father did tell me, he recounted with relish. When he was a boy he and his friends would piss into the courtyard of his building, standing at the wrought-iron railing of the fifth-floor balcony outside his apartment. Inside the building's shabby foyer, the frosted glass-sheathed elevator looked much the same as he remembered it. There was also the stairwell. The acorn-shaped brass finials atop the banister were worn and polished. I imagined my father, as a boy, rocketing down the stairs, using the finials as a pivot point to whirl around at each landing on his five-story descent. Once there was an accident. He had a huge wolfhound that knocked him over and dragged him down the steps. His father had to take him to the hospital across the street to get patched up.

Evening found us at the Citadel, the Habsburg fortress on Gellért Hill. We ate at a restaurant with game dishes on the menu and a live Gypsy band. The music was quite beautiful and unlike anything I had ever heard. The musicians played *Czárdás*, dances that are characterized by dramatic variations in tempo. The violin and *czembalom* (hammered dulcimer) are key instruments. Patrick Leigh Fermor, a famous traveler in the 1930s, described a scene very like the one we were witnessing.

> *Late at night, half a dozen Gypsies bore down on the guests like smiling crows bent on steeping everything in their peculiar music. . . . In the slow passages, the hammers of the czembalom fluttered and hesitated over the strings and the violins sank into a swooning languor, only to rekindle with an abrupt syncope when the hammers and the bows broke into double time and the czembalist went mad, as the leading violinist . . . stooped and slashed beside one listener's ear after another and closed in on his instrument like a welterweight in a clinch; passages, one might think, which could only end in ecstasy or a dead feint.*

The music moved me. I came to understand that Czárdás is the music of the Hungarian soul—the poignant juxtaposition of sorrow and joy, of lamentation and wild rejoicing. Was I stirred because there is Hungarian blood in my veins?

During a pause, my father made a request, motioning to the maestro. The musicians conferred and launched into something entirely different. There were Hungarian words to this song and I heard my father murmuring them along with the Gypsy singer. When the song was over he requested another and then another. After each one he translated a few fragments for me:

"Open your doors to me, my love. Open them quietly so the neighbors do not hear. . . ."

"The only girl in the world—she is my lover."

"Your mother, my lover, is unjust—she shouldn't hate me just because I am a drunkard!"

Never, in my wildest imagination, could I have imagined my father singing with Gypsies.

The next day he was gone. I can't remember where; perhaps home to New York or to a top-secret NATO meeting in Brussels. My cousin Pál, a kind, soft-spoken man three years older than me, invited me to stay. I moved from the Forum to a sofa in the small flat he shared with his wife, Zsuzsa, and their two small children.

Little Pál took me on a walk that was very different from the nostalgic ramble with my father. The first place we went to was the Dohány Street synagogue. With its slender Oriental–Byzantine twin towers, it was the spiritual center of Hungarian *Neolog* Jewry and the largest operating synagogue in Europe. Inside was a small museum and Holocaust memorial. In the summer of 1944, the synagogue was used by the Germans as a military command post. A forced labor battalion had been housed here, and the building had served as a detention camp.

Among the photographs on display was one of human corpses stacked against the wall of the building. A large glass case contained old documents. Pál explained to me that these were forged identity papers that Jews used in 1944 to evade deportation to the concentration camps.

I wondered why this was important for him. I asked, "Are you Jewish?"

"Of course I am, and so are you."

I found this hard to believe.

Then Pál took me back to his flat, where he showed me false identity papers for Andor, Rózsa, and Lulu that were just like the ones in the museum.

Why had my father never spoken of this?

My own reaction was mixed: incredulity followed by numbness. Then the anger that I had felt on learning I had been disinherited returned. At the same time something clicked. I had always felt, if only on a subliminal level, that there were gaps in my father's account of himself. Here, finally, was an opportunity to get to the whole story beneath the amusing anecdotes.

(From left to right) Lulu, Andor, and Rózsa Weidlinger, renamed as Henriette Hajduska, Mátyás Kaits, and Ödönné Hajduska.

When I left, two days later, Pál took me to the airport. His five-year-old son, Gábor, was with him. I had asked Pál to send me copies of the photographs he had of my father as a boy and of Lulu, Andor, and Rózsa. Making copies in those days was expensive, so I put some money in an envelope to give to Pál at the last moment, so he had no chance to refuse it.

Pál and Gábor watched over me as I ran the gamut of passport-control men. Then, when I was finally on the plane, I saw father and son on the airport's observation deck. I don't know if they saw me; but they waved solemnly as the plane taxied out onto the runway. Some-how a bond had formed between us. The secret of our Jewishness—or rather the fact that it had been kept a secret—had brought us together.

I planned to ask my father why he had hidden the fact of our origins, but I didn't see him until the next holiday season. (Natu-rally, it was Christmas that my family celebrated, not Hanukkah). He turned seventy on December 22, 1984, and I was there to wish him happy birthday. Unexpectedly, my resolve to get him to confess faltered. Behind his gold-rimmed, rose-tinted designer glasses, he looked tired and frail, his wispy hair shooting off the top of his head in all directions. His liver-spotted hands flapped like bird's wings as he told a funny story.

I posed my question very gently. "Hey, dad, while I was in Hungary, I heard some information suggesting we might be Jewish?" A strange expression came over his face. His mouth was smiling but his eyes were not. I realized I was seeing actual fear. This was new to me. My father worried about small things: whether I was dressed warmly enough when he took me out for a walk as a child, my grades in high school, my love life in my twenties. But I had never before seen that fearful expression on his face. He looked really scared. This, in turn, unsettled me, because I had always seen him as invincible, an impregnable fortress of self-confidence, the world-famous engineer, Paul Weidlinger.

The moment passed—it must have been no more than fifteen seconds—and he spoke with feigned nonchalance saying that no, we were not Jewish. He had heard that his family was descended from Seventh-Day Adventists who had emigrated from Transylvania in the nineteenth century. I knew this was a lie, but I didn't press him. My father's fear and the quality of helplessness it engendered erased my anger and, along with it, my determination to get him to confess. We never spoke of it again.

Thirty years would pass before I could open the Pandora's box of my father's history and seek a context for his denial. I began by writing to my cousin Pál. Though I had had little contact with him, he welcomed my renewed interest in family history. He sent me the Weidlinger family tree, which was both mystifying and strangely appealing. He used one of those Internet templates into which he inserted names and dates and an occasional photograph. Most relatives were simply represented by a male or female silhouette. Often dates of birth and death were left blank. The familial nouns that I grew up with were father, mother, sister, and brother. I had never met a grandfather, a grandmother, an aunt, uncle, or cousin, let alone great-aunts and uncles, second cousins, and other relatives too remote to classify. But I suddenly found that I was intensely interested in these classifications. It took me a while to figure out how I am related to Dezső Korda (1864-1919), who designed the uniquely slanted elevator in the foot of the Eiffel Tower and whose sister was Ilka Korda. Ilka married a grocer named Imre Berger. They had five children, one of whom was Júlia Berger, my grandmother.

Dezső's youngest sister died in Auschwitz with her husband and all but one of her children. There were many more connections to be made, and suddenly I found myself linked by blood and marriage to dozens of people I never knew existed.

There were also photographs, which Little Pál had carefully preserved. I matched names and faces. A family portrait taken in 1915 and trimmed to fit into a stereoscope viewer includes a serious four-year-old girl gazing frankly at the camera. She is my great-aunt Ilona ("Ili") Radó, the person whom my father went to visit by himself when I was with him in Budapest.

In her memoir, Ili recalls how the photo was made. "The photographer tortured us quite a bit," she wrote, to produce an image that was formal in composition but wonderfully relaxed in gesture.

Mother's big blue eyes were bulging a little. Maybe her corset was too tight? Klára sat next to her, the well-behaved child; her hair pulled back, emphasizing her strong cheekbones. Rózsa leaned with light elegance on an armchair, and she looked into the distance with her dreamy eyes, like a beautiful actress. On the left Dad was sitting, already old and looking at her with a gentle smile. I was the chubby four-year-old standing next to him. It is the picture of a bourgeois family in great harmony.

Though I never met Ili, I came to know her through her unpublished memoir, *Miss Porcelain*. It describes a life that is deeply linked to my father's in childhood, but in later years diverges completely. Ili

The Radó family in 1915.

became my father's contrary twin. Her story does not mirror his, but is perfectly opposite in history, beliefs, and values. Strangely, I find myself returning again and again to Ili's narrative as a way of *seeing* my father. It's like looking through the wrong end of a telescope or pair of binoculars. The image is distant and upside down, but oddly in focus.

———————

In the opening pages of her memoir, Ili described being confined to her bed with a cold when she was eight years old. Her mother gave her a box of family photographs.

> *On my blanket I separated the pictures of father's family from the pictures of mother's family, and I tried to put them in order according to age. Then I thought I should make a group for the dead and another for the living. The dead would come first, because the dead are more prestigious than the living. Then unconsciously I started putting them into groups according to love.*

Ili observed, "The people in a picture can never move away." They are forever captured, the living and the dead alike. Their lives were full of secrets that she believed could be revealed if she looked very closely. "It's like a game," she wrote. "Imagine looking deeply into the basin of a fountain. There, deep beneath the shimmering surface, every story will be replayed again in big, brightly lit pictures."

I feel a kinship with this girl in her sickbed, surrounded by the living and the dead. I, too, am playing this game, looking deeply into the waters of the past. Ili is one of my guides. There is something both exciting and immensely comforting about this. It is an antidote to that feeling of being disinherited.

There is no one alive now who knew my father as a child or even as a young man. The majority of people that I interviewed worked with him at Weidlinger Associates from the 1950s onwards. I asked them all, "Did you know he was Jewish?" All of them said no. Some had speculated.

Lorraine Whitman, an engineer who worked for him for twenty years, said, "I believed that Paul was Jewish and . . . at some point . . . he said something that struck me as implausible. He was Greek Orthodox or Roman or Russian Orthodox. I didn't know any Russian or Greek Orthodox Hungarians . . . and it seemed to me he was pulling something out of a hat."

Matthys Levy, the last surviving original Weidlinger Associates partner, told me that he only learned that Paul was Jewish when I spoke of it at his memorial service.

Another person who was present at the service was Ron Check, who had been at the firm almost as long as Levy. When I asked him about it, he said, "How honest should I be?"

I said, "Totally."

Ron said, "At the memorial service, you said something about your father being Jewish, and it was clear to me that it was the first time the general public—all the people there, became aware. And when you said it, Solveig [Paul's wife] did . . . like that." Ron made a gasping sound.

Did my stepmother not know her husband was Jewish? Or was she gasping at my public revelation of the fact? One thing was certain, her children—my half-brother, Jonathan, and half-sister, Pauline—did not know. They have told me so.

After interviewing my father's colleagues in New York, I went back to Budapest. My cousin, Little Pál, welcomed me with open arms. We were both gray-haired by then, but he was still the same quiet-spoken and gentle person I had met in 1984.

I wanted to reconstruct with Little Pál what happened thirty years ago on the day that he took me to the Dohány synagogue. Although his English had improved, I wanted to understand him perfectly, so I hired a translator. The simultaneous translation through headphones allowed me to listen and respond immediately. It's the closest I could come to having a real-time, natural conversation with him.

Pál reminded me that at first I didn't believe him and that he felt guilty for having inadvertently revealed a secret that had been kept from me. But I wanted to know more, so we went back to the flat where, again, he showed me the documents just like the ones in the museum case. In their forged IDs, my family—Andor, Rózsa, and Lulu Weidlinger—had become Mátyás Kaits and Ödönné and Henriette Hajduska, recently arrived in Budapest from the little village of Pereg.

Pál showed me other papers: the birth certificate of my grandfather and grandmother, their marriage license, and the birth certificate of my father. On every document there was a space for the person's religion. Every name was inscribed with "*Izr*," the abbreviation for Israelite—Jew. There was even a document announcing the birth of Júlia (Lulu) Weidlinger, Little Pál's mother, which formally notified the Jewish community of her arrival. It was not a legal document, but rather evidence that my grandfather, though not religious, respected the customs of the community.

After our conversation with the translator, Pál and I retraced the walk we took in 1984. At length we came again to 36 Rákóczi Street, my father's boyhood home on the southern border of what had been the Jewish ghetto. Pál thought that the front entrance to the building was outside the ghetto wall, but the rear of the building was within the ghetto's boundaries. In any case, by the time the ghetto was sealed off, my relatives had fled the building.

In the Hungarian National Film Archive, there is footage of a column of hundreds of men and women walking on Rákóczi Street and passing in front of this building. Their hands are raised and they are wearing the six-pointed Star of David on their clothes. The date is probably October 23, 1944, when the Hungarian Royal Minister of Defense ordered every Jewish male between the ages of 16 and 60 and every Jewish female between the ages of 18 and 40 to participate in "forced labor for the defense of the country." During the previous summer 430,000 Hungarian Jews, mostly from rural districts, had been sent to die in Auschwitz. But by October 1944, the Soviet army was close to liberating the concentration camp, and deportations were no longer feasible. Accordingly, most of the "defense-line Jews" were ordered to march on foot toward the western and southern borders of Hungary to dig trenches. Only a few survived.

3. THE BLESSED YEARS

BUDAPEST, 1900–1918

At the turn of the twentieth century, Budapest was the fastest-growing city in Europe. Colossal public buildings were erected as testimonials to Hungarian national pride. The parliament building, completed in 1902, was the largest parliament building in the world. Its design was an audacious mix of medieval, neo-Gothic, and French Renaissance architectural styles.

Not far away was Váci Street, the main shopping street of the Inner City. The writer Gyula Krúdy wrote:

Whoever settles in the Inner City will remain a distinguished person for the rest of his life. . . . There gleamed the hired carriages at their stations from which countesses with delicate feet had just descended; old pensioners sat on benches in their spotless clothes; the grocer with his wicker baskets and the baker smelling of his fresh Kaiser rolls kissed the hands of the chambermaids in their black bombazine. . . . It was easy to dress well from the district's shop windows, and every purchaser could have credit. The famous shops that sold the best goods from London, suits, hats, gloves, were memorable, like a grand foxhunt in autumn. The merchandise from Paris arrived directly, scented like women before a grand soirée. The barber had learned his trade in Paris ... the spice shop had the odors of a great freighter just arrived from Bombay. Blessed Inner City years! Like youth—will they ever return?

How close were the Weidlingers to this charmed world? How much did the fact that they were Jews limit their access to it? Unlike other European nations in which Jews lived as second-class citizens in fear of pogroms, Hungary's Jews could fashion their own destiny. In 1867 a law was passed guaranteeing their civic and legal equality. Unencumbered by the hidebound traditions of Hungary's feudal society and driven by the stress and insecurity of people without a homeland, they acquired the knowledge and skills of the modern professions. They became bankers, financiers, doctors, engineers, architects, scientists, lawyers, and journalists, indispensable to the formation of a twentieth-century nation. Hungary's aristocracy was glad to have them. There is a story about a nobleman, Count Mihály Károlyi, entertaining the German consul-general at his palace. At the end of the evening the diplomat inquired of the Count why no one in the Károlyi household played music. "Why should we?" asked the Count. "We keep Gypsies to play music for us, since we are too lazy to do it for ourselves, and the Jews do all the work." The arrangement seemed to work well for everyone.

The Weidlingers were not religious. During the nineteenth century they claimed the Hungarian language as their mother tongue, replacing German and Yiddish. They were proud to be Hungarian. Being a Jew was incidental. Each generation built upon the accomplishments of the last. My great-great-grandfather, Abraham Jakab Weidlinger (1820-1878), was a merchant, but his son Samuel Weidlinger (1852-1923) was a building engineer. Samuel's son Andor (my grandfather, 1882-1968) put himself through technical school in Germany and worked as a master builder and general contractor on numerous buildings in Budapest.

In 1913 Andor built a six-story apartment block, commissioned by my great-aunt and uncle, Paula and Bertalan Sebestyén. Thirty-six Rákóczi Street was inspired by the nearby Klothilde Palace, built in the 1890s for the Archduchess Klothilde Maria Amalie, daughter-in-law of Franz Joseph, emperor of Austria–Hungary. The façade had inset Corinthian columns, gracefully arched windows, and a tower with a cupola. When the building was completed, its elevator was still a rare luxury.

36 Rákóczi Street.

Great-Aunt Paula was the matriarch of the Weidlinger family. She was stepmother to four girls from Bertalan's previous marriage, and she bore him five more children. While Bertalan presided over his women's apparel shop in the Inner City, she arranged piano lessons for her children as well as nieces and nephews, including my father. In Paula's spacious top-floor flat at 36 Rákóczi, she employed not one but two piano teachers, at two pianos, as there were so many children to be taught.

I visited Paula's grave in a Jewish cemetery outside of Budapest. A fierce stone hawk is perched on her headstone. It resembles *Turul*, the bird in the origin myth of the Hungarian people. The progenitor of Hungarian kings, Turul is a messenger from God that perches on the Tree of Life with the spirits of children who are waiting to be born. Aunt Paula's Turul shelters a fledgling bird under its wing. This is how I have come to think of her, sheltering Andor, Rózsa, and Pali, who lived in an apartment in her graceful building at 36 Rákóczi. It is where that my father spent the first years of his life.

What were his earliest memories? What did he see through his own eyes? When he was eighty-two, we sat together in his living room in New York and I asked him. He dragged on his cigarette, leaned forward, and gestured with his hands, as if to grab hold of memories and haul them into consciousness: He is three years old, lying on a red Persian carpet under the dining table. He is trying hard to decipher the symmetrical patterns in the carpet . . . as if they signify something—something hidden, yet knowable. (It makes sense to me that this would be the first thing he remembered, for my father was adept at revealing patterns, symmetries, and connections between things that were invisible to others.)

Three-year-old Pál tries to explain to his mother what he sees in the patterns of the carpet, but he lacks the words. She just smiles at him. Perhaps it is the same smile she has in the photograph of her cradling her son. She looks happy and is radiantly beautiful. She is twenty-six years old, with a round face, gentle eyes, and long hair tied up in a chignon. Though the photo is black-and-white, I know that my grandmother's hair was red.

Júlia Weidlinger (née Berger) with Pál in 1914.

My father was born on December 22, 1914, six months after the outbreak of World War I, but it seems that my family did not suffer greatly from the privations of that time. Andor, an officer in the Corps of Engineers of the Royal Hungarian Army, was responsible for the city's fortifications should the front ever reach Budapest, but he was always home for supper.

In a picture taken in the summer of 1917, the Weidlingers sit in a garden at a table with a white tablecloth. It seems they have just finished a meal. Júlia, in a modest cloche hat, has an amused expression on her face. Andor, in his military uniform, sports a thick bottlebrush mustache and stares fixedly at the camera. His left hand curls around the hilt of a saber, signifying his officer's rank. My father is front and center, attended by a governess who sits with demurely folded hands. He is dressed like Little Lord Fauntleroy, the aristocratic hero of the children's novel, as popular at the time as Harry Potter. In the 1918 Hungarian film adaptation, the child star, Tibor Lubinszky, looked a lot like my father. His long golden locks, cutaway velvet jacket, and blouse with a frilly collar became a model for children's fashion among the upper middle classes in both Europe and the United States. It made perfect sense that Júlia dressed Pál as a princeling. As Jews, my family could not be admitted to the inner circles of Hungary's aristocracy, but they aspired to live life just as well, and they had the firm expectation that their son's education, accomplishments, and wealth would surpass their own. At the age of three, my father's future was all planned out.

Andor, Pál, and Júlia in 1918, shortly before Júlia's death.

Pál, age three (center), and Júlia, Andor, and
Pál's governess, seated to the right.

In the summer of 1918, the Spanish flu swept westward across Central Europe, claiming more lives than the Great War. Júlia fell ill. My father recalled that a woman with a red cross on her starched white blouse moved in with the family. In his interview with me my father touches his upper arm to show where the red cross was. Then he cups his hands above his head to conjure an old fashioned nurse's cap. Júlia must have been strong because the nurse lived in the apartment for some time. Like many, she may have survived the disease, only to die of a secondary infection. Penicillin had yet to be discovered.

My father recalled his mother's last words to his father:

"Take care of our little Pali." And, it made a great impression on me. I was completely confused and flabbergasted. I said to myself, "Why would she say that?" My father loved me all the time. Nobody had to tell him that! I was very confused by that.

What was it like to live alone with Andor after Júlia was gone? I asked Anna Valentiny, Little Pál's sister, what she remembered of our grandfather many years later. She described a tidy man who adhered to a strict regimen of daily calisthenics and took his baths in cold water. He demanded order and punctuality of the whole family. He rationed his grandchildren's sweets. When guests came to visit, Anna had to perform the ballet steps she'd learned in dance school. Andor was a martinet, but Anna seemed perfectly accepting of these traits in our grandfather. In fact, both she and Little Pál shared a deep respect for him. His autocratic ways were not atypical. In the Hungarian language two words for "husband," *férjem* and *uram*, were used interchangeably until the mid-twentieth century. But the second word, *uram*, literally translates as "my master" or "my lord."

My father insisted that Andor loved him, although he also admitted, "I was scared to death of him."

4. THE GUN UNDER THE PILLOW

In Hungary the war caused a great upheaval in the relationships between the nation's aristocracy, the working classes, and the Jews. In a newsreel from late October 1918, a few weeks before the armistice, crowds surge through the streets of Budapest under a dark sky with racing clouds and a spattering of rain. In front of the Parliament building, symbols of the monarchy are being smashed with hammers: an imperial shield, a medieval mace, and a stone laurel wreath are reduced to fragments. The footage is silent, yet it is easy to imagine the roar of the crowds as they shout their approval. Then there is a ceremony in which "Free Revolutionary Hungarian soldiers take an oath to declare their loyalty to the first Hungarian Democratic People's Republic." These events belonged to what came to be known as the Aster Revolution, because the dissident Hungarian soldiers sported the flowers in their buttonholes. I can see my grandfather putting a flower in his lapel and pledging loyalty to the liberal platform of Count Mihály Károlyi, the leader of the Aster Revolution, calling for universal suffrage and freedom of the press and assembly.

But the Hungarian Democratic People's Republic lasted just four months. It was replaced by a communist revolution that lasted even less time and was marked by violence, incompetence, and the naïve hope that Russia would step in and save Hungary from the postwar depredations and taxations of the great powers.

Then the monarchists had their revenge. Miklós Horthy, a former admiral in the Royal Hungarian Navy, rode into Budapest on a white stallion at the head of a small army of soldiers and right-wing officers who had remained committed to the idea of an authoritarian, paternalistic government. The communists fled without a fight. Horthy's initial bloodless victory was followed by brutal punishment for those who were perceived to have supported the communists. Amid this hysteria, Jews were targeted. Béla Kun, the leader of the communist revolution, was a Jew, as were thirty-two of his forty-five commissars. It was therefore assumed that Kun's communist revolution was a Jewish conspiracy that had set out to destroy the nation. In the final spasm of violent retribution the words "Jew" and "communist" became synonymous; all Jews, regardless of their political allegiances, were vulnerable. In Hungary's villages, Horthy's soldiers arrested "sympathizers" and hanged them in the public square. In what came to be known as the White Terror 5,000 people were executed, 75,000 were imprisoned, and over 100,000 were forced to flee the country.

In her memoir Aunt Ili writes about a day when it was not yet known that the communists had fled—a day when the White Terror was just beginning to spread. Her father and mother came home in the middle of the day as gunboats on the Danube started firing upon the city. The family feared their apartment would be looted.

Mother put a little canvas bag between her breasts, and Dad climbed up high to hide something above the shutter of the window. It was terrible, but I had the constant urge to look up there. If I were to be interrogated I knew I would not be able to keep the secret. At night all the men from the house took turns standing guard at the gate. Everyone in the house was scared. Mother sat on the bed and was praying. Father was pacing up and down smoking one cigarette after the other. I cried in fear under my covers.

In the end Horthy's counterinsurgents arrived and arrested their neighbor who lived on the top floor and was a communist commissar.

It is not clear whether Andor supported Mihály Károlyi's socialist republic or Béla Kun's communist republic; but it would have made no difference. He was a Jew and he was in danger. He took care not to sleep at home. My father, who had just had his fourth birthday, recalls:

> *I stayed with my father in his office. He set up a room and we slept there. . . . I remember going to bed at night, and my father would take his handgun and put it under the pillow. I remember because it made me feel safe. I knew that if somebody comes, he's going to pull out the gun and shoot the bad people.*

Andor kept his son close. When they walked together to the Rákosszentmihály Army Depot on the outskirts of Budapest, where Andor had his office, Pál no longer wore his Little Lord Fauntleroy suit. Along the way my grandfather would unbuckle his saber and let Pál wear it. The boy was so small that the tip of the scabbard trailed on the ground, raising a plume of dust.

Andor's one reckless affectation during the years of Pál's childhood was to wear a monocle without a cord. Four-year-old Pál worried it would fall out. He feared that he himself could cause this disaster by behaving in a way that would make Andor inadvertently raise an eyebrow. Like all children who suffer a terrible loss, Pál felt responsible . . . not just for Andor's monocle but also for Júlia's disappearance from their lives. How to keep in his good graces? How to earn his love?

"In desperation, or maybe as an act of contrition, I taught myself to read."

During the time when Pál lived with Andor in the room behind his office, his father barricaded himself behind the newspaper every evening. Connecting with him meant decoding the black marks on the page that held his attention, like the pattern on a Persian carpet, only more complex.

Pál enlisted his governess to help. Each day as she took him for a walk in the Inner City, he pointed to street signs, shop signs and newspaper headlines and asked her to sound out the words. (In our interview my father pointed over my shoulder, miming how he indicated signs to his nanny. It was as if he could see them still.)

It helped that advertisements had pictures. From trousers to trumpets, from corsets to bicycles, there were useful flashcards all over the cityscape. Meanings coalesced. He learned amazingly quickly. Soon, when Andor came home from his office and after he had hung up his saber, kepi, and gold-braided coat, Pál read the paper to him, seated on a green pillow at his feet. He sensed that Andor was pleased, though he never said anything about it.

Pál, age five, with his dog, a Hungarian greyhound.

Then there was a setback. At the age of six, Pál entered school. It was soon discovered that he was incapable of writing. His letters came out upside down and backwards. He could not tell the difference between left and right or up and down. Andor took him to see a specialist who recommended that he be sent to a "school for retarded children." If my father felt ashamed or stigmatized he didn't show it. On the contrary, he said, "Most of the kids looked odd and could not walk or talk too well, but I liked them, and I felt an affinity with them." Andor was probably more worried about this than Pál, knowing that education was the ticket to becoming an invisible Jew. His son's dyslexia put this in jeopardy.

June 4, 1920, was a day of mourning in Hungary. Streetcars did not run in Budapest. Church bells tolled. Shops were closed and black bunting was draped from balconies. In France the Treaty of Trianon was signed by the representatives of the winners and losers in the Great War. The map of Europe was redrawn so that seventy-one percent of Hungary's territory became part of other nations. It was a tragedy that affected people at every level of society. Three million ethnic Hungarians found themselves outside their homeland. In schools children, led by their teachers, chanted the slogan of the times. *Nem, nem. Soha!* No, no. Never!

Tens of thousands of displaced people came to Budapest looking for jobs, but found few in a city depleted by a World War and three revolutions. Suddenly those who had been largely responsible for leading the country into the twentieth century were seen as interlopers. Jews had to step aside and make room for the "true Hungarians," but it seems there were no immediate consequences for the Weidlinger family. Andor had a reputation as an honest builder and was known to be fair with both his clients and the laborers who worked for him. Nevertheless he took precautions. Pál and his governess started making monthly train trips to Vienna. There, in the cosmopolitan hub of the old empire, more fashionable than Budapest, my father was taken to a salon where his long hair was trimmed and dyed blond. He absolutely hated this.

5. ANARCHISTIC TENDENCIES

BUDAPEST, 1920-1932

"**A**h-maaaze-ingly!" My father's voice soars high on the second syllable as he tells me that, amazingly, his dyslexia simply vanished around the time he turned seven. As a result he "graduated from the school for retarded kids" and entered the Érsek Street Elementary School for Boys. His report cards show excellent marks. It is probably no coincidence that his dyslexia disappeared with the return of normalcy to family life. As government stabilized, my grandfather no longer needed to keep a gun under his pillow. The White Terror had burnt itself out. Postwar construction was booming. The Weidlinger brothers, Andor and Tibor, working with the architect Jenő Vogel, specialized in fashionable apartment buildings, many of which stand to this day. Their facades are a catalogue of Historicism, the early-twentieth-century architectural style that borrowed motifs and embellishments from previous historical periods. Some of the stylistic juxtapositions, Art Nouveau curves framed within a classical matrix, are delightfully reminiscent of a bygone era.

When Andor was at work and Pál was not with one of his tutors, he was often in Aunt Paula's apartment, under her watchful eye. Once he was old enough to receive an allowance, he was expected to honor his aunt by giving her a gift on her birthday. But one year he was broke, having frittered away all his cash. What to do? He found a shop selling expensive porcelain vases and inquired if they had any broken ones. They did. He bought a pile of shards for a few pengő and instructed the store clerk to package the broken vase and send it round to Paula's flat with a birthday card. Pál thought Paula would assume that the vase had been broken in transit and, from the evidence of the fine and delicate shards, appreciate his effort. What he didn't reckon on was the store clerk carefully wrapping each fragment separately, in tissue paper. This was how it was delivered to Aunt Paula. "I was in trouble," said my father. It would not surprise me if Andor gave him a strapping.

Three years after the end of the war, Andor felt secure enough in his prospects to look for a new wife. He courted Rózsa Radó, Ili's oldest sister. She is the one in the family photograph described by Ili, who "leaned with light elegance on an armchair and looked into the distance with her dreamy eyes. . ."

Ili writes that her first encounter with the Weidlinger relatives was a horrible experience. The entire Radó family paid a visit to the Weidlinger clan at 36 Rákóczi Street to celebrate the betrothal of Rózsa and Andor. Pál was there, as were Aunt Paula and Uncle Bertalan and their entire brood. Ili's account starts with getting dressed for the occasion. She was nine years old.

> While preparing me and patching the elbow of my checked dress, Klára yelled angrily, "This poor child will look like a beggar in this dress!" Hearing her, I became sad and ungainly, but did not say a word. I kept quiet even when Klára tried to cheer me up, putting an ugly purple flower under my collar. It made me feel even more like a beggar.

The six-room Weidlinger apartment was huge in Ili's eyes, filled with loud rich kids. Her hatred of the Weidlingers got mixed up with her latest reading, a novel by Émile Zola about the life of miners. In the book a blind horse is worked to death pulling an ore cart.

During this visit I constantly thought of this horse. I could not drink my hot chocolate with whipped cream. To the surprise of everyone, I pushed it aside with disgust after just a few sips. In this large and elegant children's room on Rákóczi Street, I felt that the horse and I belonged together and the loud rich kids were the enemies.

Andor married Rózsa in 1921, making Ili my father's step-aunt when she was just ten and he was seven. They called each other cousin. They would become the best of friends.

Rózsa had a sweet story she liked to tell. Shortly after they were introduced, Pál stood before his new mother and formally addressed her: "Madame, I kiss your hand." Then he asked leave to speak to her as a "friend." In the Hungarian language the relationship between two people is both defined and constrained by the choice of pronouns for the word *you* and the matching verb forms. Pál was asking Rózsa if he might speak to her in the familiar form. She gave her consent.

But Rózsa turned out to be incapable of taking young Pál in hand. Ili wrote that he was a "cussed boy," having been spoiled by several nannies during the three years of Andor's bachelorhood. My father, inspired by the Indian tales of James Fenimore Cooper, invented elaborate make-believe adventures for himself and Ili. Once they went on a "forest expedition." Rózsa's cabinets, tables, and chairs became boulders used to ford an imaginary raging torrent. Pál painted a forest clearing on one of Rózsa's prized silk sheets, indicating the spot where Ili should set up their tipi. He was in trouble again. Rózsa told Andor that his son was developing "anarchistic tendencies."

Budapest's schools, built in the late nineteenth century, were conceived as neoclassical temples of learning. The façade of Madách Gimnázium, still operating on Barcsay Street, features four gold panels with larger-than-life Greek gods and goddesses in studious poses. Inside is a vast staircase, flanked by Doric columns. Its marble balustrade is polished smooth by the hands of eight generations of students, including my father. On the January day in 2013 that I visited the school, the teenagers descending the marble staircase, were checking their cell phones. Ninety years ago it would have been just boys coming down these stairs (there were separate schools for girls). They would have been moving faster and wearing uniforms instead of blue jeans.

What kind of a student was Pál? In the school's library a helpful young woman takes down a stack of beautifully marbled ledgers, the student grade books for the years 1925-1931. These revealed that although my father became a student in September of 1925 at the age of nine, he was not actually present in Madách classrooms until 1927. Private tutors, hired by Andor, taught and tested him on the assigned coursework at home. This was a common practice in upper-middle-class homes. The tutors themselves were poor university students, given lunch or supper at the family table and a modest fee to give their pupil a head start in the academic marathon. Having a tutor didn't necessarily mean you were doing poorly in school. In Pál's case, thanks to his tutors, he completed two years of curriculum in one.

The academic work was hard. Basic requirements included eight years of Latin, eight years of Greek, eight years of German, mathematics courses reaching to the level of integral and differential calculus, and heavy doses of Hungarian and classical history. In most classes the hour began with recitation. Students were haunted by the fear of being suddenly called on, of being inadequately prepared, and of consequently receiving failing marks at the end of the semester. Hungarian writers wrote whole novels about gymnasiums, the relations between professors and students, the intense academic pressure, and tales of honor, loyalty, and rebellion.

Once Pál stopped being privately tutored, his performance fell off markedly. He routinely got "Ds" (barely passing) in most subjects. Occasionally he would get a "B" in math and science. He failed Latin and religion.

On weekends Ili described how, as young teenagers, she and my father would wander through the orchards and meadows of Zugliget, in the high, rounded hills above the city. Pál told her that he abhorred having to kiss ladies' hands when introduced to them. The cloying smell of benzene, which was used to clean fine leather gloves, made him nauseous. He also hated having to take fencing lessons. Andor believed they built character. Being good with a foil or a saber ensured that a young gentleman would be able to defend his honor. Pál thought this was absurd. Ili took a picture of Pál holding not a foil or a saber, but a small rifle, looking defiant. Then, as if realizing he was taking himself too seriously, Pál exchanged clothes with Ili. In a second photograph he has put on her demure flapper's dress. She has donned his jacket and short pants and added a worker's cap at a rakish angle. A cigarette dangles from her mouth and it is she who holds the rifle. (This make-believe tough-girl persona would become real in later years when Ili faced hardship and deprivation.)

Pál and Ilona Radó in 1925.

About their walks together Ili wrote:

Pali plagued me with the big questions of the world. He talked about how he would break free from his father's rigid program for him and about the amazing discoveries he would make in the future. I shared with him my inner problems and my conviction that one day I would lose my mind. We discussed the question of suicide and agreed that it is acceptable in ethical terms.

On one of their outings, the two boarded the little cogwheel train that still winds its way through a forest and up a steep slope to the top of St. John's Hill, the highest point overlooking Budapest. On top of the hill is a round, five-tiered building that looks like a wedding cake, with a crenellated turret. From Elizabeth Lookout, on a clear day, you can see for forty miles. Nearby was an elegant restaurant. Ili wrote:

At Pali's suggestion, we went into the restaurant and he ordered food and beer with manly chivalry. We sat on the terrace in the sunshine and talked about the deep problems of the world, a world that in Pali's opinion should be blown up. When the bill came, Pali didn't have the money to pay. I was ashamed. I gave the waiter my wristwatch. The next day Rózsa gave money to Pali to redeem it.

He was in trouble again. But this was nothing compared to what was to come.

In 1931, when Ili was nineteen and Pál was sixteen, they joined the clandestine communist youth movement. It was a dangerous move. Communists were outlaws; they could be arrested and even executed. Workers strikes were brutally suppressed.

The two friends were inspired by Pál's cousin Endre Sebestyén, Aunt Paula's youngest son, known as Bandi in the family. Bandi's political awakening came when he was a schoolboy returning from a vacation in the countryside. On the train platform a ragged old man approached him and addressed him in the most deferential way: "Young sir, be so kind and allow me to carry your suitcase."

Bandi continues:

> *I was seventeen. I had not yet accomplished anything in life and an old man like that was forced to ask me this favor for a few pennies. I felt that something in this society was just not right. This also contributed to my alienation from my family. Because I felt the problems of our society, I wanted to become more independent, so that the path I followed, I followed from my own conviction.*

The gap between rich and poor was exacerbated by the human cost of World War I. Misery and wealth, abjectness and power existed side by side in Budapest. Ili and my father must have had experiences similar to Bandi's. It is significant that all three were from Jewish families. As Jews they knew, on one level, that the tide was beginning to turn against them. The first anti-Semitic law had been enacted in Hungary in 1920, placing a quota on the number of Jews who could attend university. Many middle-class Jewish teenagers made common cause with the working poor against the proto-fascist dictatorship of Miklós Horthy. The Marxist ideal that all would be treated equally and each would contribute according to their ability was terrifically appealing.

I was skeptical of my father's claim that, by seventeen, he had read all of Marx and Engels' *Das Kapital* (amounting to some 2,400 pages) in the original German. But I had no doubt he was fully conversant with their *Communist Manifesto*. He told me: "I thought this was the absolute truth about everything. And it sort of opened my horizon."

Trench coats were the uniform of the movement. My father posed for a photograph of himself in one, his hands thrust deep into its pockets. Ili stopped using lipstick and wearing the "bourgeois" dresses that her mother made for her. She also had a trench coat. In *Miss Porcelain* she confesses that:

Pál in trench coat in 1932.

It bothered me that my coat was still too clean, but I pulled it tight with a leather belt. I wore socks rolled down and men's shoes with flat heels, but somehow my peers could still sense the bourgeois girl in me. . . .

Wearing her trench coat, she tried to explain "capitalist exploitation" to five rapt working-class boys as she paced back and forth on the tree-shaded sidewalk of Andrássy Avenue.

The boys were thirsty for knowledge. They wanted to understand the causes behind their miserable lives, so they liked listening to me. Yesterday I felt I understood [capitalist exploitation] completely, since I had carefully read Kautsky's book, but now when I tried to explain it like a teacher, I felt a little confused. I felt like a swindler, who tries to lead others on a very thin path that she has just made.

In 1931 the underground Student Socialist Council established twelve cells in Budapest gymnasiums. In my father's cell at Madách there were ten members. Four, including Pál, belonged to the outlawed Hungarian Communist Youth Union (*KIMSZ*). The activities of the cells consisted of organizing demonstrations, collecting money for the Red Aid [*Vörös Segély*], and rallying students in other schools. They met on weekends for walks in the hills above Budapest under the cover of "the Association of Nature Worshipers." Most of the adult leadership of the Communist Party in Hungary (those who had not been executed during the White Terror) were in prison. The remaining activists were kids like my father. What they lacked in experience they made up for in zeal.

Pál's cell decided to collect signatures protesting the execution of two Hungarian communists who had fled to the Soviet Union during the White Terror, only to be arrested on their return to Budapest. The boys went canvassing in the poorest, outer districts of Budapest, where tenements stood among breweries, slaughterhouses, mills, and factories. In the tenements people lived ten or twelve to a room, without a toilet. Fourteen-hour workdays were common. My father said, "I had read all about the proletariat but I had never seen them. It was the first time I saw those people. They existed."

Pál and Ili recited movement poetry and sang revolutionay songs. Pál helped to write and distribute an illicit newspaper, *The Red Student* [*Vörös Diák*]. It contained, an article explaining Marx's theory of dialectical materialism, anarchist declarations, and a condemnation of Madách professors' authoritarian practices. Among my father's papers I found a scrawled manuscript for an unpublished piece titled *Jobs and Bread*. It describes a workers' demonstration that is brutally attacked by mounted police. Escaping from the melee is a young boy whom I can easily imagine as Pál.

> *Two cops rush after the skinny boy. He swerves into a back street, and jumps on a passing tram. The policemen curse, but let him go. The boy sits in the tram, catching his breath. He is scared. The passengers are also scared. They whisper, "Demonstration!" The conductor hesitates. Should he stop the tram?*
>
> *A fat, confident man slaps the boy. "Snotty little rascal! I will teach you politics! You will not make any progress in life like this." The passengers are on his side. Someone says: "He got away easy." The boy is scared and speechless. On his face is the red handprint of the fat man. "Be happy," says the man, "that I did not give you up to the police, you'd have got more from them." And he looks around with a self-satisfied air.*
>
> *At the next stop the boy creeps from the tram. He feels himself a coward not to stand up to the fat man, but he runs to the square where they had all agreed to meet. Others are already arriving. Then more and more. And once again, like music, it rings out sharply and threateningly: "Jobs and bread!"*

My grandparents lived in fear of the knock on the door that would bring bad news; that their son would be caught doing something that would bring disgrace upon the family. It came in January 1932.

Pál had just turned seventeen. His cell had already experienced a few close calls with the police, but he seemed oblivious to the danger. Ili remembers telling him of her own narrow escape from the cops, to which he replied, "All right, but don't shit yourself."

Then, one day, Ili got a call telling her that the group's meeting place had been revealed to the police. She warned Pál, but he went to a meeting anyway. He was arrested on January 12, 1932, along with several others. Ili wrote:

At 4:00 a.m. that night, Rózsa's servant called to tell me that Pali had been arrested and his father's flat had been searched. I went over there. The flat was completely torn up. Rózsa was pallid, but calm. Andor was in a rage. She could barely keep him from beating me as he blamed me for what happened to Pali. I told them I had warned Pali but he didn't listen.

My father said:

I was in the police station when they told me that I was under a death sentence. It didn't worry me. What really worried me was that I was in school and would be unable to get my baccalaureate. That's what really concerned me. I said, "The hell with a death sentence. If I die, I die. But if I don't die I want my baccalaureate." That really worried me.

I heard this story several times while growing up, and I was suspicious of it, but I found corroboration in historical sources. The police had renewed their arrest and prosecution of communists at this time, owing to the suspicion that leftists had been behind the sabotage of a railway bridge. Under a new martial law, communists were being arrested and imprisoned. Some were executed.

So why was my father laughing when he said, "The hell with a death sentence!" Perhaps it was simply because at seventeen one feels invincible. Pál could not conceive of his own end but the consequences of failure at school felt so much more tangible.

He continued:

They beat us and tortured us and afterwards they gave us a cigarette. That was where I smoked my first cigarette. I was amazingly lucky. The Chief of Police was some sort of a relative of an aunt by marriage. And she came and begged him to let me go.

But Pál was only out on bail. He still had to face a trial.

On January 14 newspapers reported the arrests. The right-wing paper *The Evening* (*Az Est*) stated that the police "had eliminated disturbing elements in the student body." The left-wing *People's Voice* [*Népszava*] said, "Police are harassing students for writing factual articles. They are frightened that children will disturb the social order."

In the Budapest city archives, the court documents of the Red Students' trial include a list of banned communist literature that was confiscated when the police raided the Weidlinger apartment, statements of the accused, sentences handed down, and reports by court-appointed social workers who investigated the family background of each defendant. Most interesting is the profile of Pál Weidlinger (referred to as "the minor") written by his social worker.

The minor's parents tried to ensure for their only son a future appropriate to the social standing of the family by providing him with an education beyond elementary school. However, in the beginning there were problems because the minor suffered from neuroses with symptoms of compulsive head shaking and cracking his knuckles. His mind worked with difficulty, so he was under the guidance of a tutor for six years. As long as the tutor was responsible for the intellectual development of the minor, there were no problems. However,

after the private lessons ended and the minor became a teen-
ager, everything changed.

The first indication of this change was when the minor got
in touch with the far left-wing organization of "Nature Wor-
shipers." Their misleading teachings disturbed his judgment
and awakened his interest so that he bought printed materials
from them. Under the influence of these materials, he couldn't
resist the second challenge [to become actively involved in the
movement].

I visited his homeroom teacher, whose opinion about the
minor is not at all flattering. In the beginning he was a well-
behaved, cooperative boy. However, he changed. He tended to
be disruptive in class. Like a narcissist he prides himself on
his below-average knowledge, and he responds to his teachers'
warnings with a mocking smile. Letting him go back to school
is problematic, because the teachers fear that the minor would
be of bad influence on his peers. Signed: Emil Vankó.

Three of Pál's codefendants in the trial were found "guilty of
attempting to destabilize and disrupt, with violence, law and order
in society" and given jail sentences of six months to one year. Pál,
because of his family's connections, did not have to go to jail. The
impression presented in the court papers was that he was a neurotic
and impressionable young boy who had been led astray by the older
ringleaders.

Ili recalls that when Pál came back from the trial, he was sullen.
He made a contemptuous comment about Ili's boyfriend, Ferenc
Pándi, who was also part of the Red Student group. Pál said that
Ferenc was a cowardly Social Democrat, less committed and willing
to take risks than his communist comrades. Ili writes that she became
angry: "I said, 'Pándi is not a Social Democrat—and he wasn't scraped
out of the crap by his father.'"

Pál was indeed scraped out of the crap by his family. But banned
from school it was not clear if he would be able to sit for his baccalaureate exams, without which he could not advance in the world. Andor

was devastated. All those tutors, all that effort spent on trying to keep his son on the rails seemed wasted. Fortunately Pál was allowed to finish his studies elsewhere, take his final exams, and get his diploma in the late summer of 1932.

And then:

That's when I finally ran away. I felt very different from our family—from my background. I was ashamed that they were middle-class or upper-class. I had the feeling that my future was completely planned by them. They knew what I should do and whom I should marry, and I think that was part of my rebellion.

6. THE FOREIGNER

BUDAPEST AND BRÜNN,

CZECHOSLOVAKIA, 1932–1934, 2014

On an unseasonably warm day in late January 2014, my translator, my Hungarian production assistant, and I arrived at an art gallery in the Inner City to film the first gathering of an association of the children of Hungarian Jews who attended the German Technical University in Brünn, Czechoslovakia, in the 1930s. I am one of those children. It is one of several uncanny coincidences on this project; I just happened to be visiting Budapest at the time that this group coalesced.

My father's *Meldungsbuch* (school enrollment book) was my passport, the credential that identified me as a legitimate member of the gathering. It states that Pál Weidlinger matriculated in the Deutsche Technische Hochschule of Brünn on October 8, 1932. The *Meldungsbuch* declares my father's area of study as engineering and architecture. The two disciplines were combined in a single course of study, which also included the construction of railways and bridges. Stamped diagonally across the first page of the book is the word *AUSLÄNDER*, foreigner. In his ID photograph on the cover Pál looks even younger than his seventeen years. He's a beardless boy with slicked-back hair

Pál Weidlinger's school enrollment book,
German Technical University of Brünn, Czechoslovakia, 1932.

and protruding, vulnerable ears. Behind perfectly round, owlish glasses, his eyes seem both sad and defiant.

Each year, between 1928 and 1938, about 250 Hungarian Jews enrolled in the school. They were part of a much larger Diaspora that was shut out of universities by a law that severely limited Jews' access to higher education. Known as the *Numerus Clausus* Act, it was part of the backlash against Jews who had filled the ranks of the skilled professions before World War I. Accordingly, thousands of Hungarian Jewish students, those who could afford it, went to school in Czechoslovakia, Switzerland, Italy, France, and even Germany.

At the gathering of the children of Brünn alumni, my father's *Meldungsbuch* is passed from hand to hand, around a big circle of gray-haired men and women seated on folding chairs. I have a shot of myself sitting on the edge of my chair. I was expecting new and wondrous revelations. My translator whispered into my ear, recounting everything that was being said. But while everyone present was as eager as I, we were all astonishingly ignorant of the formative years in our parents' lives. Over time I came to understand the reason for this.

I then discovered that there were six people here whose parents actually knew my father. We made a date to meet separately and, a few days later, gathered around a large kitchen table at the apartment of Anna Perczel. Anna's father had been part of the Red Student Movement and was arrested and expelled from gymnasium at the same time as Pál. The parents of Anna Erdős and Katalin Talyigás did not cross paths with Pál in Brünn, but they knew and worked with him later, as did the uncle of Gabriella Bartos. András Szurdi, the only man in the group, is the nephew of Endre (Bandi) Sebestyén, my father's close friend and leader in the communist youth movement. András was gently protective of Ágnes Sebestyén, the daughter of Bandi and the oldest and frailest among the six gathered around Anna's kitchen table.

What I learned was that the life of a foreign student in Brünn in the early 1930s involved hard work, cramped quarters, and meager meals, all of which were endured with a kind of sly hilarity. Katalin told a story about her father and his friends looking for a room to rent.

> *They found a suitable room. The landlord offered them coffee and asked if they liked the room. They said, "The room is OK, but we'll be needing breakfast with it. But if what we are drinking is coffee then we would prefer tea with breakfast. However if what we are drinking is tea then we would prefer to have some coffee."*

Photographs were passed around. Boys in ties and jackets, each with a handkerchief folded in the breast pocket, lounge in the window frame of their classroom. Boys in heavy coats huddle around tiny tables in a canteen. In one unusual picture two boys hold a classmate horizontally in midair, while he mimes a breaststroke, swimming, while another pretends to reel him in, like a fish.

My father appears in some of these photos in the most amusing poses. He is in serious conversation with a horse. He is a pirate with a polka-dotted kerchief tied around his head. He is engaged in a duel, but instead of brandishing a saber, his weapon is an artist's palette.

(Top) Unidentified students in Brünn, Czechoslovakia.
(Bottom) Pál and horse.

Many of the classes that the boys took involved drawing and painting. Pál's architectural renderings were finely wrought—but what is more interesting are the doodles and cartoons he drew. He used his pencil to make sense of the world through the lens of his political convictions. He drew the gauntfaces of the poor, and he imagined a new Garden of Eden as the destination of the revolutionaries' road.

Pál Weidlinger, March to Paradise, *1932.*

A group of friends with similar political convictions called themselves the Gang of Thirteen. Some of them had been involved in the Red Student affair back in Budapest, and they renewed their commitment to the communist movement in secret meetings in Brünn. Endre Sebestyén (cousin Bandi) was their leader. Bandi recalled that although my father was a "sympathizer," he no longer participated in movement activities. It could be that he was resented; his bourgeois family connections had protected him from jail when many others had to do time. Certainly the Brünn group was censorious. Anna Perczel's mother had been chastised for bourgeois materialism and banned from meetings for wearing a conspicuously pretty dress.

Instead of going to meetings, my father wrote poems. They are what you'd expect from an angst-ridden teenage boy, but there is one, "The Ballad of the Sick" that stands out:

> . . . but they [the Sick] just hate in secret
> As their souls grow cold, their blood goes white,
> Panting for vengeance against the great society of the Healthy.
> The secret organization of the Sick will rise up,
> And throw a bomb amid the Healthy.
> Crutches will turn into rifles, thermometers into bayonets
> Sickbeds will become tanks and their dying desires will
> be reborn. . . .
>
> They will attack in perfect formation.
> Their frantic pain. their burning fever,
> Will eat at your bodies,
> Woe unto you, the Happy Healthy!

I sat with this poem for a long time in the belief that it would reveal something profound about my father and the forces that propelled him from adolescence into adulthood and onto the trajectory of a most extraordinary life. Who are the Sick? Who are the Happy Healthy? Are the latter the happy complacent generation of Pál's parents? Are the Sick the young communist students or the poor masses? The writer does not seem to identify with the Sick: "lepers and epileptics with foaming mouths, cardiac cases with despotic hearts, the lunatics, idiots and neurotics coordinating the grand attack;" or with the Healthy: "treacherous renegade hordes . . . [who] healed in apostasy will be executed."

Nothing clicked for me. Then I realized that my confusion is also Pál's confusion. He is not unlike teenagers of a later generation who emblazoned their black clothes with winged death's heads and skeletal riders of the Apocalypse. Sometimes the search for mean-ing and identity requires a journey though darkness and absolute nihilism. I also understood that a certain part of my father, his vul-nerability and a capacity for empathy will get detained, left behind on the battlefield between the ranks of Sick and the Healthy.

In his diary from those days he wrote: "I am writing because I am lonely." And yet he hardly dared to write down his true feelings lest "somebody should read what I have written." On another page he described himself wandering the streets of Brünn "waiting for a miracle." The miracle was a girl, but she did not come. He wrote: "I am not in love! Yet, in contradiction with my every statement, I would be able to love very much. Or perhaps I couldn't love at all. . . . I would break into tears of self-pity. Fortunately these days I am steel-hearted."

I feel a great tenderness toward this boy who, in the midst of his crowded student lodgings, found himself completely alone. The external circumstances of his exile (being not only a Jew but a communist with an arrest record) seemed to mirror perfectly his self-exile from family and from boyhood friends who shunned him for his shameful privilege—for getting "scraped out of the crap" by his influential father.

Pál needed to separate completely from Andor, to create an iden-tity for himself away from his father's expectations and influence. He claimed he ran away from home to go to school in Czechoslovakia and that his parents did not know where he was for two years.

> I put myself through school. I don't know how the hell I did it, but I remember I got a scholarship and I supported myself mostly by tutoring other students. We lived, four or five of us in one room, but I didn't feel underprivileged. I wasn't starving or anything. I thought this is what you did. Amazingly I was there without my parents' knowledge for two years."

In creating his identity Pál created this narrative to support it, modifying what actually happened. In reality, Andor did know where his son was and may even have given him money for his tuition. I have a photograph of Pál posing with Andor in Brünn, amidst a group of classmates.

The other omission in my father's account of himself is his motivation for "running away" to Czechoslovakia. To be sure he wanted to get away from Andor; to be sure it was an act of rebellion; but he left out the fact that he was a Jew and that his chances of continuing his education in Hungary were slim. Why did he not or why could he not say this to me?

I asked the group sitting around Anna Perczel's kitchen table, "Why did my father never tell us he was Jewish? Has anyone here experienced anything similar?" Anna said that it simply didn't matter to her parents. They were communists first, then Hungarians, then Jews. Anna Erdős says she learned she was a Jew when she was eight. She found her birth certificate and asked her mother about the abbreviation *Izr* (Israelite) inscribed in the space for religion. Gabriella Bartos "accidentally" found out she was Jewish when she was twenty. Why was she not told? She said:

> *I think my parents knew what happened to my family during the Holocaust. . . . They probably thought that if they just turned their heads and didn't talk about it, then the whole thing didn't happen. Just like when a guest comes to visit you and you don't want to clean the whole flat so you just sweep everything under the carpet. They didn't want to talk about it. It never happened.*

A couple of days later I was introduced to a distant relative, whom I will call István, who did not wish to be identified. István's father was a boy during the terrible autumn and winter of 1944-1945, when Jews were hunted and executed on the banks of the Danube by Hungarian fascist gangs, known as the Arrow Cross. When István was eighteen and studying to become a historian, his father told him his family's story but made him promise to speak of it to no one. This was why, when I do an interview with István, his face is hidden from the camera. Together we speculate on the trauma his father (who is still alive) must have experienced, a trauma that has not loosened its grip on his heart to this day.

But rationally speaking, what about us, István and me, here and now? Surely being a Jew in Hungary, whether religious or assimilated, carries no stigma, no hint of angst or anxiety? Anti-Semitism exists, as it does almost anywhere, but surely it is relegated to a tiny minority of right-wing troglodytes? István smiles and, almost apologetically, explains that when he was engaged to be married, his future mother-in-law said to her daughter, "I'm not an anti-Semite, but you may want to consider the possibility that your future husband *could be a Jew*. I am just saying." In fact it is not uncommon for well-educated, intelligent and apparently tolerant Hungarians to remark in casual conversation that so-and-so is a Jew or may be a Jew—as if this information provided a lens through which the other known attributes of said person, whether positive or negative, could be seen and understood. As if blood mattered as it once so clearly and tragically did.

Cousin Bandi observed that Pál was the most brilliant of the Hungarian students in Brünn—in marked contrast to his sorry performance at Madách Gimnázium. In June 1934 Pál took his *Staatsprüfung I,* the universal exam given to students at the end of their first two years of study. Among the subjects he was tested in were architectural morphology, geology, history of architecture, elements of higher mathematics, and the mechanics of materials. Passing the exam, Pál felt vindicated in the choices he had made. Meanwhile, in Andor's eyes, Pál had redeemed himself from the scandal of his exploits as a young communist. Reunited in the summer of 1934, the whole family went on a vacation to the Italian Riviera. Despite the worldwide Depression, Andor could afford it. He and Tibor had just completed a modernist villa for a wealthy private client. It was the third luxury house they had built in three years.

My grandfather then attended to the matter of his son's ongoing education. Pál had completed just two years of the four-year course required for a diploma in architecture and engineering. Andor himself had dropped out of technical school, never receiving the diploma that would have certified him as an architect. He wanted to ensure that his son would go further. He wrote to the Federal Technical University in Zurich, Switzerland, petitioning that Pál be accepted as a third-year student in the architecture department, specializing in high-rise structures. The school, also known as the Polytechnic, was *the* national university of Switzerland. Its students were exposed to the world's best and brightest in science, industry, and technology. Six Nobel laureates, including Einstein, were either alumni or professors.

Curiously, Andor's letter to the university was written on the professional letterhead of his younger brother, Tibor Weidlinger, who *was* a certified architect and engineer, thus giving the impression that Andor himself had these qualifications. The letter is simply signed: *Weidlinger.* Andor also invoked the name of our illustrious relative, Dezső Korda, who had both taught at the Polytechnic and designed the slanted elevator in the Eiffel Tower. A letter of acceptance from the university arrived within a week. By the end of October 1934, Pál had taken up residence at 58 Universitätstrasse, Zurich, according to his alien registration with the Swiss police.

7. THE LITTLE SAILOR

ZURICH AND LONDON, 1935–1937

"Every intelligent person spent a part of his youth in a café . . . without that, the education of a young man would be imperfect and incomplete," observed Jenő Rákosi, a prominent turn-of-the-century Hungarian playwright and statesman.

In Zurich Pál made up for what he had missed out on in Budapest, having left home too young. There was a little café on the north bank of the Limmat River, not far from where it flows out of Lake Zurich, bisecting the city with its green waters dotted with swans. It was called Au Petit Dôme, and it was where Pál could be found when he wasn't attending lectures at school.

> *Whenever I had some free time I spent it in the café. I rarely had enough money to order a dinner but once in a great while I could. I still remember the vol au vent avec petits pois. That was a feast. Usually I would just go there and have coffee and play chess. The waitresses were like surrogate mothers to me.*

Only a few blocks upriver was the much grander Café Odéon, where in the 1920s and '30s, a whole congregation of famous writers and political figures gathered. Among them were James Joyce, Erich Maria Remarque, Somerset Maugham, and Stefan Zweig. In high-ceilinged, marble-clad rooms with Art Nouveau brass fittings, the thinkers of the age had their espresso, smoked, held forth, fell in love, schemed, expostulated, wrote poems, manifestos, and novels, and imagined the future. Would the twenty-year-old Central European student dare set foot in there? If not he certainly felt the allure, the gravitational pull of the West, of London, Vienna, Berlin, and Paris. And this may be what contributed to his falling in love with Madeleine Friedli, the woman who would become my mother.

> *I remember one time, at the bar, I saw this very glamorous-looking French woman. She was very tall and slender and she had short dark hair. I immediately fell in love with her. I knew very little French but I told my friends, "See that woman there, I'm going to marry her." Everybody laughed at me but I said, "Absolutely this is the woman I'm going to marry. I managed to have somebody introduce me and . . . then it was very immediate. The first time I talked to her I walked her home. I didn't go in but I walked her home and I kissed her goodnight. I remember that very well.*

I asked my father what he found so alluring.

> *First she was Western European and I was from Central Europe. I hated where I came from. Also, here was a woman who was independent, who spoke French, and who had a job.*

Describing his *coup de foudre*, Pál wrote on stationery from Au Petit Dôme to Vera, a cousin in Budapest. The tone of the letter suggests they had been intimate.

> *Dear Vera: I feel a bit ashamed of my last letter, not because of what I wrote, but because of the change of mood I went through in just a couple of weeks. Actually this is not a change of mood;*

Pál Weidlinger and Madeleine Friedli.

I believe that I went through a deep and serious transforma-
tion. What is this transformation? I am happy, inexpressibly
happy, after a long, long time I met a woman who I love. How
banal does it sound, now that it is written down, but for me
it means a lot. My dear Vera can you understand this? I am
happy, and now I see everything differently.

My mother was not glamorous in the romantic way that Pál saw
her, but she was beautiful, smart, and very tall. Describing her early
life she wrote:

I was a child grown tall too fast, and everyone could see that I
was a "brain." I had it easy at school because I absorbed what
was taught like a sponge. I wanted to become a teacher, but
in those days a woman lost her teaching job when she became
married, and I wanted more than anything to have a family.
Therefore, at fourteen, I abandoned plans for years of study
and entered a vocational high school. At sixteen I was offered a
job which I accepted because of economic difficulties at home,
and because I was impatient to have the world for my teacher.

The Friedlis lived in the town of La Chaux-de-Fonds. The name
translates as "meadow at the end of the valley." Nestled in the Jura,
the foothills of the Swiss-French Alps, it was an idyllic place—and
not only because of the grandeur of the landscape. Settled by exiled
French Huguenots in the sixteenth century, the town became famous
for its watchmakers and clockmakers. These artisans developed a
unique system of working together, pooling skills and resources. This
non-exploitative, worker-driven industry was so successful that at one
point, half the watches used in the world came from there. The utopian thinker Jean-Jacques Rousseau visited and extolled the virtues
of La Chaux-de-Fonds, as did Karl Marx in *Das Kapital*.

My mother was seventeen and working as a secretary at the
workers' cooperative at the time of the 1929 Wall Street Crash. It
had a huge impact. The worldwide demand for fine Swiss watches

plummeted. My mother's job was to certify workers' unemployment compensation claims. The "world" had indeed become her teacher.

Day in, day out, I listened and spoke to those men and women, stunned, discouraged, worried. The older ones, who all their life took pride in turning out [watches], those little marvels of precision, were suddenly idled. The young ones, unbelieving and angry, finally left to take up pick and shovel in the government road-building programs. In four years the city's population decreased by 25 percent.

My mother left home in 1933 at the age of twenty-one. She polished her school German with a three-week immersion course and then traveled to Zurich. There she began a job as an accountant managing the books of a metalworkers' union. Someone told her it was a man's job, but this did not faze her.

Madeleine described Zurich as a city at the crossroads of Europe, bustling with people and ideas. Religious and political refugees poured down the roads from the north. For the first time in her life she was on her own and she felt "as free as the wind." There she met my father. German was their common language.

On one level Pál was both a religious and political refugee from the north. As a Jew and a communist, there was no way he could go home to complete his studies. On another level, having gotten back into Andor's good graces, and probably receiving money from him, Pál was just another relatively well-off foreign student. While he was attracted to Madeleine because of her perceived Western European, cosmopolitan traits, she esteemed his status as student communist who had acted on his convictions and been exiled for it. There was also an endearing and puckishly defiant quality about Pál. He treated money with contempt. Sometimes he would buy my mother flowers with the last sous in his pocket. He rented a boat and taught her how to sail on Lake Zurich. He said, "Madeleine liked that, and we would go to expensive places where they would look very suspiciously at us, and I would order these things as if I was a millionaire." For

Madeleine, raised in an atmosphere of bourgeois propriety, there was something romantic about Pál's penchant for spending his last francs on flowers or an expensive meal.

My father had a camera, a tiny one that took tiny pictures. Most of them are of buildings, as if he were making a catalogue of architectural styles that he would later draw on or reject. Then there are some extraordinary pictures of my mother. She sits or reclines on a bed. She is fully clothed in a woolen dress, chastely buttoned to the neck, yet the images are erotic. She looks at the camera with a gaze that is so serious yet so completely unselfconscious. She is aware of her beauty. She makes no effort to promote it but neither does she seek to hide it. In one image, taken from overhead, she is looking up into the lens as if to say to her lover, "Well, are you coming to me?" In another her hands are outstretched, toward the camera—as if she herself were framing the picture.

Pál and Madeleine were in love. They did not talk of marriage. My father says they both saw it as an outmoded, petit bourgeois institution. Despite this they were committed to each other. Certainly they were both romantics.

> I recall in the early times of our relations coming home (she lived somewhere else, then); I found her sitting in front of my door and crying. She said, "I came to see you and you were not here." And I said, "I didn't know you were coming." And she said, "I expected you to know." She had sort of mystical ideas. She counted very much on me reading her mind.

Even as Pál and Madeleine settled into their relationship, my father had the urge to travel and explore. In the summer of 1935 he and some student friends took a road trip from Zurich to Brussels. Pál kept a log of the trip, noting place names, dates, and distances. They hitchhiked. Sometimes they were on foot, sometimes in cars. Pál filled an album

Madeleine in Pal's room above the café, Au Petit Dôme.

with the postage-stamp sized photographs from his camera: a customs checkpoint at the French border, a student sitting on the running board of a truck playing a ukulele, Notre Dame and the Eiffel Tower in Paris. He sketched rooftops and the cathedral in Langres and a pastoral landscape in Chaumont. In Brussels the boys ran low on funds and had only bread to eat. On the return trip they crossed the southwestern tip of Germany, north of Basel. There they encountered a friendly group of young people, about their own age, and were invited to a meal at a summer camp. Since they had only bread to eat, this was greatly appreciated. The camp was a Hitler Youth camp.

The people were just wonderful people. They were idealistic young people and I was very disturbed: I expected the Nazis not to be humans and I remember that meeting these young boys and girls so very upset me. . . and there was this lovely girl. . . .

The lovely girl, who was named Ursula, took a liking to Pál, and she later wrote several letters to him, care of the Petit Dôme. She signed each letter "Love, Ursula 88." Eighty-eight was a code. "H" is the eighth letter of the alphabet. Two "H"s is 88. This meant "Heil Hitler."

That September the Nazis enacted the Nuremberg Race Laws that excluded Jews from citizenship in the Reich and prohibited them from marrying or having sexual relations with persons of "German or related blood." Clearly the lovely Ursula did not know she had a crush on a Jew.

My mother also traveled on her own and took pictures. Her prized possession was her Leica, a professional's 35mm camera. She had an excellent eye for composition, much better than Pál's. She put her pictures in carefully labeled photo albums. She documented her trip to the Socialist International Youth Congress in Liège, Belgium, where she made many friends. There were photos of a parade with bicycles festooned with flowers, a sit-down strike on a cobblestone street, and a portrait of "Mary who works at a socialist newspaper in Brussels." On another page she wrote, "We speak of trade unions!" and "Europe is full of hope for the Popular Front" (a left-wing political

Pál gets food at Hitler Youth camp.

coalition that swept French elections in 1936). When it came to politics, my father and mother were very much of the same mind.

That winter Pál took courses in the construction of high buildings in reinforced concrete, high buildings in steel, structural analysis, city planning, and art as an elective. In the summer of 1936, he was given an internship working for the Congrès International d'Architecture Moderne (CIAM). It was a feather in his cap. Convened by the famous architect Le Corbusier, CIAM formalized the principles of the modern architecture movement and was devoted to improving the world through urban planning.

But while working in the CIAM office, Pál completely neglected his studies and failed his final exams at the Polytechnic. My father said to me, "I remember Madeleine was very upset about it, and she was afraid I would never amount to anything." Her concern motivated him. It was not the first or the last time that she acted as a guiding and sobering influence. He knuckled down for another semester, passed the final exam, and was awarded his diploma in architecture and engineering on February 11, 1937.

Around the same time Pál graduated, he wrote to cousin Ili about Madeleine.

> *My dear Ili: I am writing you for selfish reasons. I am inter-*
> *ested in your opinion regarding what my family's reaction will*
> *be if what I am about to write becomes public knowledge. I*
> *plan to be married in a short time by entering into a serious*
> *morganatic commitment!*

Morganatic is a curious word. It dates from the seventeenth century and was used to describe a marriage between a person of royal or noble birth to a partner of lower rank. Simply by using this word Pál identifies himself with aristocracy. He continues:

> *There is every reason for my family to be indignant, since the*
> *woman I plan to marry has been my girlfriend for some time.*
> *She is one year older than me, very poor, and is the daughter*
> *of a worker in the printing business. What's worst of all she is*
> *a secretary for a metal industry union! I am quite aware that*
> *all these reasons are enough to cause a huge scandal. I am*
> *turning to you for advice, since you are more familiar with the*
> *atmosphere there. Please write about this honestly!*

What a snob! How could he profess to be a Marxist and worry about entering into a morganatic relationship? Despite all he has done to distance himself from his parents during his years in Brünn, despite denouncing their petit bourgeois values, he still cared about his father's opinion. He was a young man divided within himself. He was aware of this in his interview with me.

> *In some ways, because I broke with my background, I had no*
> *standards. I didn't know what one does. I only knew what one*
> *does in the milieu which I didn't want to belong to.*

Going back to Hungary to face the stifling expectations of his family was the last thing he wanted; but finding employment anywhere, with Europe still recovering from the Depression, was hard. Andor suggested that he go to London and try to get a job with the Hungarian film producer Alexander Korda, whose movie *The Private Lives of Henry VIII* was a smash hit. Andor believed that this Korda was a relative, belonging to the same side of the family as Dezső Korda of Eiffel Tower fame. He would therefore feel bound to give young Pál a job, perhaps as a set designer.

I was the envy of everybody. I had this dream of working in his film studio. I imagined I could be—who knows?—maybe a famous movie actor or a director or . . . anything.

Pál embarked for London just a few days after receiving his diploma. Madeleine remained in Zurich. Her steady job was too precious to give up. She wrote to him on February 17, saying how she laughed at his account of his travels passing through France and how she looked forward to his impressions of London.

He arrived via the Calais–Dover ferry and train at Victoria Station. Advised to seek cheap lodgings in the vicinity of the British Museum, he made inquiries in broken English at what appeared to be a bed and breakfast, but turned out to be a brothel. The pleasant woman who answered the door asked: "How long would you like to stay?"

"Permanently," replied my father in his thick Hungarian accent. This elicited howls of merriment from the working ladies who, once they stopped laughing, directed Pál to a lodging house at No. 3 Bedford Square. It was run by Quakers.

It turned out that Pál's chances of getting a job with Alexander Korda were nil. Korda had two box-office flops after his hit movie and was not hiring. Furthermore he was not, in fact, related to the Weidlingers. The film producer had been born Sandor Kellner, a Jew who chose the more Hungarian-sounding name Korda as his *nom de plume.*

Andor tried to come to the rescue by providing more London connections, but Pál made no use of them. He told me, "I just resented it.

I got introductions, very high-level introductions, and I just resented it. I didn't want to do anything with those people."

Alone and jobless in London and isolated by his pride as well as his poor grasp of English, Pál seemed to be crossing an internal frontier. He had been independent in Brünn and Zurich, but his life was circumscribed by the demands of school. Now he was completely free. Not knowing where he was headed, he had a kind of mystical idea that events and circumstances would unfold to show him the way. But weeks passed without a sign and, in this gap in which nothing happened externally, Pál had the time to observe the world around him and his inner self. In the box of papers that came to me after his death were several scraps of paper torn from a notebook with scrawled notes from this time.

London, 22 March 1937. I have been here a month. Today, when I woke up, I thought that all this is just a dream. It seems improbable, how I live without understanding the language and not knowing, each day, what I ought to be doing. Is it a good or bad dream? Reality seems to be at times depressing and pointless. How will I feel in a year when I think back on this time?

He wandered around the city. He became fascinated with beggars who made drawings on the sidewalk with colored chalk.

They sit on one side of their pictures, their hat on the other. After a few days they lose their place. The colorful landscapes, trees, houses, and flowers gradually disappear beneath the feet of pedestrians. The rain washes the sidewalk clean. Then the beggars come back and. . . .

It is possible he imagined himself as one of them. When he arrived in London he had just enough money to rent a room for two weeks. Fortunately, the Quakers took pity on their young Hungarian guest and gave him credit. His room came with breakfast, which he lived on. He did buy cigarettes, which he shared with a young Hungarian woman who lived on the floor above him. She was Éva Károlyi, the daughter of the idealistic Count Mihály Károlyi, the leader of the ill-fated 1919 Aster Revolution that caused Andor to sleep with his pistol. Pál and Countess Éva sat and smoked on the stairway between the third and fourth floors. It was a comfort to speak Hungarian.

At night he listened to the sounds of the Bloomsbury neighborhood:

Here on this little street (far from the crowds on Oxford and Piccadilly Streets) everything seems to have fallen asleep. Like in a village, one can hear the barking of dogs and the love cries of cats on the roofs. The song of a mandolin breaks up the silence, but the silence and loneliness of the night soon swallows the sound, as water swallows a pebble that is thrown into it.

Pál's loneliness is manifest in his story about an encounter with a girl in Hyde Park. It takes place on an unseasonably hot day. People are lying in a stupor on the grass with copies of the *Evening Standard* strewn about them. A few have paid tuppence to rent a reclining chair. Pál is not among them. He writes:

If only I knew what to do this afternoon. (The problem is the same every day, and yet it is still a novelty.) If I met some acquaintance, I could at least enjoy a cup of steaming hot tea somewhere. I would tell him about my life story. I would relate everything; how I traveled through all of Western Europe without any money. I started "telling" the story even as I walked along and I could hardly wait to sit down in the tea shop. I whistled a little ditty: Wir haben die ganze Welt gesehen, die Welt ist überall rund. . . .

"We have seen the whole world—The world is round everywhere!" The words are from a ribald sailor's shanty ("Hamburg on the Elbe," made famous by Hans Albers, the German John Wayne of the 1930s). While the narrator is whistling this tune and dreaming of regaling a friend over a cup of tea, a real girl appears before him. From a distance she looks like a "modern statue, polished to smoothness." She has a German shepherd that has slipped its leash. She asks him to hold her purse while she pursues the animal.

The two get to talking and walking together and the narrator vacillates between excitement, awe, and contempt. He observes: "How open and uninhibited this girl is! It is impossible to find proletarian girls like this back East." By contrast he is quite shy.

"What's your name?" she asks.

"Pál," I reply, surprised.

"Yes, but your other name."

"I only have one name."

"That's impossible, everyone has two names."

Now I have to say something. Why should I tell her my name? Not as if it were any secret, but why is she asking? I simply don't answer but then I finally say: "I am not anybody. I am just Pál."

She smiles. It seems she is satisfied with this answer.

I suddenly ask: "Would you be angry if I kissed you?" Her eyes well up with tears. They become sad, so sad. I say, "Don't worry, I won't kiss you. There is too much lipstick on your lips."

Maybe I just imagined it, but it seems to me that the girl is smiling though her tears. She is much smarter than I am. She does not consider events to be tragic.

––––––––––

Meanwhile two or three letters arrived from Madeleine each week. They are filled with the most passionate endearments. On March 7, 1937 she wrote:

> I would give up the sun for a whole week just to feel you near me, to have your head on my shoulder, even if it were only for a few minutes. You know, sometimes the blood suddenly stops flowing in my veins when I think about how long we have to be apart. If only I could see you.

Three days later she asks if he has enough money. Also: "I am so proud: My little sailor is truly a fabulous sailor, so seaworthy." This line triggers a memory from my own childhood. One of my parents, I am not sure which, is singing a bedtime song to me with a strangely haunting refrain:

Ohé ! Ohé ! Matelot,
Matelot navigue sur les flots…

Ahoy! Ahoy! Sailor,
Sailor sailing on the high sea. . . .

The words are from a macabre French children's song. A little ship is lost in the vast ocean. Food runs out, and the sailors draw lots to see which of their number will be eaten. Fate decrees it is the smallest and youngest of the ship's company who will become food for the rest. The little sailor climbs the mast and prays to the Virgin for a miracle, which comes in the form of many small fishes that leap onto the deck, providing food for the starving sailors and sparing the life of the boy.

Mon cher petit matelot (My dear little sailor), is how Madeleine began all her letters to Pál. She ends them with *ton petit bateau* (your little boat).

The endearments are significant. On a scrap of paper from that period my father has written the refrain of the song . . . and then, in Hungarian, he plays around with the words:

I know a man who has never, never gone out to sea.
He stood in the dirty harbor and wished for infinity.
He wished for a little ship that he could steer, far, far away. . . .

But the little ship did not have the courage
To face the big, big waves
Because it had never been on the sea
Ohé, ohé! Called the sailors to the little ship. . .

Then there are the drawings, pencil sketches on cheap paper, which reveal more than his words. They have a yearning, melancholic quality. A sailor sits in the bow of a ship named *Desire* and stares into the water. Beneath the surface is a woman.

There are sketches of a muscular, broad-shouldered man; a bold sailor. His shirtless back is toward us and we do not see his face. He looks over the rooftops of a town, as if he owns it . . . and yet there is something wrong with the composition: in the pictures his legs are cut off at the knees by the edge of the paper.

The same shirtless figure reappears in several sketches with a woman sitting on a bed, who resembles my mother. He holds out his hand like a beggar asking for alms. The pockets of his pants are turned out, showing that he is penniless. In juxtaposition with the female figure the male figure is diminished—no longer hulking and muscular, but an awkward teenager, standing stiffly.

I think my father never meant for these sketches to be seen by anyone. It would be easy to infer too much; to reduce him to a boy with an Oedipal complex; an unresolved desire for his lost mother. But the pictures are haunting.

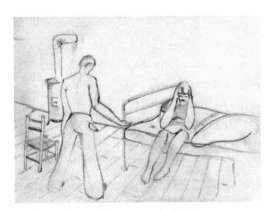

Pál Weidlinger, Three Untitled Sketches, *1936.*

8. ART AND BEAUTY

In his interview with me, my father confessed that after five or six weeks in London he was at his wits' end. He sat on the bed in his room at No. 3 Bedford Square and leafed through the pages of the London telephone directory. Having nothing else to do he occupied himself with a pencil, filling in the "o"s in people's names. He came across a name with three "o"s, László Moholy-Nagy. It was a Hungarian name that Pál had heard before—someone, it seemed, involved with design. Perhaps this was the sign he was waiting for.

Pál didn't telephone. He figured his chances were better if he showed up in person. So he wrote down the address and spent his last pennies to take the tube from his boarding house near the British Museum to the Belsize Park station in Hampstead. From there he walked to the building in which Moholy lived, which looked "just like a giant ocean liner which ought to have a couple of funnels."

I rang the bell and he said, "What do you want?" I said, "I'm Hungarian!" And he slammed the door in my face. Then he must have felt embarrassed, and he opened it and again said, "What do you want?" And I said I was looking for work. And he said, "Well, what can you do?" And I said I was the best draftsman in the whole world, and he said, "Well, come back after lunch." And then I walked around for two hours and came back, and he gave me a job.

My father's life would have turned out quite differently had he not had the great good fortune to discover Moholy in London and then act on his instinct. Between the young man and the older one there was a shared cultural experience and a way of facing the world with a mix of defiance and optimism.

Moholy was a twentieth-century Renaissance man, versatile, charismatic and accomplished in many fields, though he would have hated the term Renaissance because it derives from a past historical period. By the time Pál knocked on his door, Moholy already had an international reputation as a painter, sculptor, typographer, designer, photographer, and filmmaker. He was also an essayist, lecturer, and social critic.

For five years in the 1920s, Moholy-Nagy taught the foundation course at the Bauhaus School in Germany. Out of the school grew a philosophy, a way of approaching issues in art, craft, design, and architecture that reverberated throughout the twentieth century. The 1919 founding proclamation of Bauhaus was the Modernists' call to arms:

Let us then create a new guild of craftsmen without the class distinctions that raise an arrogant barrier between craftsman and artist! Together let us desire, conceive, and create the new structure of the future, which will embrace architecture and sculpture and painting in one unity and which will one day rise toward heaven from the hands of a million workers like the crystal symbol of a new faith.

Moholy collaborated with the founder of the Bauhaus, the German architect Walter Gropius, on fourteen books, which applied their philosophy to the entire range of creative and productive endeavors. Stating this philosophy, Moholy wrote:

A human being is developed only by the crystallization of the sum total of his experiences. Our present system of education contradicts this axiom by stressing preponderantly a single field of application. Instead of extending our milieu, as the primitive man was forced to do, combining as he did in one person; hunter, craftsman, builder, physician, etc., we concern ourselves only with one definite occupation—leaving unused other faculties.

Moholy exhorted his students not to be intimidated by "tradition and the voice of authority" or specialists who, "like members of a powerful secret society," obscure the path to authentic individual instinct and creativity. This was balm to young Pál's soul. He had audaciously thought of himself as an artist, a poet, a social activist, an architect, and an engineer. After his struggle with the career-track dictates of the Swiss polytechnic, the Bauhaus view of the interrelatedness of art and technology was profoundly liberating.

There were other things, experiences that had shaped Moholy's life, which seemed synchronous yet different from the Weidlinger family history. Like my grandmother, Júlia, Moholy had become gravely ill in the Spanish flu epidemic of 1918, but he survived. Like Andor, Moholy had been a soldier in the Great War. Unlike Andor, Moholy had directly experienced the carnage of war. Using colored pencils and crayons, he sketched intimate scenes of life in the trenches on the backs of military-issued postcards. He made portraits of peasants in their fields in Galicia and of his wounded comrades in hospitals.

Sergeant Moholy-Nagy's postcards echoed the creative voices of artists, writers, and photographers who had turned their attention to the plight of Hungary's dispossessed. It is not surprising, then, that right after the war, Moholy joined the Communist Party and supported Béla Kun's Hungarian Soviet Republic.

To the teenage Red Students of Budapest, including my father, Moholy could have been an icon. It was precisely his fellow travelers, Hungarian communists who had fled to Moscow (and who, in 1932, had made the mistake of returning to Budapest), whom my father and his schoolmates were petitioning to save from execution. Fortunately, Moholy had fled to Vienna. He would most certainly have been killed in the White Terror, the monarchists' counterrevolution, had he not had the good sense to do so.

Another synchronicity is that Moholy had worked on special effects for a science-fiction movie produced by our putative relative Alexander Korda. *Things to Come* was one of the flops that had put Korda temporarily out of business, but it is possible that Pál found it playing in a London cinema in 1937. The film depicts an alternate world history, diverging from reality in the 1930s and ending in the year 2106. A devastating plague wipes out most of humanity, but out of civilization's wreckage an elite fraternity of engineers and mechanics build a utopian society. "The brotherhood of efficiency! The freemasonry of science!" proclaims Cabal, the engineers' leader, when speaking to the denizens of a ruined city called Everytown. I can see Pál taking pleasure in the idea of a utopia built by engineers.

Things to Come *poster and special effects props created by László Moholy-Nagy.*

For all these reasons, when Moholy opened the door to his London flat to young Pál in March 1937, there was a mutual feeling of déjà vu, a recognition of shared history and ideals. Pál had found a mentor. He wrote to Ili:

I am starting again to hope. Moholy is so unbelievably kind. I really like working for him, although his studio is a madhouse. It is full of fantastic pictures and models. Moholy himself puts his sentences together in three languages: Hungarian, German, and English, and so it is very difficult to understand his complicated thought processes. Despite this, I consider him an exceptionally smart person. What is truly unique is he is also exceptionally honest. I am only now beginning to see how well-known he is. He just had an exhibit of his paintings in London and one at the Constructivists' exhibit in Basel. Just yesterday he was invited to give a lecture in Oxford. Meanwhile, he makes films, designs posters and exhibits, and works on his inventions.

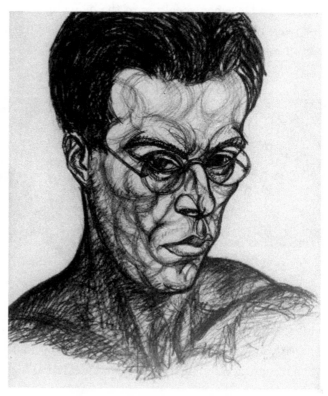

László Moholy-Nagy, self-portrait, 1920.

Moholy was a refugee from fascist Germany. In 1934 he had been ordered to submit three of his paintings for censorship by the Reich's Chamber of Culture. In 1935, when he arrived in London, Nazi denunciations of modern art and architecture reached their height. The fascists mounted "instructive" exhibitions in which Modernist paintings were hung next to photographs of deformed and diseased human beings. The message was: "Modernism is a sickness."

I wonder if this is what Pál's poem, "The Ballad of the Sick," referenced earlier, is about. Perhaps it was more than just adolescent nihilism.

But they [The Sick] just hate in secret
As their souls grow cold, their blood goes white,
Panting for vengeance against the great society of the Healthy.
The secret organization of the Sick will rise up,
And throw a bomb amid the Healthy.
Crutches will turn into rifles, thermometers into bayonets,
Sickbeds will become tanks and their dying desires will be
reborn. . . .

Whatever the case, once Pál got the job with Moholy, he didn't have much time for poetry. He worked principally as a draftsman on commercial projects. At that point, Moholy was designing posters for the London Transport System and designing window displays, Modernist dioramas, for the menswear store Simpson's of Piccadilly. There was also a commission from a travel agency, which Pál was immediately put to work on.

He had this idea of making a big head out of neon, and out of the brain these ideas would come . . . of travel. He came to me and said, "Well, Master Pál, I want you to draw a brain machine now." Then he walked out. I was so depressed because I thought, "Jesus Christ! Everybody probably knows what a brain machine is except me." Kepes was sitting across the room and he was laughing! (György Kepes, another Hungarian, who became a famous design theorist and a lifelong friend of Pál's.)

Pál had been working for Moholy for about three months when he wrote an incredibly long and convoluted letter to Madeleine. He made several drafts, which is why it's one of the few he wrote to her that has survived. It is a manifesto on art and beauty.

> *My little darling, here is the letter I promised you. It was an easy promise to make, but I don't think it will be so easy to keep it. I want to tell you all of my thoughts on Art and Beauty so that you will give it as much thought as I have and then tell me later whether or not you agree with me. I want to approach things the way one would a revolution; by this I mean tearing down the old—whether it be buildings or ideologies—and then constructing a new world in the ruins.*

There follows a passionate treatise in which twenty-three-year-old Pál denounces Plato and Kant as the allies of bourgeois capitalists. He rejects the idea of a divine constant underlying all that we perceive as beautiful. He offers instead the Marxist view that beauty is only an idea that stems from the ideology of a particular time and place. This is important because those who shape the ideology of an era—writers, artists, and architects—can enlist art in the service of that ideology and in so doing guide the world toward a brighter future. Wading through the dialectical twists and turns of my father's arguments, I imagine a cartoon in which a classical Greek sculpture (representing Timeless Beauty) and a cathedral's stained-glass window (representing the Divine Constant) give way to visuals of the sleek functionality of the industrial age, culminating in an apotheosis of Soviet propaganda posters.

———————

To use one of my father's favorite words, there is something touchingly naïve about his letter, as if the entire history of mankind's creative endeavor could be summed up so simply. Yet it is important to understand that Pál was writing his letter to his beloved in a time of manifestos—increasingly urgent calls to action as the shadow of fascism spread across Europe. There was nothing that was not political, not art, and not beauty. In the Europe of the 1930s, there was no space in which to be simply "an artist" or "an architect."

Pál's mentor, Moholy-Nagy, echoes this in his own writings. To Moholy machines are beautiful, and it is from them one should take inspiration because of their pure functionality. There is also a rationality to machines that do the work they were designed to do: a sewing machine, a water pump, a locomotive. . . . Their simple predictability was a comforting antidote to the social dysfunction that appeared to be tearing the world apart. Moholy, writing in the journal *Today: Activist Art and Social Issues*, declares:

> *To be a user of machines is to be the spirit of this century. It has replaced the transcendental spiritualism of past eras. Everyone is equal before the machine. I can use it, so can you. It can crush me; the same can happen to you. There is no tradition in technology; no class consciousness. Everyone can be the machine's master or its slave.*
>
> *This is the root of socialism, the final liquidation of feudalism. It is the machine that woke up the proletariat. . . . This is our century: technology, machine, socialism. Make your peace with it; shoulder its task.*

There is one machine that my father relished explaining to my mother: the lift that carried passengers from the ground to the second stage of the Eiffel Tower.

During 1937 my parents met for romantic weekends in Paris when they could scrape together the train fare. Pál came from London via the Dover–Calais ferry; Madeleine came from Zurich. They made love in a Left Bank pension and visited the Eiffel Tower on a Sunday, when lift tickets were discounted.

In a photograph Madeleine appears self-possessed in her white trench coat, while Pál seems to be trying to match her long-legged stride. They bought paper cones of hot roasted chestnuts from a street

Pál and Madeleine in Paris.

vendor on the steps of the Trocadéro. Then Pál explained the workings of the *Fives-Lille* elevators installed in the east and west piers of the tower in the year 1900. Designed by my great-uncle Dezső Korda (who was both a mechanical and an electrical engineer), each was powered by a gigantic hydraulic cylinder that animated a system of cables, sheaves, and counterweights. It was part elevator and part inclined railway, since it did not just rise vertically but followed the curvature of the tower's legs. The elevators incorporated the elegant feature of self-leveling cabins, which automatically adjusted as the pitch of the ascent changed. While the tower's original American Otis elevators were removed, Uncle Dezső's machines remained in use until the 1980s.

To those seated in the lift car, rising diagonally at a rate of 400 feet per minute, a majestic view of Paris opens up as the steel latticework of the tower's western leg sweeps past and falls away. In 1937, looking northwest, across the Seine, was a miniature city within a city. "The International Exposition of Art and Technology in Modern Life" was an ambitious World's Fair, with pavilions showcasing every type of commodity and activity. The organizers of the Paris Exposition embraced the audacious idea that it was possible to create a model of *modern* and future civilization in one place and time.

For a young man trying to formulate his own unified theory of beauty and art, this had a profound resonance. Pál wrote a long and detailed critique of the Paris Exposition's pavilions and its overarching concept. Written in Hungarian (instead of the German he had used for school papers), it is a letter to countrymen who are unable to make the journey to Paris. In this my father was also following in his uncle's footsteps. When Dezső Korda was twenty-five, he had written a critique of the Paris Exposition 1889 for the *Review* of the Hungarian Engineers' and Architects' Association.

Pál's account of the 1937 Expo is circumspect and scholarly, yet it does not hide his excitement. "Nowhere else does an architect have so much space to experiment with new building materials," he wrote. "We admired colorful *thermolux* and *vitrex* glass in metal frames in the Czech architectural exhibition," as well as the use of "fiber-cement" in the Swiss Pavilion, opaline glass panels in the French pavilion of Saint-Gobain, and see-through *rhodoïd* (cellulose acetate plastic) incorporated into the aeronautics pavilion.

But stepping back to take in the whole experience, Pál observed that instead of a world exhibition of art and technology, the Expo was more a marketplace of each nation's commodities.

It was also an arena into which were projected the warring ideologies of the era. Two monumental buildings, the Soviet and German pavilions, faced each other across the broad avenue that stretched northwest from the base of the Eiffel Tower. It appeared that the principal function of the Soviet Pavilion was to serve as a plinth for a six-story statue of a male factory worker and thinly draped woman farm worker, raising a hammer and sickle between them. Opposite this colossus, Hitler's architect, Albert Speer, had built a fifteen-story tower in a severe classical style, topped by an eagle on a swastika. The monumental nature of both structures was designed to frighten and belittle the onlooker, and they succeeded in doing so.

So what did young Pál have to say about these pavilions? Ignoring the forms as symbols of power, he judged them by their functional-

A postcard from the 1937 Paris Exposition. The German Pavilion, (left), faces the Soviet Pavilion, on the right.

ity, the way people were led to move through the space. About the German building he wrote.

> *A tower without proportions reaches up to the sky. Inside the whole exhibition is one big room, too narrow for its height and length. It is illuminated with lamps which stand like soldiers and chandeliers that were fashionable in petit bourgeois salons twenty years ago. The objects of the exhibition are displayed in shop-keepers' glass cases arranged in long straight lines. The dominant design is of a boring neatness and symmetry that is truly dismal.*
>
> *The Russian exhibition, just across the street, is also quite terrible as an architectural work. Here are chaos and confusion. The building's front facade is as high as the German tower, but the structure diminishes, in stages, toward the back.*

This doesn't make sense because the ceiling of the interior space rises in the opposite direction. The walls are covered with pictures, most of them quite bad. While in other pavilions the promotional effects of a few big companies give the sense of a commodities market, here in the Soviet Pavilion one feels that a whole nation is being advertised.

For anyone who cared to see, the Soviet and German pavilions were the heralds, in glass and stone, of the coming World War. But war had already broken out in Spain. German warplanes sent by Hitler to support the Nationalist forces bombed the defenseless civilian population of the town of Guernica on April 26, 1937. Pablo Picasso, who had been working on a mural for the Spanish Pavilion, abandoned his original idea and began his "Guernica," arguably the most important artistic statement on war in the twentieth century. With Picasso's huge mural as its centerpiece, Spain's pavilion became the platform for the Loyalist government's plea to the world to stand against the fascists.

Pál liked the Modernist architecture of the Spanish Pavilion but mentions only the existence of "a fresco by Picasso decorating the wall in the hall of the first floor." By contrast he is deeply intrigued by a gigantic square tent devoted to the theme of modern city planning, called the Pavilion of New Times. The tent-pavilion was the work of the architects Pierre Jeanneret and Le Corbusier.

Le Corbusier, who was perhaps the most famous architect living at that time, proclaimed that if architecture could be wrested from the styles and dictates of the past, it could save the world. His book, *Toward a New Architecture*, was *the* manifesto of Modernism. Like Moholy-Nagy, Le Corbusier saw the pure functionality of machines (including steamships and airplanes) as models for architecture. Hence his oft-quoted declaration: "A house is a machine for living in."

Artist, architect, city planner, visionary, and iconoclast, Le Corbusier was sometimes called "Pope Corbu." Some felt he was a megalomaniacal crackpot. In 1932, when France announced its plan for the '37 Expo, Le Corbusier proclaimed his intention to stage an alternative exposition, the International Exhibition of Modern Dwelling. Le

Corbusier's idea for a utopian city complex was a grand fantasy that would have required the demolition of a vast swath of historical Paris.

It's a measure of Le Corbusier's status among Modernists that the official Exposition's planners, instead of cutting him loose, offered him 500,000 francs to build a modest, temporary building. After months of jockeying for a permanent edifice and a bigger budget, Le Corbusier finally accepted his partner Pierre Jeanneret's more realistic proposal for a large building with canvas walls. Inside would be what Le Corbusier called "*un grand livre des images*" (a big book of images)—pictures, plans, blueprints and text that promoted the architect's vision of the utopian city of the future.

Pál wrote about the Pavilion of New Times:

The building is ideal for an exhibition like this. It is light, economical, and easy to install and disassemble. The first impression a visitor gets is of spaciousness. Light filters through the canvas walls. The shadows of trees surrounding the tent animate the space. One does not feel cut off from the outside world.

Here Le Corbusier lays out the four functions of city planning—"Habitation, Transportation, Work, Leisure"—in a convincing way. Going up a ramp one passes images and blueprints offering solutions. The visitor can see both the plans and the finished works of Le Corbusier and his colleagues, as well as the results of analytical work on cities around the world.

As we ascend the ramp we are drawn more deeply into these topics. There's a clever correlation between one's position on the ramp and one's depth of exposure and understanding. The blueprints, models, and montages are presented with the precision and beauty Le Corbusier is known for.

Pál was less impressed by the ideological content of Le Corbusier's big book of images, which he called "obviously utopian, mistaken, and full of false economic arguments."

The Pavilion of New Times at the 1937 Paris Exposition.

9. WORKING FOR GOD

Pál worked happily for Moholy-Nagy for a year. Then Moholy received an offer to move to Chicago to start the new Bauhaus American School of Design. He generously offered to take Pál with him. It was an incredible opportunity, but my father refused. When I pressed him he said merrily:

> *Who the hell wanted to go to an uncivilized country like America? And Chicago? I had this vision of a gangster city. I felt so sorry for them!*

Graciously, Moholy-Nagy then offered Pál a letter of recommendation to Le Corbusier. What aspiring young architect could resist a chance to sit and learn at Pope Corbu's feet? Well, my father, for one.

> *I said to him [Moholy] I didn't want to go to work there because I heard that he [Le Corbusier] would probably never even talk to me. And then Moholy said something very sensible. He said, "Doesn't matter. You go there. Maybe he will never talk to you,*

but you will be there in that atmosphere, and you will see other people doing things, and just breathe in the air and it will be good for you."

Because Pál seemed programmed to do the opposite of anything that was proposed, he did not immediately act on this advice. Instead he found another job in London making good money. He and Madeleine began to discuss the possibility that she would quit her job and join him.

This was in February and March of 1938. On March 11, Hitler annexed Austria. In Vienna, the city where six-year-old Pál had gone to have his hair dyed blond, nightmarish scenes unfolded. A *New York Times* correspondent, G.E.R. Gedye, wrote about what he saw:

A brown flood was sweeping though the streets. It was an indescribable Sabbath: Storm troopers, lots of them barely out of the schoolroom, hooting furiously, marching side by side with police turncoats, men and women shrieking the name of their leader, embracing the police and dragging them along in the swirling stream of humanity . . . men and women . . . shouting and dancing in the light of smoking torches. . . . The air filled with a pandemonium of sound in which in the intermingled screams of "Down with the Jews! Heil Hitler! Sieg Heil!" and "Perish the Jews!" could be discerned. "Today we have Germany; tomorrow we have the world."

In the following weeks, Viennese mobs looted Jewish shops and businesses and forced their way into private apartments to "requisition" money, jewels, furs, and furniture. Jewish men and women, young and old, were dragged from their homes to participate in *Reibaktionen* or "scrub parties," in which they were forced to go down on their hands and knees to remove anti-fascist political slogans from the pavements of the city. Victims were sometimes made to scrub the pavements with toothbrushes for the amusement of their tormentors.

Tens of thousands of Jews tried to flee from Austria and Germany. Anticipating a flood, England tightened restrictions on immigration and moved to deport illegals already within her borders. In London, British immigration authorities finally caught up with Pál. His visa had expired. He was given forty-eight hours to leave the country. He went to Paris and Le Corbusier.

Most young architects who worked for Le Corbusier were not paid. They came from all over the world for the privilege of sitting at the drafting tables in the long narrow room of the atelier at 35 rue de Sèvres. My father insisted that some actually paid Le Corbusier for the privilege of being his disciple. But thanks to Moholy-Nagy's introduction, he was invited to breathe the air in "God's" office for free.

Le Corbusier photographed by Ida Kar.

He moved to Paris in early April 1938 and found a room at a flophouse called Hôtel des Colonies at 20 rue Oudinot. It was a fifteen-minute walk on the Left Bank to Le Corbusier's office, located in a disused wing of a Jesuit monastery.

Le Corbusier's collaborators in the studio at 35 rue de Sèvres in Paris.

To get to the second-floor atelier, one had to pass the scrutiny of a suspicious concierge and climb a dark staircase. At the head of the staircase one encountered an enigmatic symbol, a modernist's glyph. Red, hand-painted letters on a hand-shaped blue metal plaque read *Atelier Le Corbusier*. A door opened onto a long, narrow, high-ceilinged room flooded with light from windows that overlooked the monastery courtyard. The space was only wide enough for a single row of a dozen drafting tables, each with its own black, adjustable lamp clamped to the work surface. A large stove was situated in the middle of the room. Every horizontal surface was covered with plans and drawings.

Le Corbusier was not an easy man to work for. He was quick to anger and could get nasty in a sarcastic way when someone misunderstood his instructions or failed to grasp a concept. He kept to a rigid schedule, working at home in the mornings and arriving at the atelier at two o'clock every afternoon. Jerzy Sołtan, a young Polish architect who worked there for four years, wrote:

> *Every day, just before his appearance, a cloud of panic hovered over the atelier. . . . He brought from home new ideas, new*

sketches, new notes. They were not easy to decipher. Corbu had the ability to communicate clearly . . . but he also had his own sense of how much information to give, where to stop. The sketches at some point became fuzzy . . . a sign that they represented more his digging into the subconscious, his guessing, than a finished proposal. He would pass them on to us with a mischievous smile. . . . The role of the team was then to interpret, clarify, and present the concept for his scrutiny in a precise graphic form, sometimes as a model. The more intuitive his thoughts, the more difficult it became to decipher his notes.

My father's ability to decipher Le Corbusier was further compromised by his poor grasp of French. One day the master forgot his pipe on the edge of Pál's drafting table. Pál mistakenly assumed that his boss wanted him to draw the pipe, which he did with great care and precision. We have no clue as to the master's response.

The short period, April to August 1938, during which Pál worked at the atelier did not coincide with the production of any of Le Corbusier's great works. It was a bleak time for Modernism. Le Corbusier, Moholy-Nagy, and Gropius were under attack in the fascists' propaganda war, and most of the work at the rue de Sèvres consisted of proposals rather than paid commissions. The two Le Corbusier projects that Pál worked on were a fifty-story skyscraper planned for Algiers and a city planning project that involved the reconfiguration of municipal structures and roadways converging at a bridge in Boulogne-sur-Seine, a western suburb of Paris.

At the same time, the atelier was occupied with the design of a model house to be installed in London's Ideal Home annual exhibition and a prototype for a children's board game to be marketed in Europe and the United States. The game, called *Ville Radieuse* (Radiant City), was a utopian Monopoly. It was based on Le Corbusier's great vision for a city that would hold its inhabitants in a well-ordered environment. The city drew upon the shape of the human body, with a head, spine, arms, and legs; humans living in a city shaped in their own image. The city included high-rise housing blocks perched on columns, or *pilotis*, with abundant green space and pedestrian paths. Le Corbusier never got to realize his plans for a utopian city, but perhaps, one day, children would roll their dice and move their markers on its colorful map and become inspired.

As we shall see, Pál did not unquestioningly accept Le Corbusier's utopian notions, but the master and his acolyte did have a couple of things in common. 1) They both wore perfectly round eyeglasses. 2) They shared a belief in solitary intellectual heroics. As a young man, Le Corbusier had been deeply influenced by Friedrich Nietzsche's philosophical drama *Thus Spoke Zarathustra*. In the book a prophet descends from his mountain cave to foretell the coming of the Superman *(Übermensch)*, a being free from all the prejudices and moralities of human society, a being who creates his own values and purpose. This Superman is a rugged loner. He must destroy conventional order and wisdom before he can realize his own revolutionary genius. He may be an enlightened captain of industry, using his wealth and power for the betterment of mankind. He may be a scientific prodigy or even an engineer, like the hero in Korda's science fiction film, *Things to Come*, who has made it his task to redesign the cities of the world.

The Superman's struggle is often symbolized as climbing a mountain. I am reminded of Pál's drawings from his early, lonely days in London: the muscular, broad-shouldered giant who looks over the rooftops of a town. My father did become a sort of *Übermensch*, and not only in his own mind. Many years later, young engineers who worked for him called him "The Wizard."

10. THE JOY OF SPACE

While at Le Corbusier's atelier, Pál was working out his own ideas about architecture. Scribbling in cafés and on park benches on long summer evenings and weekends, he wrote a rambling manifesto. Its introduction is a call to battle, rising to a crescendo of righteousness.

> *After much study and little experience, one already has a few thoughts about architecture and enough qualifications to express them. Perhaps the soft voice of the inexperienced may now be allowed to join the deep bass voices of the authorities? After you have heard it, you will say: This voice is dissonant! Possibly! But it is after all a very soft voice and does not wish to disturb.*
>
> *We see the starkest struggle of two irreconcilable worldviews in the history of people. Victory belongs to an advanced movement, far-reaching and battle-tested, which is built on thinking freed from useless traditions. But it is not yet definite. Our buildings that reach for the sky, our airy constructions, our bridges that float bravely over their gorges—a "harsh reality" could still shatter them all. Then, instead of sunlit houses rising up out of*

the ruins, we might find dark cellars and palaces bursting with
gold and silver. We must, as never before in history, feel our
bond in this struggle along with the compulsion to take a stance.

Though Pál shared with Le Corbusier the idea that architecture could improve, even save society, he questioned the architect's vision for mass-produced housing. He rejected the credo that "a house is a machine for living." Working out his own theory in juxtaposition to Le Corbusier's, he came up with an idea that was both transcendent and truly radical for its time. But he only arrived at this idea at the end of a long and tortured journey.

To begin with, Pál was trained to write in the incredibly long-winded and obsequious German academic style, in which one must bow, scrape, and tip one's hat to every recognized theory in the field before making one's own modest contribution to the discourse. Pál was naturally influenced by Marxist thought and by the Modernism of his mentors, Moholy-Nagy and Le Corbusier, but he was also deeply enmeshed in the *anti-philosophical* philosophical movement of Logical Positivism. The Logical Positivists (known also as the Vienna Circle) were a humorless bunch who wanted to "erect a unified structure of science in which all knowledge would be built up from logical strings of basic experiential propositions." According to Logical Positivists, language should be cleansed of "ornaments," all metaphor and subjective impressions. Each sentence should be "proven." This anti-philosophy had a huge impact on the disciples of the Bauhaus school of architecture. A new house should be purely the product of rational science(s), the synthesis of work done by economists, statisticians, hygienists, climatologists, and engineers. The architect became a kind of rationalist traffic cop, concerned with organization and coordination of the myriad disciplines brought to bear on the problem of creating dwellings for human beings.

Pál laid out this view but then challenged it.

Let us build a building with a floor plan that works well; its
construction is perfect, its colors and proportions are pleasing.

It can be a model for mass production. Experts do the design, builders erect the structure, and "artists" are brought in to beautify it.

This is familiar, we know it well. We also know that it is not right. The result is merely a concatenation of rooms. There is something missing. What is missing is the creation of space (Raumgestaltung).

What is this "creation of space" that young Pál insisted is an essential part of the package? In attempting to define it, he went to great lengths to avoid using unprovable subjective language, language that is unacceptable in the system of Logical Positivism. Yet he finally surrendered and declared:

The only common characteristic in the creations of modern architecture is a highly enhanced level of spatial experience, a joy of space.

In architecture we experience relationships in space. This experience is both active and passive at the same time: We move through the space and experience its effect upon us. The clearest form of spatial experience is dance. It is space creation done with the simplest methods.

Three simple words: joy of space. A mysterious experience that defies measurement, classification, and deconstruction. It is one thing to build a house that is perfectly functional. It is something else to build a house that is perfectly functional and, at the same time, elicits a sense of well-being and joy through the arrangement of its volumes. This is something that industry cannot produce, something that requires the spatial intuition of the architect responding to a unique set of circumstances. It follows that architecture is more an art than a science, since it must relate and respond to unquantifiable human experience. Pál conceded that some "prototypical characteristics of humans can be defined, but individual instances do not always conform to collective definitions." Therefore "the architect must always deal with the *individuum* (from Latin, meaning the unique, individual instance). In fact, it seems unlikely that architecture will ever become an exact science." Pál seemed almost apologetic that, in the end, architecture cannot be described as a pure science; a conclusion that would be so much more compliant with the absolutist anti-philosophy of Logical Positivism or the pure, machine-inspired functionalism of Le Corbusier's "A house is a machine for living in."

Pál rejected this formula. With his idea of the "joy of space," he asserted that great architecture needed to embrace the indefinable and convey an expansive sense of freedom.

11. PARALLEL LIVES

BUDAPEST, PARIS AND ZURICH,
APRIL–SEPTEMBER 1938

Pál was broke, since Le Corbusier paid nothing. In Paris he shared a room with his cousin Bandi (Endre Sebestyén), who was equally poor. In the three years since they'd been students together in Brünn, Bandi's ongoing commitment to the underground communist movement in Hungary had got him into serious trouble. He had been arrested and beaten several times while in police custody, in an effort to make him betray his comrades. He did not talk. But as a criminal who had committed "crimes against the state" he was barred from getting a job in Hungary as an engineer. Then he tried to enlist in the fight against the fascists in Spain. He came to Paris because it was the recruitment center for the communists' International Brigade. But joining up was not easy. To be accepted one had to have bona fides from the Communist Party and be interviewed by a Soviet NKVD agent. I don't know why Bandi was not accepted, but it is how he came to share a room in Paris with Pál. Not only did they share the room, they shared a razor and slept head-to-toe on a narrow, single bed.

I wonder what their relationship was like. Bandi was a true believer, a hero for not breaking under torture, and willing to give

Cousin Endre Sebestyén (Bandi) and Pál in Paris, 1939.

his life for the cause in Spain. In contrast, Pál's involvement with the movement was a student's infatuation. Did Pál look up to Bandi? During the day, Bandi rode around the city on a bicycle and scrounged used spark plugs while Pál worked at the atelier. In the evenings they would clean and polish the plugs so Bandi could resell them for a few sous. Then they lost their room. My father said to me:

> *It was an odd sort of life because I had a job from eight to five, and then I had no place to go. Sounds grim but it wasn't. I had a terrific life. Sometimes I found places. I remember I knew a girl who owned a dance studio, and sometimes she would let me sleep there, except that it was so cold, it was colder than outside. Because outside on the street I could find a grate, which was warmer.*

Once in a while Madeleine took the train from Zurich to spend a weekend in Paris, but for Pál, entering into a serious commitment, morganatic or otherwise, seemed less and less possible. In one of Madeleine's letters she expressed relief at the arrival of her period, having feared she was pregnant. They both felt the precariousness of their situation.

> *I couldn't imagine that I could ever earn a living. I mean just surviving was such an unlikely thing for me. I thought if I get married, I'm going to support my wife and we'll have children. I just couldn't imagine that. It didn't look feasible.*

Overshadowing everything was the news of Republican defeats in Spain and the continuing panic resulting from Germany's annexation of Austria. Hitler's aggression seemed to threaten all of Europe as France and England followed a policy of appeasement.

In May Madeleine wrote to Pál that she was ashamed of her pleasure in viewing the just-released film *Olympia*. The documentary about the 1936 Berlin Olympics used sweeping, dynamic camera moves never before attempted in a nonfiction film. It was also a masterpiece of fascist propaganda. Madeleine observed: "It shows the effort of each nation to be the strongest, not merely in sport, but way beyond that." To see such strength and beauty edited to a symphonic score in the service of the Nazi creed was chilling.

Meanwhile in Vienna, in the weeks following the Anschluss, thousands of Jews flooded the US Consulate seeking immigration visas. Only a few hundred had the remotest chance of succeeding. The total annual quota for Austrian immigrants to the United States stood at 1,413.

In Paris Pál went to the US Consulate and submitted an Application for Registration as an Immigrant. The "uncivilized country" was starting to look pretty good. On the application he listed Edmund Bokor, a cousin in Chicago (the city of gangsters), as his nearest friend or relative in the United States. On May 28 he wrote a letter to Bokor. Bokor replied:

When you get your quota number, we will do our best to get you brought out. Your father sent the data requested, and if you arrange the issue on your part, we may obtain the papers within one week. . . .

Pál also got some less encouraging advice from Marcel Breuer, whom he had met in London. Breuer was a Hungarian architect and furniture designer who had immigrated to the United States a year earlier to teach at Harvard with Walter Gropius. "As far as I know," wrote Breuer, "the Hungarian [immigration] quota is full for years."

———————————

The telling of Pál's story becomes more complicated at this point. It divides into two strands, two concurrent narratives. The first concerns the adventures of Pál during the war years. The second is the story of our relatives in Budapest during the same period. I pieced together the latter only recently from my interview with Little Pál and the discovery and translation of letters written to my father from Andor, Rózsa, and Lulu.

Because Pál was not in Budapest, what happened to our Hungarian family did not happen to him. But I believe he was haunted by the knowledge of their experience, and that this influenced many of the choices he made in his life.

On the same day that Pál wrote to Bokor asking him to sponsor his immigration to the United States, the Hungarian government enacted the first of four anti-Semitic laws. It stated that "for the sake of economic and social balance, certain white-collar professions," including architects and engineers, could only be practiced by those who belonged to a professional chamber. The number of Jews in a professional chamber could not exceed twenty percent.

In Hungary every citizen had to document their origins so that Jews could be distinguished from non-Jews. To facilitate this process, government offices waived customary fees for copies of birth, marriage, and death certificates. The birth certificates for Andor, Rózsa, and Lulu that Little Pál showed to me were issued during this period.

In spite of this, in the summer of 1938, most Hungarian Jews believed that the sanctions against them would never reach the extremes of laws in Germany and Austria, which had already stripped Jews of the rights of citizenship, completely banned them from many professions, and severely limited their freedom of movement.

My grandfather was not so sure. The first Hungarian anti-Semitic law must have impeded his ability to do business, and he was worried enough to plan an escape route for the family should it become necessary. He understood that an effective strategy depended on having a place to go just as nations all over the world were shutting their doors.

There is a photograph of Andor, Rózsa, and Lulu sitting around a table with Mr. and Mrs. Alan Robertson, Australians who had agreed to act as sponsors for the family's immigration to their country. Robertson was a young architect who had befriended my father in London. He asked Pál for someone he could contact in Hungary while on an architectural tour of European cities. Andor became his guide to Budapest, and Robertson became the family's sponsor to Australia.

From left: unidentified man, Alan Robertson and his wife,
Lulu, Rózsa (behind Lulu on opposite side of the table),
Andor, and two unidentified men.

Meanwhile in Paris, Pál's days were numbered. The French immi-gration authorities had already taken an interest in Bandi, and it was only a matter of time before he would be deported. Pál figured he would be next. Le Corbusier gave him a few introductions and he wrote letters to architects in New Zealand, Mexico, Argentina, and Uruguay, countries where he assumed he might be able to get a visa. He also wrote to Madeleine proposing the idea that they immigrate together to South America. She responded:

> *My dear companion, my great friend . . . I didn't answer your letter immediately because I needed to give the whole situa-tion a lot of thought. . . . Dearest, I would like to tell you now that I am in total agreement with you and completely ready to emigrate with you as soon as possible. You see, dearest, I am ready for anything. The thought of being with you forever gives me courage and strength. I am so happy. I am happier than I have been for a long time.*
>
> *I don't feel sad or disillusioned about all of these things at all. On the contrary. I am still quite hopeful that you won't give up your career. Or perhaps just for a short time. I am so convinced that you truly have a lot of talent.*

Then, in Paris, the inevitable happened. The police caught up with Pál, and he had to leave France and Le Corbusier. What to do next? Madeleine wrote:

> *I have to tell you right away, dearest, that everything looks so damned uncertain, nothing at all positive about it, and I wait and don't know how to get started. I have a strange feeling, one that tells me that we should not stay in Europe. I am afraid of the war, and if the war comes, then I will become so small, lost, and powerless.*

Pál went to her in Zurich and, for the first time, they moved in together, sharing a flat with a friend. Feeling uncharacteristically homesick, Pál wrote to Budapest asking for the recipe of his favorite goulash soup.

I remember sending an express letter home to my parents asking them for the recipe. And I got this very indignant letter from my father and he said, "You don't have a passport, you don't know what you're going to do, you don't know where to go, and you are worried about the recipe!" [Laughing.] And that was about the shape of things.

It may have been Pál's evident unconcern about his life's circumstances that prompted Andor and Rózsa to pay him a visit in Zurich. Anticipating their arrival, Pál said, "We were so scared. Madeleine moved into Jean's (their flatmate's) room, and I pretended that Jean was my landlady." But contrary to Pál's fears, Andor and Rózsa did not disapprove of Madeleine and her working-class roots. They quite liked her.

In Zurich Pál had managed to get a job with the Swiss architect Herbert Roth, who was just putting the finishing touches on a book of case studies of Modernist buildings worldwide. In order to be able to compare and contrast these structures, Roth employed draftsmen to draw elevations of the completed buildings in a uniform style. Pál was one of these draftsmen.

But events in Europe kept drawing Pál's attention away from his drafting table. In Germany on the night of November 9, 1938, Nazis torched synagogues, vandalized Jewish homes, schools, and businesses, and killed close to one hundred Jews. In the aftermath of *Kristallnacht*, the "Night of Broken Glass," 30,000 Jewish men were arrested and sent to concentration camps. Kristallnacht marked the point at which the persecution of Jews turned violent in Germany.

Pál renewed the political contacts he had made while a student at the Polytechnic and worked with them to smuggle anti-Nazi tracts into Austria. When Pál asked Madeleine to help, she readily agreed.

As a citizen of neutral Switzerland, she was less likely to attract attention at border crossings than a Hungarian Jew.

I remember preparing her suitcase. We sewed the illegal papers into the seams and she took the train to Austria and amazingly enough, at the border, they began to search the suitcase and they found this literature, and the SS wanted to arrest her. But she was still on the Swiss side of the border and the Germans could not take her. But the Swiss authorities put her in a cell. She didn't stay very long, and the only thing I remember was while she was in jail, she knitted a pullover for me. And I had that for a long time.

Madeleine's letters to Pál showed, over and over, that she was deeply devoted to him. This devotion was not hindered by the fact that she fell in love with others, both men and women. Both she and my father wrote about one woman in particular. Her name was Lili, and I have found photographs of her in my mother's albums and among my father's papers.

Darling, I cannot imagine having a better companion than you. Lili and I spent quite a bit of time together. I already liked her when we met the first time, when you introduced her to me. Do you remember? It was at a community theater show. The more I know her, the more I admire her. Some feelings that I have in her presence remind me of feelings I had when I was with Jean-Pierre or Karl. These are hard to explain. The harmony of gestures and movements of people like them, the rhythm in the form of their body, have a calming effect on me, so much that I would never feel sad or depressed when I am with them. Can you understand that, darling? I know that feelings like this are somewhat peculiar, and are often misunderstood. This kind of admiring of a woman toward another woman is considered "unnatural."

Lili

I asked my father about this. He said:

She used to sort of fall in love with women, and then she wanted me to have them.

Tom: And did you?

Only just one time. There was this tall German blonde woman and her name was Lili. Madeleine was just absolutely in love with her, and she always arranged for me and Lili to be alone together. And she had other girlfriends like that, and she would make me want to get involved with them.

Other girlfriends? There are intimate photographs of Madeleine with other women named Ruthy, Baby, and Miquette. In one picture Madeleine holds Ruthy's head in her lap.

In the wake of *Kristallnacht*, Jews from all over the continent tried to escape the Nazi juggernaut. Leo Spitzer, a historian writing about this moment in time, compiled fragments of several letters all on one subject: "Visas! We began to live by visas day and night. When we were awake we were obsessed by visas. We talked about them all the time. Exit visas. Transit visas. Entrance visas. During the day we

Madeleine, Miquette, and Ruthy

tried to get the proper documents, approvals, stamps. At night, in bed, we tossed about and dreamed about long lines, officials, visas. Visas."

Seeking to stem the tide of refugees into Switzerland, Swiss authorities demanded that the passports of all German and Austrian Jews be stamped with the letter "J" to distinguish Jews from "regular" German nationals who would not be seeking refuge.

Then, *amaaazingly* . . . Pál got a visa to Uruguay. Among his papers is an affidavit signed by one Juan Magyar, a barber in Montevideo, who had paid 1,000 Uruguayan pesos (about $47) as a bond against his acceptance of total financial responsibility for the Hungarian immigrant Pál Weidlinger. The document seems fishy. *Magyar* translates as "Hungarian." There is no other correspondence with Mr. John Hungarian and no evidence that we are related to such a person. The visa that was supported by this affidavit turned out to be a fake.

In those days high prices were paid for forged documents that proved worthless. In 1939 hundreds of Jews crossed the Atlantic to South American ports only to discover on arrival that their documents were invalid. Refused landing, they were sent back to Europe, where many of them perished in the Holocaust.

I wonder how much Pál paid for his forged papers. In any case he was lucky. His fake visa was discovered as soon as he attempted to board a ship in Cannes. It was a disappointment but not a disaster.

A month later Andor paid the central Catholic Parish of Budapest for a document certifying that he had been baptized and become a Christian. He was one of about 100,000 Hungarian Jews who attempted to evade the restrictions of the anti-Jewish laws by "converting" to Christianity.

12. THE RUBICON

Time was running out for Jews trying to leave Europe. Most of the Gang of Thirteen, the young communist Jews who had been friends at Brünn, had returned to Budapest after completing their studies. In early 1939 they were in the habit of meeting at Kis-Ilkovics, a café and pastry shop near the Margaret Bridge. After the Anschluss and Kristallnacht, they foresaw the dangers of staying in their country. Imre Erdős, who had recently completed a tour of duty as a conscript in the Hungarian army, wrote in his memoir:

> As a freshly trained soldier, I marched off to Czechoslovakia. It was clear to me that being a Jew, they would use me as canon fodder. So our "Gang of Thirteen" (young communist engineers) decided that we wouldn't accept this role, but would rather sail to calmer waters.

Erdős ironically thanked the repressive Hungarian government for forcing Jews to leave home to seek an education abroad. They were already experienced as exiles and had become men of the world, fluent in German and other languages. The same was true in a deeper sense for Pál and Bandi, members of the Gang who were barred from returning to Hungary because of their arrest records.

But where would the gang find "calmer waters?" Bandi telephoned from Paris with an answer. Bolivia was giving visas to engineers. With no other options, and fueled by a great respect for a hero who had withstood arrest and torture in service to the underground movement, the group began preparations to go immediately. No one knew anything about where they were headed.

Meanwhile, thwarted in Cannes, Pál decided to go to the gambling tables of Monte Carlo. He believed that his math acumen, combined with a photographic memory, would enable him to transform the small sum he had saved for his trip into a fortune. But before he could put his plan to into action, Bandi tracked him down.

And we began to talk and he said, "Why don't you come with me, I'm going to Bolivia." And I said to him, "What's Bolivia?" He said, "Don't be stupid, that's the country with triangular postage stamps." This one piece of information sounded so convincing that I checked out of the hotel, went to Zurich, and told Madeleine, "I'm going to go to Bolivia and you're going to follow me there after I arrive."

Triangular postage stamps? The practiced insouciance with which my father always told this story made it hard to credit. Of course there were other reasons. Bolivia needed technical expertise for mining and infrastructure. For engineers there were good jobs to be had, jobs that were not off-limits to Jews.

Pál laid out the plan for Madeleine, and she told her parents in La Chaux-de-Fonds that she would be leaving Switzerland. She wrote, "Papa even cried when he heard. My mother, too, is sad but says she is glad that her daughter has found a man to be with her."

Andor was furious. He wrote and said:

How can you do something like that? This woman you love so much; she has a job at a union, she will get a pension and you just tell her to leave everything? How can you be so irresponsible?

No matter. Pál stuck to the plan. He met Bandi and two other Hungarian engineers, György Bartos and János Varga. Together they formed the vanguard of the Gang's migration across the Atlantic. In Paris Bandi got everyone real visas through his connection at the Bolivian consulate, although a bribe still had to be paid. Then Bandi, Bartos, Varga, and my father booked passage on the Pacific Steamship Navigation Company vessel *Oropesa*, bound from La Rochelle, France, to the Panama Canal and beyond. Someone took pictures of the friends before they embarked, clowning around, in high spirits. There is a sense of anticipation, as if they were setting off on an adventure.

From left: Pál Weidlinger, Edith Wagner, and György Bartos in Paris.

Around the time of my father's departure from Europe, another young Jew crossed the Atlantic on board the *Orduña*, also a vessel of the Pacific Steamship Navigation Company. Egon Schwartz, an Austrian, wrote:

This was no ordinary ship but a transport of displaced and vanquished people. Our ship was populated not only with fugitives from every corner of Greater Germany, but also by Spaniards who fought on the side of the Republic in the Civil War and who now, after their defeat, were searching for a land of refuge where their language would be understood. Here were people who had been in concentration camps, whose pianos had been thrown out of the window into the street on Kristallnacht, and people who, at the cost of unimaginable casualties and privations, had put up resistance against Francisco Franco. Here were North German university professors who spoke in cultivated prose and Bavarian country boys with their broad dialect who (God knows how) had come into conflict with the Nazis. Here were Jews from Galician shtetls, impoverished Austrian aristocrats still trying to cling desperately to a little bit of distinction, and folk from widely dispersed places who had become intimately acquainted with unclean jails and the pitiless immigration police of every nation.

In March 1939 Pál, Bandi, Bartos, and Varga found themselves immersed in the same desperate polyglot society on their ship, but they did not think of themselves as refugees. They might be displaced, but they were not vanquished. The four friends shared a Spanish grammar book and a typewriter. They used the typewriter to keep a collective account of their voyage, which they titled *The Adventurous Voyage of the* Oropesa. To judge by their account, these four young Hungarian Jews, crossing the ocean to an unknown land while the fascist noose tightened around Europe, had not a care in the world.

Bandi: March 13, 1939—Pál is sketching his tragedy in twelve chapters. He is done with missing the boat in Cannes and is now recording his sharp turn, which is taking him to La Paz. But it could not have happened otherwise; who would we laugh at all day if he was not here?

János Varga, György Bartos, Endre (Bandi) Sebestyén, and Pál in The Adventurous Voyage of the Oropesa.

Pál's sketches have survived. They show my father, with his round glasses, standing on a quay in Cannes, watching his ship to Uruguay steam away, then a confused Pál in Paris, suitcase in hand, flanked by the Eiffel Tower and Notre Dame, and then Pál with a gigantic question mark above his head as he receives his Bolivian visa. Anticipating success in the New World, my father drew a cartoon of himself as an architect-saint with a halo, rubbing shoulders with the builders of pyramids and cathedrals. His friends shared his optimism.

The Architect's Dream.

On board Bartos discovered a piano, which he started to "caress in his usual tender way." His music attracted an audience of Germans, Poles, Czechs, and Hungarians in the third-class lounge.

"Even though we were from different backgrounds, we all had one big thing in common. We really were *all in the same boat!*" This observation was made by Julius Wolfinger, a passenger on the same route a few months later. He continued:

> *People played games, cards, chess. Lots of conversation. Stories about how everybody got out. Arguments sometimes. Boredom sometimes. We younger ones flirted and entertained ourselves. We laughed, but there was also sadness and ten-sion in the air. It came from leaving Europe and the relatives who stayed behind. I couldn't help thinking, "What is going to happen next?"*

If the four friends had such wistful thoughts, they didn't share them. They had long since adapted to exile as the normal state of affairs. In their diary they wrote about more immediate concerns:

Bartos: The notion of seasickness did not even occur to us, and our friend Pál assured us that he has a full bottle of oil, which can tame the biggest waves. Just a couple of drops in the sea and there will be no trouble.

Pál: But the ship was pitching like crazy. Because it's an old model it has no emergency brake.

My father's sketches depict a tiny ship pitching on a vast sea, then the four friends leaning over the rail, vomiting violently, and finally all prone on their cabin bunks. Pál said that he remained horizontal except for an argument with the ship's doctor, who "stated that an English gentleman does not vomit even when seasick."

It's true that the crew and staff on the ship were not sympathetic. Egon Schwartz observed that "the service personnel confronted us with unmitigated contempt" and that allegedly the ship's captain had expressed profound pity for the nations that would receive his human cargo. The third-class dormitories and cabins were deep in the bowels of the ship, saturated by humid heat. The food was inedible. Regarding the latter (once he recovered from seasickness) my father wrote.

We are getting used to the food. Today we took only two portions instead of three. The waiter asked in concern if we were seasick again? Not wanting to upset him—while he went back to the kitchen—we emptied our plates out of the porthole. This had two results: 1) The waiter was satisfied. 2) The sea started to foam and all the fish got gastric poisoning.

It's significant that, unlike other refugee accounts, *The Adventurous Journey of the* Oropesa never referenced the world that was left behind. In his interview Pál recalled: "I said to my friends, one great thing about Bolivia—there are no relatives!" All the baggage of family expectations, allegiances, and obligations seemed left behind, growing small and utterly insignificant in the churning wake of the *Oropesa*. The feeling of crossing a threshold, of moving forward into a new reality, was bolstered by political convictions. The Gang of Thirteen were communists and, as disciples of Marx, they disdained looking backward. Nostalgia was self-indulgent sentimentality: escapist, reactionary, and a betrayal of history. It was a weakness.

All this explains why the four Hungarian friends did not feel much connection with their fellow passengers on the *Oropesa*. Rather, they were regarded as a source of entertainment. Mealtimes provided abundant material. Pál described a nice German couple:

> *The lady denounced Bartos as a dodderer because accidentally he sat in the chair of her little boy (twenty years old) who must sit at his mommy's side so that she could cut up his meat. The gentleman's profession turned out to be a retired Social Democrat.*

"Social Democrat" was the same insult that Pál hurled at his cousin Ili's boyfriend, who was part of their teenage Red Student group. Social Democrat = political wimp.

Another target for mockery were the *hitsorsos*, which, literally, translated as "coreligionists." *Hitsorsos* were all the Jews on board fleeing Europe. But the *hitsorsos* were not a homogeneous group. German-speaking Jews from the nations of the old Austro-Hungarian Empire looked down upon Yiddish-speaking Jews from Poland, Russia, and other parts of Eastern Europe and vice versa. Varga wrote:

> *The sharks appeared today according to schedule and had a review of the passengers. Pál kept desperately pointing out to them one of the most disagreeable Polish coreligionists, but they turned up their noses and left.*

At dinnertime arguments between coreligionists were a favorite sport, each opponent creatively cursing the other's place of birth

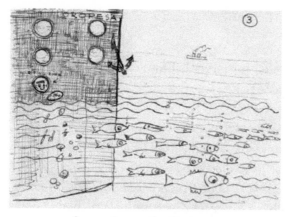

Suppertime on the Oropesa.

and race. Varga says that Bartos risked getting beat up because he repeatedly deplored the other passengers' unbearable manners and behavior. "Soon he will be the biggest anti-Semite on the ship."

One day, in the third-class lounge, the four boys were invited by a group of observant Jews to help form a *minyan,* the quorum of ten adults required for public prayer. They politely declined. Sometime later my father made a drawing of his "coreligionists" on the *Oropesa.* It shows a huddled group under a flag with the Star of David. Most of the figures have large, grossly exaggerated noses. These figures are clearly *Polacos,* a derisive term widely used by Central European Jews for their Eastern European coreligionists. The *Polaco* stereotype was loud, coarse, uneducated, and untrustworthy. They were viewed as embarrassing reminders of ghetto Jewry from which most middle-class Hungarian Jews, including my father's parents and grandparents, distanced themselves in their process of assimilation.

It is interesting that my father could not leave behind, in the ship's wake, this class prejudice, which should have been erased by all the Marxist principles and proclaimed love of the proletariat of his student days. To let go would have clashed with what I believe to be his honest declaration, written in a diary that he believed no one would ever read: "How I hate those people who arouse pity in me!" and "Woe to the defeated, because he feels defeated."

———

Three days after my father left for South America my mother wrote to him from Zurich.

> *Dearest, I want to write you again how much I love you. I will not let anything keep me from being able to be with you soon and be with you forever. I can still earn a bit more money, so I will work for another twenty-four days. Then I will spend a week at home before my departure, so I can comfort my parents.*

During her week in La Chaux-de-Fonds, she took photographs and later put them in her album. Here were her parents and friends with the Alps in the background, and also her brother, Pierre André, sitting in a café. She must have handed her Leica across the table to him because he took a picture of her in the same location. She was wearing a new hat similar to a man's trilby, only softer. She gazed out of the café window as if contemplating the far horizon of a new life.

Madeleine, in a portrait by her brother, Pierre André Friedli.

She wrote to Pál:

The situation in Europe is extremely tense. Last week I wrote to your father, but I have not got an answer yet. I would like your family to follow us as soon as possible. I told my own parents that you have found a good situation over there, so they will not worry. They send you greetings.

Then she copied out a lengthy description of Bolivia written by emigrants who had gone before. They described the country's climate, geography, economy, and industries. They reported that La Paz was an El Dorado, a promised land with no unemployment, where one was promptly paid for goods and services.

In early April 1939, Madeleine's ship followed in the wake of the *Oropesa*. The world she sailed into was completely unlike anything she had experienced before. When she passed through the Panama Canal she had time to go ashore. She made a photograph of ragged brown children peering in through the open window of her hired car. It was the first time she had seen people with brown skin.

Madeleine found letters from Pál in each port of call. "They were like lighthouses that greeted me all along my journey." On April 29, 1939, she wrote to him from Arica, Chile's northernmost port.

> *Dearest, I am here now. I have only one wish: to be in your arms. Just a few more days and then that will come true. I received all of your letters, and I believed only what you wrote to me and followed your advice. And it all went well. I still don't know how and when I will travel. On Monday there is a train, though no tickets with sleeping accommodations. There is a plane on Tuesday, which would only take an hour and twenty minutes, but it costs $35 American. Or I can wait another week and travel on Monday in eight days; such a long time without you does not work for me.*

Almost all European refugees bound for Bolivia took the same route as my parents, sailing across the Atlantic, through the Panama Canal and down the west coast of South America to Arica, Chile, where they boarded a train for the interior. Arica was chosen by authorities as the point of disembarkation for Europeans because of its isolation. Dry, hot, and surrounded by desert, it had no roads connecting it to other towns. There was no possibility that a European without papers could simply "disappear" into the Chilean hinterlands.

My mother took the train because the airfare was beyond her means. The train from Arica to La Paz, Bolivia, climbed from sea level to 14,500 feet, up the desolate flank of the Andes' Cordillera Occidental. The route was so steep that for most of the way a special cogwheel locomotive was needed to engage cogs in a central third rail. A children's ditty that was sung about this train went:

Arica La Paz, La Paz, La Paz. Tres pasos p'atrás, p'atrás, p'atrás.
Arica La Paz, La Paz, La Paz. Three steps back, back, back.

Three steps back may refer to the actual slippage of the train as worn cog-rails slowed its progress. The journey took two days when the tracks were not blocked by landslides.

The route in the Andes.

I wanted to see what my parents saw from this train: the desert and the mountains. I wanted to know more about the four years they spent in Bolivia. I wanted a framework within which to try to correlate the wild anecdotes my father told me and the meager facts contained in surviving correspondence from that time. I flew to La Paz in the summer of 2015. Tracing the route of the Arica–La Paz railroad and visiting the land it passed through was no easy matter. The train had stopped running long ago, and roads through the rugged land were few and far between. After studying Bolivian military topographical maps, I hired a guide and a driver to take me to the tiny outpost of Charaña near Bolivia's border with Chile. It was here that the steep climb up the Cordillera leveled off and the trains crossed the border. The cost of my trip was exorbitant because smugglers, bringing electronic goods from Chile, use the same route and pay high prices for transport. The 150-kilometer drive from La Paz on bone-jarring dirt roads traverses one of the highest deserts in the world. The villages we passed were dirt poor, surviving on subsistence agriculture and llama herds.

I tempered my expectations of what we would find at Charaña. I did not expect to find railroad tracks, assuming that once the train stopped running, the steel would be considered too valuable to be left in the desert. The first evidence of the outpost was a mile or two of rubbish, mostly plastic bags, snagged on rocks and brush. The town itself was an unpaved grid of ten square blocks of brick and adobe houses, most of them unfinished.

Then, on the far edge of town . . . railroad tracks! Not only were there tracks, but the tracks led to a train yard and a seemingly abandoned station, like a set from an old Western movie. Here the twin, snowcapped peaks of Pomerape and Parinacota rose from the desert like sentinels, with their western slopes in Chile and their eastern flanks in Bolivia. This was the Rubicon, not only a frontier outpost, but a demarcation point between an old life and a new.

Had Pál and Madeleine disembarked and shown their precious Bolivian visas to the border guards while the cogwheel locomotive was being shunted? What did they feel as they crossed this isolated frontier? Relief? Anxiety? Disorientation? Walking the tracks with Chile at my back, I mused out loud to my camera in much the same way as I am writing here. On the soundtrack I can be heard gasping for breath in the thin air of 14,000 feet. Breathlessness, both literal and metaphorical, may be the answer.

Two other German Jewish refugees, Heinz and Hanni Pinshower, who followed on the route a few months after my parents, described their journey:

> We absolutely didn't know what was awaiting us. We didn't know about the people, their customs or traditions. We did not expect the altitude to be so oppressive. On the train from Arica to La Paz, people's noses and ears were bleeding. Some were hemorrhaging.
>
> The Indio. We never had seen anything like them. Already on the train, at stops, a real novelty; we looked at them; they looked at us. I noticed I was in a black land. Not that the people were Negros, but so many men and women were dressed in black or dark clothing.

13. EL DORADO

The rest of the Gang of Thirteen soon followed my father, Bandi, Varga, and Bartos. Time was running out to leave Europe. One who hesitated, András Tömpe, spent two years in a concentration camp in France for political prisoners, because he had committed the crime of fighting against the fascists in the Spanish Civil War. But the men who made the Atlantic crossing did not seem daunted by their strange new circumstances. Arriving in La Paz, they immediately put into practice their idea of a utopian communist community. They lived together in a boarding house and shared both their earnings and household expenses. My father told me that "it was quite a lovely boarding house with big windows and a balcony overlooking a main street." I have a photograph of seven men in their pajamas on the back stoop; they are all polishing their shoes, sharing a tin of polish.

My father started using Paul as his first name, instead of the Hungarian Pál. Henceforth, in this narrative, I will do the same.

When Madeleine arrived, she was welcomed at the boarding house. Though my parents had ideological objections to matrimony, they prudently bowed to the conservative mores of the country they found themselves in. They obtained a marriage license at the La Paz city hall.

Bandi and Varga served as witnesses. "It was over in about ten minutes," said my father. "Afterwards we went out for a cup of coffee."

Over time, the arrival of women in the young men's utopia changed things. Erdős wryly observed that on laundry day, if a man ended up with the same number of pairs of underwear that he had put in, it didn't matter who the original owner was. But one could hardly expect women's stockings to be accounted for in the same way.

Everything turned out well for my parents. Two days after Paul's arrival in La Paz, he was hired at the Sociedad Constructora Nacional. He told me: "I was just incredibly lucky." It wasn't just any job. Sociedad Constructora Nacional, better known as Soconal, was the only company in Bolivia devoted to the design, engineering, and construction of large urban structures. Paul's bosses, the brothers Luis and Alberto Iturralde, had received their education in France, and they revered Le Corbusier. They dreamed of bringing Modernism to Bolivia. The fact that twenty-five-year-old Paul had actually worked with Pope Corbu was deeply impressive. His training statics, the analysis of loads acting on fixed structures, and the engineering of multistory, reinforced concrete buildings made him the perfect man at the perfect time. Initially he was hired as head draftsman.

> [The Iturralde brothers] kept asking me: "Can you do this? Can you do that?" And whatever they asked, I said that I could. And pretty soon they just left me to run the office.

After several months, he had become the chief architect in charge of all reinforced concrete construction. His personal letterhead read: *Profesor Pablo Weidlinger, Arquitecto-Ingeniero, La Paz, Bolivia*. In his interview he said:

> In Bolivia they were so much in need of people with technical skills that when they heard you were an engineer, they

assumed you were a god, that you could do everything. Of
course I couldn't, but they just assumed that I could. I remem-
ber on a construction site, if the cement mixer didn't work,
they expected me to know exactly what to do with it. I remem-
ber when we built our first tall building, I had to install the
elevator. I didn't have the vaguest notion of how to do it, but
I figured it out.

The office where Paul went to work every day was in an unusual building. The story of its construction reflects the primitive conditions of Bolivia's building industry in the 1930s, conditions that Paul and the Gang of Thirteen fought to improve. Four fifty-one Avenue Villazón, also known as *El Atelier*, was conceived and built by Luis Iturralde, one of Paul's bosses. Influenced by Le Corbusier and the sleek, unadorned facades of New Architecture, Iturralde wanted to use reinforced concrete. However, when construction began in 1931, cement did not exist in Bolivia. So he set about using available materials to devise a structure that would at least *look* like a modern, reinforced concrete building. For beams he used steel rails salvaged from a city tramline that was being decommissioned. For the walls he used stone, covered with an adobe skin and smoothed to look like concrete slabs. In the end the building had only four stories, not five, as Iturralde had dreamed, but it was high enough to outrage the local gentry, who claimed it was a sacrilege to erect a structure which, from a certain angle, blocked the view of Illimani, the snowcapped Andean peak above the city.

By naming the building *El Atelier*, Iturralde was paying homage to Le Corbusier. When Paul came to work in the building, he was aware of the irony. *El Atelier* was a building that pretended to be something that it wasn't. If this weren't bad enough, it was an homage to Le Corbusier, who had vigorously fought against what it represented, namely the old ruse of using materials to emulate other materials in the name of style. "Styles are lies," he famously proclaimed, yet here was an architect turning the ethos of Modernism into a style.

El Atelier turned out to be my parents' first real home. The Iturralde brothers gave my father the use of a six-room apartment on the top floor in appreciation of his work for them. He and Madeleine left the boarding house commune and were soon living in the lap of luxury. From their narrow balcony they could see Illimani to the east. To the northwest was El Prado, a majestic avenue lined with stately homes. It was here that the upper classes came to stroll and be seen. There were few automobiles, but elegant boxlike trams trundled down the west side of the avenue—passing the Hotel Sucre, also built by the Iturraldes and known for its imported, modern European bathroom fixtures.

El Atelier (451 Avenue Villazón) is in the right foreground.
El Prado stretches out behind. Around 1938.

Pictures from the 1940s of the building and neighborhood where my parents lived bear little resemblance to the modern city today. But in 2015 *El Atelier* still stood as a derelict hulk, slated for demolition. I was able to get inside. The windows were covered with soot, but the Modernist frames were recognizable from old pictures. The balcony that overlooked the elegant tree-lined El Prado was also still there; but the grand avenue was now chaotic, flanked by electronic billboards and every conceivable enterprise. With the roar of La Paz's twenty-first-century rush-hour traffic in my ears, I tried to imagine the space as my parents had occupied it. It helped that my father drew two cartoons labeled "The Bedroom and Living Room of Señora and Señor Mouqui and Pouqui, La Paz, Bolivia, South America (On the Pacific Side)."

Pouqui and Mouqui were my parents' love names for each other. Transliterated into Hungarian, Pouqui becomes *puki*, a child's word for "fart." Mouqui/*muki* is the short form of *mukikám*, slang for "women and children."

In the cartoons we see Pouqui and Mouqui ensconced in their new digs. Furniture and personal effects are carefully labeled. In the bedroom the big double bed is labeled "a project of Pouqui." The blankets have been purchased for 340 *bolívianos* (about $17). In the bedroom my mother's tiny handbag contains "lots of money," and my parents' clothing is strewn on the floors and furniture. Mouqui's lingerie is contained in a wardrobe drawer, but there is so much of it that the drawer cannot be closed. In the living room sketch, Pouqui, with his big round glasses, listens to Radio Condor from La Paz while Mouqui hunches over the typewriter she brought from Zurich. She is seated close to an electric heater identified uniquely as hers. There is a mysterious piece of furniture ("No one knows what it is for") and an imaginary cat. My father's sketches are a joyous boast that seem to proclaim: "Look, we have arrived!"

Another image, a photograph made by Madeleine, has been lovingly staged. It is of Paul and the architect István Haász. It reminds me of the make-believe adventures that my father invented with Ili when they were children. Paul, wearing a colonial pith helmet, grips a bamboo pole in one hand and a live kitten in the other. Haász, in a silly paper hat, has slung a draftsman's T-square over his shoulder like a big-game hunter's weapon and holds a lighted candle. Both men peer off camera with intense concentration, eyes fixed on an exotic horizon.

Details of the Bedroom and Living Room of Señora and Señor Mouqui and Pouqui.

Paul Weidlinger and István Haász in a photo staged by Madeleine.

Paul's story is interwoven with the exploits of the Gang of Thirteen. Paradoxically he was both integral and peripheral. He participated in the life and business of the commune, yet he had his own apartment and his job with Soconal. The latter was crucial. The Iturralde brothers desperately needed reliable subcontractors— carpenters, electricians, and plumbers—as well as prefabricated windows and doors. So the Hungarians founded their own company to meet these needs, Compañia Nacional Alfa. Paul made sure that Soconal's business went to them.

I have some invoices with Alfa's beautiful logo, depicting a pitched roof with the Greek letter alpha (α) framed between the rafters and A-L-F-A parading down the slope of the roof in Art Deco font. Alpha: first letter of the Greek alphabet. Alpha: first in order of importance. An audacious name for a company that started out with odd carpentry jobs.

Paul said, "The boys worked full time and I worked at night with them, and we had great fun at the beginning." A bookshelf, a wardrobe, a table with wheels, and an antenna installation are some of the items on the first invoices. The work was done in a rented apartment with a few tools brought from home. As the business grew, it was possible to acquire more tools and a real workshop. A group picture shows the boys posing with Alfa's first truck. On Sundays the whole gang piled in for excursions to La Titicaca, which, they soon discovered, was too cold for swimming.

The company grew quickly. The carpentry shop made doors and windows. Then it was decided to make metal-framed, double-glazed windows better suited to the Bolivian climate. Templates were obtained from the United States, the boys taught themselves how to weld, and production started. A building inspector threatened to shut down the operation, claiming that the workshop was unsuitable for window production but he was mollified when Erdős repaired his wife's kitchen stove. In general Alfa was well received. Erdős wrote:

> There was this perception: "Let's trust them, that they can do everything, they are European engineers!" We would have caused disappointment if we turned down a project with an excuse that "We can't do it." It is true that there was a wide variety of engineers within our "Gang of Thirteen."

A vivid recollection of Alfa's exploits, told by both Paul and Erdős, is the saga of an electrical generator that the company contracted to provide to a client, outbidding the big American company, Westinghouse. Paul's and Erdős' accounts vary somewhat. My father boasts that the generator was destined to power the entire town of Copacabana. Erdős gives the more plausible scenario that it was destined for a hotel within the town. Erdős writes:

> On the shores of Lake Titicaca, where young Bolivian married couples went to ask the Virgin to give them healthy children, a hotel was built. Alfa was hired to provide the electricity. We asked companies for bids to provide a generator, but they were extremely expensive and could not be delivered on time. So we looked for a used one.

Paul, continuing the story, said:

One of our guys (István Roth) was a born wheeler-dealer, and he went out and he found a huge diesel generator in little pieces. He bought it for two hundred dollars, which was pretty much Alfa's entire operating capital, and he piled it in our truck. He said, "Look what I bought for two hundred dollars! We can compete with Westinghouse if we manage to put this together!"

"Then," said Erdős, "we started the ugly work of assembly and repair." It is typical that the boys were confident that they could fix the huge machine, although none of them had ever repaired a generator before.

The pressure was on. The hotel that had contracted for the generator had invited government ministers and the upper crust of Copacabana to a ceremony at which the lights would be turned on. "We spent many nights trying to put this goddamn diesel engine together," said my father. "And we finally did, but we couldn't get it started. I remember you needed compressed air to start the generator and there was just one compressed air factory in town and we used to buy their total output day after day." A cloud of despair settled over the Alfa team. One of the boys, drowning his sorrows in a pub, recounted the tale of woe to a man on an adjacent barstool. The man was a diesel mechanic. Paul says:

We brought him to where we were working. This guy saw the engine and tears started streaming down his face. He said, "This is my diesel engine. I used to supervise this." And he went to the engine and fiddled around and it started, and we delivered it.

Erdős continues:

After desperate work, the machine was ready on the day of the grand opening. We held our breath and turned it on. The hotel lit up. Then there was a huge crash and everything went dark. The timing belt had snapped. We fixed it and five minutes later the lights went back on. Fortunately the official guests . . . were all still in church for the blessing of the hotel.

The lights stayed on just long enough for all the guests to retire to their rooms and then they went dark for good. Erdős observed: "The wiring of the building was so full of shorts it was not salvageable." Fortunately the blame was not pinned on Alfa, as it had not done the wiring.

The common quality of Paul's and Erdős's account of the adventures of the Gang is one of insouciance and careless good fortune. Lucky things just kept on happening. The men actually worked incredibly hard to make a life in Bolivia but downplayed their efforts. Certainly there were hard times, but to make much of them seemed in bad taste. Self-pity was the greatest sin. The words my father wrote in his journal as a teenager still resonated: "Woe to the defeated, because he feels defeated."

Keeping a low profile was another part of it. Never did the Gang of Thirteen identify themselves as Jews or as communists. They could

(From left to right) Cini Szenes, Ödön Szenes, Paul Weidlinger, János Varga, and Endre Sebestyén—members of the Gang of Thirteen.

have savored a taste of the old Austro-Hungarian Empire at one of many German/Jewish establishments opened by émigrés in La Paz. They might have indulged in a slice of Sacher torte at Elis Confitería or a meal of Wiener schnitzel at Café Vienna. They might have seen a cabaret show at Kleinkunst Bühne or listened to the live chamber music performances of Mozart and Beethoven at the Collegium Musicum, but if they did any of these things, there is no mention of them.

At the end of 1939, a virulent wave of anti-Semitism swept through the country when it was discovered that Bolivia's foreign minister had colluded with consular officials in European capitals to sell thousands of visas to Jews, pocketing millions of US dollars. The timing of Bandi's purchase of visas for the Gang of Thirteen at the Paris consulate corresponds perfectly with the period in which the minister Eduardo Diéz de Medina and his cronies were raking in the cash. When Medina was put on trial in La Paz, spectators in the galleries kept up a steady chant of "Death to the Jews." A bill was introduced in the Bolivian congress to expel all Jews from the country, stating that "Jews are an unhealthy element due to their selfish social, racial, and moral principles." The newspaper La Calle, in one of its editorials supporting the bill, lamented the "inundation" of the country by people "with very beaked noses . . . members of the Jewish race who were waiting to fall like a ravening horde on the cities of Bolivia."

The closest that Erdős comes to dropping his jocular tone when writing about his friends and implying their collective vulnerability is when he observed:

> About a hundred Hungarians live in La Paz. It is like a small town back home, only worse. People are much too eager to know each other, and too many are full-time gossips. This is not the case with us. I was often surprised when, upon introducing myself, one would say: "You are that Erdős?" Certain individuals have a lot of free time. We don't have much of a social life because apart from our own company, we keep in touch with other Hungarians quite sparingly. We don't need

more company as there are plenty of us, and among others
there are just a very few people that have similar social and
[communist] political views.

A short walk from my parents' apartment down Avenue Villazón
is the Universidad Mayor de San Andrés. It was here, at the city's
only university, that Paul went to present himself to Emilio Villanueva, Bolivia's most famous architect and a member of the country's
oligarchy.

There is a story about Villanueva as dean of the university's
School of Architecture. At a faculty meeting he sacked a professor
over an argument about closets. Built-in closets were a new idea
in 1940. Before closets there were wardrobes, large free-standing
wooden cabinets, often with intricately carved ornamentation. Villanueva was a supporter of wardrobes and did not want closets to be
introduced into the curriculum. Ernesto Privero, the young professor
who championed closets, protested, "I don't agree with you, Señor
Architect. And if this does not change, I will leave."

Not deigning to reply directly to this upstart Modernist, Villanueva addressed the assembled gathering, "Members of the advisory
committee . . . you have just heard that the architect resigned, and we
thank him for his service." He named Privero's successor on the spot.

How was my father granted an audience with this intimidating
personage? My guess is that it was his letter of reference from Le
Corbusier that opened the door. The letter stated that he had worked
in Le Corbusier's atelier for five months, accomplishing his "assigned
tasks with devotion." He was particularly occupied with city planning
projects for Paris and Boulogne.

This was hardly a glowing recommendation, but any association
with Le Corbusier carried weight, and the fact that Paul had worked
on city planning projects was useful. Villanueva was trying to promote his book, *Evolution of City Planning in America and Europe,* and
he saw an opportunity. He asked young Paul, a "collaborator" with
the famous city-planning theorist Le Corbusier, to write a preface. It
would help sell the book in Europe and the United States.

The original manuscript of the preface, in Paul's papers, was dated May 22, 1939. It is a broad summary of the problems faced by city planners. It only briefly congratulates Villanueva on his work. Nevertheless it was sufficient.

The week prior to the date on the manuscript, there was a flurry of letters between Dean Villanueva and the chancellor of the university, first recommending, and then offering my father a job as a professor of modeling and perspective. Paul Weidlinger was "uniquely competent" according to Villanueva, thereby releasing him from the usual requirements of submitting a résumé and syllabus in competition with others. Quid pro quo.

Paul taught at the university while continuing to work for the Iturralde brothers and collaborating with his friends at Alfa. His hours were minimal, as was his salary, but he relished the title of "professor" at a place where people bowed their heads and took off their hats as they passed through the portals of the institution.

But this was just the opening act in the drama of the young, cocksure Hungarian and the elder statesman of Bolivian architecture. The plot thickened in the fall of 1939.

Under Villanueva's direction, the university published a request for proposals for the design of a new campus. The winner would have the distinction of being the creator of the first modern, twentieth-century campus in Bolivia. To protect against favoritism, entrants remained anonymous, identified by code names, to be revealed only when the competition jury chose a winner.

Paul entered the competition with his friend István Haász. The code name they selected for themselves was "Two Circles." The comic photograph (see page 127) that my mother took of Paul and István as jungle explorer-architects commemorated their audacious partnership.

Why had Paul never mentioned this amazing project? I only learned of it indirectly in a letter he wrote to Le Corbusier in which he refers to the university's call for projects to which he applied despite some "laughable inconsistencies" in the guidelines.

I asked my Hungarian Bolivian researcher in La Paz, Etelka Debreczeni, to look into this. After weeks of appealing to authorities, starting with the current chancellor of the university, she came at last to the cluttered desk of Pedro Callisaya Hinojosa, a modest man in charge of the institution's central archives. We affectionately called him Don Pedro. The basement of the university's principal building was his realm. There were no computers. Surely there was a catalog system? However, I believe that if we had been allowed access to it, we would have given up in despair. Immense ledgers and folio books, some of them two feet square, were arranged on shelves or stacked on the floor in precarious columns. It was a challenge simply to clear an area large enough to put down my tripod and camera so I could interview Don Pedro.

Like Alfa's man discovering the diesel mechanic in the pub, Etelka's befriending of Don Pedro was a serendipitous development. Don Pedro took a liking to Etelka (on one of her visits she brought him tea cakes), and he was also genuinely interested in the story of my search for my father. He made it his business over several weeks to find every document in his archive referencing the name of Paul Weidlinger.

The competition guidelines were for a modern, North American style, university campus with separate buildings for the varied academic disciplines, a sports complex, and green open spaces. Don Pedro found the original architectural drawings that were part of the Two Circles' submission. Paul and István must have dedicated many long nights and weekends to creating them. They are beautiful. There are separate pavilions for the humanities, social sciences,

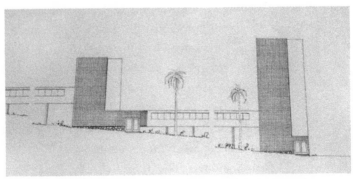

University campus building elevation from the Two Circles submission.

mathematics, biology, and medicine. There is a library, a film theater, and a planetarium for the astronomy department, as well as an amphitheater for scientific lectures and demonstrations.

The competition jury found the work to be a "very modern and original design" which fulfilled the requirements of the competition. It was also cited as "the best presentation of new ideas." Paul and István had won, but they did not get to see their dream realized.

Imre Erdős wrote in his memoir that:

Their plans were set aside and the dean [Villanueva] of the engineering school made his own plans. . . . The old university building, which used to be a military academy, was built in the shape of a horseshoe, enclosing a large yard. They decided to keep the old building until a new one was built, so they came up with the brilliant idea of building a huge skyscraper in the middle of the horseshoe. After the new building was built the old one would be demolished.

Villanueva had completely swept aside the concept of a spacious campus with multiple buildings in favor of a single monolithic structure. He justified this decision with the explanation that the university did not have enough land to build on. So why launch a competition with guidelines for a multi-building campus? The answer to that question remains a mystery.

Villanueva was then asked by the chancellor to come up with a design for his thirteen-story "skyscraper." Although Villanueva had designed several of La Paz's palatial public buildings and a sports stadium, he had never built a high-rise. There were no skyscrapers in Bolivia. His would be the first. So Villanueva asked Paul Weidlinger to design one. Paul was already handling all the reinforced concrete construction for the Iturralde brothers, so he was a good candidate for the job.

Paul did not like Villanueva's skyscraper concept, already dubbed the "Monoblock," so he wrote to Le Corbusier asking the master to back up his argument for a counterproposal.

The dean of the Engineering Department (Villanueva) is one of your fans and sincerely believes that he subscribes to your ideas. Yesterday he presented to the University Council a sketch, which is supposed to be the basis for my work.

In Paul's mind Villanueva's idea was completely in opposition to Le Corbusier's Modernist precept that stipulated that a building's design should derive from its function.

I disagree with the idea of putting in one building with a single entrance and a single staircase to reach classrooms, clinics, and laboratories. On the contrary, I envision putting them in different buildings, especially because there is a lot of space on the university property. Since the dean (Villanueva) is using your name for his idea to prevail, I would very much appreciate it if you could tell me what you think about this project so that I may justify myself. I am concerned about a false interpretation of your ideas. Even though I am far away, I still consider myself one of your students.

Le Corbusier, Paul's ace in the hole, did not come to his defense. Instead he wrote to Paul telling him "not to get too excited." He suggested some ways of locating elevators and using the spaces around the building to handle pedestrian and automobile traffic and concluded his letter to Paul saying:

I understand your situation: You gave birth to an idea, you believe in it; however sometimes a good idea can come from outside. Our duty as an architect is to know how to change our tune when it is for the good of the solution. A tall building can very well be a solution. Therefore, courage! And best regards. Le Corbusier.

In Villanueva's account of the matter, he simply says that he offered the job to my father and my father refused. Villanueva then went to Buenos Aires, where he employed architects and draftsmen to come up with plans for his building.

Perhaps Paul did not tell me about the Two Circles affair because it did not end well. It did not fit his narrative of "amaaazing" good fortune. Yet he held true to his understanding of the Modernist ideal of "form follows function," in that the small skyscraper was no container for the multitude of purposes it was intended to serve. In this he seems to have been proven correct. The Monoblock, completed in 1948, with an Art Deco façade decorated with pre-Columbian motifs, is an imposing structure. It has been dubbed "a masterpiece of Bolivian architecture," but the distribution of interior rooms is chaotic. A structure designed for 1,800 students now must now serve 10,000. It's poorly maintained. The rooms are dirty and desolate, missing latches, light switches, and blinds; 90 percent of the restrooms are out of order. Poignantly, it was in the basement of the Monoblock that Don Pedro showed me Paul and István's drawings—drawings of the university that might have been.

In the ensuing months Paul lost interest in his classes at the university, sometimes not even showing up to teach them. There is a letter of admonishment from the dean and documentation showing that his pay had been docked.

———

Alfa's motto was "We can do anything." Gifted young men with the education and opportunity to realize their gifts can develop a sense of invulnerability. The men in the Gang of Thirteen believed they would prevail on the basis of their gifts and their merits. Paul and István won but they did not prevail. However, my father was in no way defeated. He simply redirected his energies with redoubled vigor. At the same time, his relationship with my mother was suffering.

14. A DIFFICULT PLACE FOR A WOMAN

LA PAZ AND COCHABAMBA, 1940-1942, 2015

It was deeply moving to follow my parents' footsteps, going to the places they had passed through seventy-six years earlier. Walking breathless along the railroad tracks in the desolate landscape of Charaña, standing in what had been their home in a now derelict building, and watching as Don Pedro unfurled the Two Circles blueprints, I felt an intimate connection.

While planning my trip, I had been warned not to expect too much. In a nation that has endured 190 revolutions and political coups since its creation in 1825, the historical record is fragmented. Archives are hard to access and poorly organized. Permission is needed to do almost anything, including filming, and getting it depends almost entirely upon having the right connections. The person whom I hired to smooth the way was my Bolivian researcher, Etelka Debreczeni. She took a special interest in my project because her father was also Hungarian, having arrived in La Paz at about the same time as my parents. Etelka started to lay the groundwork for my visit two months prior to my arrival, but even after I landed in La Paz it was not clear her efforts would bear fruit.

Then wonderful things started to happen. The fact that Don Pedro Callisaya Hinojosa had made it his personal project to research my father's story seemed miraculous. Manuel Iturralde Jahnsen, gave me original blueprints drafted by my father for buildings that still stand in La Paz. I interviewed Janet Barriga, an architect who knew the entire history of 451 Villazón, because she had fought to protect it as an historical monument..

The leap of faith I had taken when I began the search for my father was validated, and I found myself respecting him for his own leap of faith, working hard and being rewarded for it, not looking back in nostalgia but shaping his own destiny.

For me there was also the problem of altitude, which led to certain insights. La Paz is at 12,000 feet. People from lower elevations have a hard time breathing. Walking up a flight of stairs feels like extreme exercise, but after a few days the body adjusts to the lower level of oxygen. A few people are unable to adapt. I was one of them. I experienced breathlessness, a bronchial infection, and sleep apnea for six weeks. I mention this because physiologically I take after my mother. I wonder if she had the same difficulty adapting that I did. Though she came from Switzerland, she grew up in the low foothills of the Alps. In Bolivia she often went alone for extended stays in Cochabamba, at an altitude of 8,300 feet, where she could breathe much more easily. For me the worst thing was sleep apnea. Exhausted, I would drift off, only to be jerked awake, gasping for breath. This would happen again and again, with the possibility of sleep ever more remote. It was crazy-making, inducing black thoughts. Extreme symptoms of altitude sickness include psychosis.

The high Andean landscape, described in the 1940 diary of an immigrant, Dr. Heinrich Stern, was a canvas upon which dark thoughts were projected:

The path was rocky, rough, steep, and lonely . . . thorny shrubbery, tall cactus, stones and stones. In the distance two wretched huts; mountains all around, giant furrowed mountains. Loneliness, frightful loneliness, and strangeness.

In the distance two women, wrapped in red ochre shawls, climb uphill. . . . Dark thoughts waltz through my brain. They torment me. They repeatedly knock and sting against my forehead. They circle about the horizon and want to penetrate the distant mountain wall; and they search and they ask, "The sky above me, is it not the sky of the old homeland?" No, it seems to me—or am I only imagining it?—more glaring, more poisonous.

In one of the letters my mother wrote to Paul from Cochabamba, she said: "I am puzzled because during this trip I have a deep feeling of *ennui*." The French word implies a world-weariness. "This is a feeling that I never experienced back in Europe. . . . If I start analyzing it deeply, then I come to strange discoveries!"

Madeleine had given everything up for Paul—her job, her family, and (despite her fears) her relatively safe existence in the single neutral country in a continent headed for war. Her deep love for Paul eclipsed everything familiar except him. In her photo album there is a picture of Paul, standing at a ship's wheel. Underneath it she has written: "Paul Weidlinger, *au gouvernail . . . de ma vie*"—at the helm of my life. But there was not much to do in Bolivia for a European woman. Paul said, "It was Victorian. They were expected to just keep busy with the household, to dress up and play bridge in the afternoon. She really didn't want that." Never mind that financially "it was like heaven."

Settled in their spacious flat at *El Atelier* and attended by maid and a cook, my parents lived very well. At a certain point Paul was making so much money that he started gambling. He lost $2,000 in one night at a casino. This didn't seem to faze him, but Madeleine spoke to him:

and she said that this is immoral, what I was doing. And you know, I could see her point, because I know it had a bad effect on me.

A page from Madeleine's photo album with her typed caption.

If only money could buy happiness. Despite Paul's newfound success, or perhaps because of it, my parents were drifting apart. Trying to come up with an explanation for this distancing, my father said in his interview with me:

> When I started out I was very much interested in mathematics. When I met her I became interested in art. But while we were in Bolivia, I began to go back to my original interest. She resented that because all of a sudden I was doing something she didn't understand. I had a close friend who would come over in the evening, and we would discuss mathematics. She resented it that all of a sudden she was excluded.

I believe it went deeper than this. Having lost his own mother at the age of four, Paul's ability to develop an intimate bond with a woman was limited. He replaced intimacy with a sense of responsibility as a husband, which basically meant providing for and taking care of his wife in a material sense. This was not at all unusual for exiled men of his generation and circumstances.

Madeleine went through a period of depression during her first year in Bolivia. In retrospect my father wondered if it was the harbinger of the mental illness that would plague her, intermittently, for half of her adult life. The one thing that gave her pleasure was her cherished camera, with which she was free to explore her environment. Alone, she traveled to the hot springs resort of Urmiri, where she captured European expatriates and their children frolicking around a swimming pool with a sheer mountain wall rising behind them. On a rugged mountain road she encountered an aristocratic Bolivian lady being carried in a palanquin by four Indians.

Copacabana, Bolivia, on Lake Titicaca.

From a high vantage point above Lake Titicaca, she photographed Copacabana (where Alfa had supplied the generator for a hotel). It is one of her most remarkable compositions, juxtaposing the immensity of the landscape with an isolated human settlement.

My mother also took pictures of Indians: barefoot Quechua women with woven, knotted shawls and bowler hats, as well as road workers, street vendors, and musicians at a fiesta. The images are typical of the photos taken by European émigrés: the Indian is the exotic, the other, existing in a world separate from the world of the white person behind the lens.

There are, however, two images made by my mother that suggest she was not blind to deeper truths. One is of a beggar. In the foreground is an outstretched white hand offering a coin between thumb and index finger. This is the only image in which white and brown are juxtaposed, and the relationship is very clear. The second photograph, taken at the Urmiri hot springs resort, is of a young Indian woman with her child bundled on her back, folding a crisp white tablecloth. In the background is a white marble statue in a classical pose. A geometrical fence with cross-bracing separates the earth-brown mother from the white marble icon. There is no crossing the line.

A beggar in La Paz in a photograph taken by Madeleine.

My sister was conceived in January 1940, although until she was born, my parents firmly believed that they would have a son. They called him Jack. In March my mother wrote Paul from Villa Mercedes, a rustic country hotel outside Cochabamba.

I have knitted a little jacket for Jack. It is blue, my friend. I also bought a warm sheet for his little bed for 20 bolívianos. I could also buy a blanket for 50 bolívianos from Ms. Kemperer, who has two little girls. It is very nice; white lambskin. But I do not want to buy it before I hear your opinion. Would you like to see little Jack bundled in his lambskin blanket? I hope you do not think that I am wasting money.

Tomorrow evening I am invited for dinner at the Aalfelds. They are expecting visitors, including a Mr. Iturralde. This must be your Alberto (one of Paul's bosses). I will quarrel with him because he did not bring you with him!! Is it really not possible for you to come? You should have a break at Easter, shouldn't you? Or is it because you are very busy with the competition?!

Jack is well. He takes a lot of space now! You should not expect a fat lady, but a black woman!! I spend the whole day here in the garden, sometimes in a swim suit, always without stockings. I acquired a tan, but did not put much weight on. Little Jack put all the extra weight on!! I hope you will not be upset with me because of that.

Chéri, I love you. Really, you do not need to send me more money. Send me more wool instead. Chéri, I am so happy that I will see you again soon. Little Jack is also looking forward to seeing you, and we both are sending you kisses. I dream almost every night about you. Love, your little boat, M.

Madeleine stayed at the Villa Mercedes for almost a month. At least one guest politely expressed surprise that she was traveling alone in her condition, unattended by her husband.

My sister was born on August 19, 1940, in a hospital run by American missionaries. After giving birth, my mother asked the doctor: "Where is my boy?" The doctor said, "Your boy is a girl." My parents did not seem disappointed. In photographs of them holding newborn Michèle, they each seem utterly enchanted. "It was nothing but joy," my father told me.

My mother's depression lifted. She now had a clear purpose in life and she took charge. My father did as he was told.

Paul with his newborn daughter, Michèle.

I didn't understand what it meant to have a child. I didn't know that men had any role with a little baby. I didn't know that one can enjoy having a baby. I didn't know that you could die for your baby. I learned all these things from her.

Then Madeleine saved the life of another child. In my mother's photo album, little malnourished Márta Szenes shares a crib with my sister. In his memoir Erdős states:

Ödön Szenes' wife, Cini, died. Soon after giving birth she got stomach typhus, and her weakened body could not recover. They were in Atocha, a third-class mining town, without a physician or modern medications. We took Márta, a skeletal skinny baby, to La Paz, where Madeleine Weidlinger took care of her. To our joy, we managed to save her.

I never dreamed that I would meet Márta, this person who had nursed at my mother's breast, along with my sister, seventy-six years ago. But one day I got an e-mail from the daughter of another émigré

Márta Szenes and Michèle.

and friend of my father's living in Bolivia telling me that she was alive and well, living just a half-hour's drive from my home in the Bay Area. Our meeting was both strange and sweet. We were strangers to each other and yet connected. Márta slowly turned the pages of my mother's photo album with pictures of Madeleine and Cini before she died, as well as herself as a skinny baby. Márta said in her short, on-camera interview with me:

> *Your mum fed me, along with your sister, with mother's milk, and it saved my life. She seems very beautiful outside and from inside. I say thanks to her for the rest of my life.*

Márta wept, missing the mother she never knew, and I wept, missing my mother, whom I lost in the labyrinth of schizophrenia.

It seems part of the Hungarian ethos, call it pride or protectiveness, never to speak of the past, especially when it is painful. Márta and I have in common the fact that our fathers withheld from us essential facts about our origins. Until she was an adult Márta did not find out that the woman who raised her (her father took a Bolivian wife) was not her birth mother. I did not know my father and his family were Jews.

As Madeleine took responsibility for the lives of Michèle and Márta, she came back into her own. In her short autobiographical statement she wrote:

> In 1939 I followed my husband to South America. I had along with me a solid set of democratic principles, a profound respect for human beings, a fierce need for freedom of thought and freedom to inquire, and that indispensable womanly endowment: compassion.

In October 1940 two of the bachelors in the Gang of Thirteen needed lodging. Madeleine gave Imre Erdős and István Haász rooms in the apartment at *El Atelier*. Alfa's carpenters made the furniture. My mother made sure that meals were thoughtfully prepared and served at regular hours. She also helped with Alfa's bookkeeping and found time to teach French at the Progressive School in La Paz. In an effort to bring culture to the Gang of Thirteen, she organized weekly musical evenings featuring recordings of classical music, which she borrowed from the La Paz Columbia Record Player Company. Erdős recalls: "That's how I actually got to like classical music."

15. DREAMING OF AMERICA

Around the time the Gang of Thirteen was crossing the Atlantic, cousin Ili made a haunting drawing in charcoal and pastels. It is of a young girl in a green shift standing in a narrow cobblestone street. Her arm is flung protectively over her head, and the gesture has caused her shift to hike up, revealing the tops of a cheap pair of stockings. The girl has dropped an earthenware pitcher on the cobbles. Her gaze is fixed on the dark sky. Ili's memoir is in two sections. The first is titled *Miss Porcelain*. The second is *Miss Porcelain, Shattered*. The painting of the girl who has dropped the pitcher in her distress heralds the second part. It is prescient of the dark years to come.

Paul and Madeleine had been in Bolivia for five months when the war broke out in Europe. Germany invaded Poland on September 1, 1939. In La Paz mail from Europe came once a week. Erdős reports that the men in the Gang of Thirteen who still lived together had dinner at 8:00 p.m. unless it was European mail-sorting day, in which case all eyes were on Alfa's post-office box. The news from home was not good.

Untitled drawing by Ilona Radó.

My grandfather Andor's plan to emigrate to Australia, with the Robertsons acting as the family's sponsors, was thwarted. In 1939 he had received a letter stating that he, Rózsa, and Lulu had been granted Australian landing permits, but Andor hesitated and did not leave Hungary immediately. In May 1940 his request for a visa extension was denied. Six months later, Lulu wrote a desperate letter to my parents. Uncharacteristically, she wrote in broken English rather than Hungarian. I believe she wanted to appeal directly to Madeleine as well as to Paul.

> *Dear Madeleine and Pál: We are all right of course but in need of help. Our greatest ambition now is to reach you as soon as possible because for Father and Lulu it is not possible to work here. We made our application to the American Quota on 17 December 1940 under numbers 36525, 36526, and 36527. We ask you to do your <u>best now</u>, so make as possible to start immediately in case of any possibility. . . . Hoping you are healthy we are longing to see you all and are sending this letter on the way of the American JOINT Distribution Committee.*

Ili also asked Paul for help. He did not keep her letters but she wrote in her memoir:

> *I wrote secretly to him asking for his help. I wanted to save Ferenc, but only those with a local sponsor could get immigration clearance in Western countries. Pál already had a good sponsor in America, but he didn't help.*

Ferenc Pándi, Ili's fiancé, was in grave danger. As a Jew, he was drafted into a forced labor battalion in support of Hungarian troops fighting on the Russian front. There was little that Paul could have done for his own family or for Ili and Ferenc. The "American Quota" in Lulu's letter referred to the annual quota of Hungarian immigrants allowed into the United States, which in 1940 was 5,000. At 36,525, Andor, Rózsa, Lulu, and Ferenc didn't have a chance.

In his interview with me, my father said something that made me incredulous:

Until the last moment, I didn't think there was going to be a war. In fact, when . . . the war broke out, I wanted to go back. I was desperately trying to get a visa. I just knew I had to be back there. There was too much going on there, and I wanted to be in it.

He said this to me on tape with evident passion, but it was hard to credit. He was a highly intelligent, farsighted person. He knew what was going on in Germany, Poland, Czechoslovakia, and Hungary. Was he trying to compensate? Did he feel guilty about having escaped while the rest of his family had not?

He *was* trying to get a visa—not to go back to Europe, which would have been suicidal, but to the United States. Because he had applied for immigration at the US Consulate in Paris three years earlier, he now had a chance. I don't know his quota number but it must have been relatively low. Paul renewed his correspondence with Edmund Bokor, whom he had asked to be his sponsor. Bokor instructed him to open a bank account in a US bank, in order to demonstrate his financial solvency, a requirement for visa approval. Paul did this. His statement from the Security National Bank in Los Angeles for May 1941 shows a balance of $1,550.64, equivalent to about $22,000 in today's dollars. Six weeks later, Bokor wrote to Paul:

I am happy you have so much money in the bank. It makes this easier, but unfortunately on July 1st they made the immigration process harder. We have to start over. I have attached thirteen questions, which should be answered by you and your wife. Please answer me ASAP because we will be very busy in the near future, and these issues require much time for me.

There follows a series of four letters from Bokor spanning five months. Each sounds hopeful . . . but is ultimately inconclusive. Then on December 8, 1941, Japan attacked Pearl Harbor, and the United States entered the war. The letters from Bokor stopped coming.

In the meantime, the Iturraldes, Paul's bosses, had made a bid to buy Alfa from the Hungarians. The Gang of Thirteen was eager to sell because war embargos were making it difficult to obtain building materials. The Iturraldes did buy the company but then failed to pay the asking price, claiming that the company had been overvalued. The Hungarians took them to court . . . but the system was stacked against the foreigners. Paul did not speak of this except to say that he divested himself of his shares in Alfa sometime in 1941.

It is a fact that my father got bored quickly. He was restless. He hated the very things (like a steady, predictable job) that gave most people a sense of satisfaction or security. He was never happier than when he was doing something completely new. If the odds were against him, so much the better.

In the summer of 1942, he learned that Bolivia's Bureau of Reclamation was looking for an engineer to work on dams. Corruption had been rampant in this agency, so it was decreed that only non-citizens could occupy key positions, as they were more easily monitored and insulated from bribery. Paul saw this as a perfect opportunity. Never mind that he knew absolutely nothing about building dams.

So I applied for it, but they told me I had to take a test. I remember I studied every night for about six weeks. I sat at home and studied hydraulics because I didn't have the vaguest notion. Madeleine brought me coffee and fed me. Then I passed the test and I became the chief engineer of the Bureau of Reclamation.

My search for my father's dam is another of the synchronicities that kept occurring in Bolivia. The only clue I had was a few words from his interview with me. He said that his project manager was also a foreigner, a Mexican and "a marvelous person with whom I became good friends." Etelka contacted the Department of Reclamation. There was not a trace of my father. Then she acquired a database of dams, their GPS coordinates, dates of construction, and project managers. One, in the planning stages during the period my father was employed, was built by a Mexican contractor. Bingo. I plugged the GPS coordinates into Google Earth and then zoomed down to La Angostura Lake and the dam that created it, about 15 kilometers south of Cochabamba. The daughter of one of the Gang of Thirteen grew up in Cochabamba. I wrote to Julie Vargas and she confirmed that both our fathers had worked on the dam. She had a photograph of it under construction.

La Angostura Dam under construction in 1946, Bolivia.

Felicitous things kept happening. I had my camera in the cabin on my flight to Cochabamba. On its approach my plane pivoted neatly around La Angostura Lake with the dam at its head. The angle of light was perfect. I could not have asked for a better shot had I hired a helicopter. On the ground I arrived at the dam at what cinematographers call the magic hour, before sunset when shadows are long and the land is golden. La Angostura had become a destination for Cochabambans, a place to cool off and enjoy a meal in one of the restaurants that ring the "Lake of Eden," a pond just downstream of the dam. My search ended in incongruous hilarity. In the foreground of my shots, swan boats, pedaled by tourists, glide sedately beneath the towering massif that is Paul's dam.

Paul was only chief engineer for a short time. In late September 1942, he had another letter from Bokor:

> You might think that I forgot you. I didn't write because I had no news. Now I am pleased to inform you that the committee in Washington approved your immigration. The American consul will advise you. Please write when and from where you will come. I had started to give up on this as a lost cause.

A large wooden crate weighing 441 pounds, self-addressed to my parents in Chicago, left Arica, Chile, on December 19, 1942, via the Chilean Line steamship *Aysen* to Callao, Peru, where it was transferred to the South American Steamship Company's *Aconcagua*, headed through the Panama Canal and thence to New Orleans. In New Orleans it was consigned to the Mississippi Shipping Company, which brought the shipment up the river and then overland to Chicago. During wartime shipping was a risky proposition. The *Oropesa*, the ship on which Paul had come over, had been torpedoed by a German U-boat several months earlier. The epic journey of my family's worldly belongings took over two months, arriving in Chicago on March 1, 1942.

It is significant that there was such a large crate. Paul had come a long way from his hand-to-mouth student existence. I was not yet born, but the crate contained artifacts that were both familiar and exotic to me growing up: a small, carved wooden bowl with a pair of yoked oxen inside, a large black Zapotec vase—more like an amphora, really—with a round bottom that rested on a woven basket base, and a heavy, wood-backed linoleum printing block with an incised design, so the surface could be inked and printed onto paper or fabric. The design was taken from a Mayan bas-relief that my mother had photographed.

The family got to Chicago before the big wooden crate, via steamship to the eastern terminus of the Panama Canal, then a Pan Am flight to Miami with a connection to Chicago.

The Bokor family welcomed the Weidlingers with open arms. Michèle walked in snow for the first time and Madeleine immediately got a job in the photo darkroom for the catalogue division of Montgomery Ward. She earned $24 a week and felt fortunate that she did not have to work on the weekends.

It was harder for Paul. He went to New York to look for work. Madeleine wrote to him two or three times a week. Amazingly, her letters are suddenly in English.

> *March 7, 1943. Chéri, first I want to kiss a thousand times the "unknown friend" who left some beautiful roses in my room. As I came home this night, it was so full of fragrance and color that I hardly recognized it. I felt suddenly much gayer. . . . I hope that we will do all right, all three together in NY and that we will not have to pack our things within 24 days for another country!! I think I shall like the States very much, much more than I did Bolivia. Michèle is crazy about going to school. . . .*

At three and a half, my sister Michèle had lustrous blond curls and a gentle, inquisitive expression in the photos that Madeleine took. In one shot, standing on my father's shoulders, she seems utterly fearless. She learned English quickly and had a deep curiosity about the world around her. She was precocious. The Bokors, who doted on her, were glad to take care of her while Madeleine went to work.

In March 1943 the government had just started food rationing and Madeleine instructed Paul:

> *Buy all the canned and dried food, like peas, asparagus, fruits, dry Sun-Maid raisins, beans, etc. as you can and keep them carefully. Sugar too, if you do not need all. I shall be glad to have them when I come over. Tomorrow by the same mail, I shall send you a parcel with your laundry. Do not forget to take*

Michèle, age three.

out the candies . . . instead of kisses. Also do not forget your
coat at home, even if it is nice and warm outside. You know
the temperature changes so quickly. . . .

Meanwhile my father wrote from New York that he was consider-
ing a lease on an apartment for $70 a month. Madeleine was swift to
curb his spendthrift ways.

Seventy dollars a month is too high a sum! NO, really Chéri,
just imagine you or me losing our jobs and having a contract
for a flat we cannot pay. I was thinking of it the whole night
and day. First there is the fear that you could be fired really
soon.

My mother was eager to be reunited with Paul but the war was
very much on her mind. In New York she said she would be "very
scared about air raids."

I am glad you had a nice time looking at the George Washing-
ton Bridge. Very soon we will all three go together and have a
look if it is not bombed yet!! I am sure you could build some-
thing like that, but where? The future will tell us.

Madeleine and Michèle joined Paul in New York in an affordable
apartment he had rented in Queens. His first job was as a structural
engineer for the architectural firm of Fellheimer and Wagner for
which he was paid sixty dollars a week. Later he became an engineer
for the Atlas Aircraft Products Corporation, working on airplane
hangars. Madeleine found a job as a darkroom assistant for a commercial photographer. She kept some of her favorite images of elegant
models, showcasing the latest modern housekeeping appliances: an
iron, a toaster, and a vacuum cleaner.

16. THE WAR

During the months that my parents were making a new life in the United States, the tide of the war began to change. The Battle of Stalingrad, the first major defeat of the German army, began in August 1942. In November, US and British forces launched the invasion of North Africa, which was ultimately successful. But the war was far from over, and the suffering of the civilian populations across Europe increased exponentially. Amid the broad historical movements, what news from home? There are no letters to Paul from his parents and sister in Hungary. Ships were torpedoed in the Atlantic. Lines of communication were broken. I wonder if Ili wrote to Paul after her plea to him to help save Ferenc? Would she have shared with him the story that she recounted in her memoir?

Ferenc was drafted into a slave labor battalion in late 1941. He was sent to the Ukraine, where Jewish battalions were used to support Hungarian army units in the fight against the Russians. After several months at the front, he was briefly reunited with Ili when she was able to visit him in a military hospital. He described his experience in his diary that he later gave to her. He wrote about a starvation diet, typhoid fever, lice, and men committing suicide in despair. He gave this detailed description of being beaten in a railroad tunnel.

I got beat up seriously one night. I was doomed because I wore a white shirt that stood out from the rest. That was stupid, because a different outfit is a good target. "Why don't you work, you there with the glasses, you there with the bandaged hand, you there with the green scarf, etc.?" we heard many times. Sergeant Serák, this little fat man with pig eyes, did not wait long: "Why don't you work, you there with the white shirt?" I started swinging my pickaxe as hard as I could. Then he told me to get closer and asked my name. I told him. Then he slapped me. Not too strong, but his fat, soft palm burned my face. I knew he had no reason to slap me, because I was a good worker. "Where did you work until now?" he asked. I told him, then I looked sharply into his eyes and answered that wherever I worked my supervisors were always satisfied with my work. My tone and confident look was enough for him. Serák started yelling at me and then he started hitting me. He hit me wherever he could. With his fist he hit my head and my back. He climbed on a rock above me and he jumped at me from there. His boot hit my chest. I fell back and hit my spine in a sharp rock behind me. He struck me harder and harder becoming drunk on his own power. His anger just grew as he yelled. I did not say a word, just tried to protect my face with my arm and fist. Everyone was silently watching us. Ervin turned away and blindly and helplessly whacked the ground with his pickaxe. After this incident I could not stand straight for days. I got beaten on other occasions, by others as well. No one took notice of it, because everyone was beaten.

Ili and Ferenc saw each other once more after he was released from the hospital. He had been recalled to his labor battalion for a second "tour of duty." On New Year's Eve, 1942, they had a forbidden meeting in a room in the Hungarian border town of Csap. Ili writes:

When we women learned that on the last night of 1942 the boys would be leaving the country, we took the risk to go to Csap. Trains to the front left from there. Our trip was dangerous; being in Csap was even more so. That night I stood on the corner where I was instructed to wait. The icy wind blew through my coat. I was terrified that we might not be able to see each other. All of a sudden a soldier appeared. He waved to me and I followed him on the cobblestones. I knew with all my senses that Ferenc was near.

My heart jumped when I noticed two policemen standing in a doorway. The one with the purple face grabbed me and asked: "Where are you going, Miss?" "Please, don't!" I cried and broke free, turning into an alley. It seemed that the policeman could not leave his spot because he did not follow me. In the alley I was breathing hard. I thought, "Oh my God, Ferenc has lost my trail and the policemen will capture him." But at the other end of the alley his very thin silhouette appeared. The blond mustache he grew made him look strange.

In the room, where we found refuge for a couple of hours we looked at each other without words. "What hell this man with these hollow blue eyes has gone through already," I thought, "and what more my most precious Darling must still endure." I washed his feet with mutilated toes with warm water in a basin. I gently stroked his feet as I dried them, while Ferenc held my shoulders with his thin hands.

Strangely, only on this last night we spent together did I feel I was ready to become a woman, to experience the enjoyment of my female body. When I prepared our bed, Ferenc knelt down and buried his head in my lap and wept. It was terrifying. His whole thin body shook like a leaf. At this moment I could not weep but somehow my tears seemed to fill my heart. Ferenc whispered, "I want us to have a child, a daughter. We will name her Kati and she will wear red ribbons in her hair! She will resemble us. I have imagined so many times how you will lead her holding hands and talk to her about me!" And then with a gentle hug I lay with this tortured body that would be mine for a few hours.

When Ferenc put on his clothes, his face was calm, "I will be the first in the front line. I will have the advantage that I can escape to the Russians more easily. But you, take very good care of yourself!" I could not let him go, but he started for the door. "I cannot get the other soldier into trouble who helped me to get here." We just stood for a minute holding hands.

It was exactly midnight when the railroad man waved his little red flag and the box cars rumbled out of the station. The rooster feathers in the helmets of the policemen along the tracks waved in the wind. I felt the earth move under my feet. The station did not seem real. Perhaps it was only a theater set. Dizzy, I leaned against the wall and thought that the curtain would roll down in any minute. My father would take me by the hand and bring me home. Then he would say to my mother: "This child is so sensitive. Each opera aria stirs her up!"

But my legs were shaking and I thought, for a moment, I should throw myself under the wheels of the train. Then the

Ilona Radó and Ferenc Pándi.

train was gone and the world around me slowly became real.
I started walking; in my hand was Ferenc's diary, which he
gave me at the last moment. "I am doomed to live!" I thought.

When I first learned about Ili's and my Hungarian family's experience during the war, I was fascinated yet strangely disconnected from the horrors they endured. "Ili's passionate anecdotes make a good story," I thought, and "they are in interesting juxtaposition to Paul's experiences at the same time." Then many months later, when it came time to incorporate these "stories" into the manuscript, I was stopped in my tracks. I could not go forward. I was in crisis. I was also in deep pain from a back injury, which seemed weirdly appropriate. Previously Ili, Ferenc, Andor, Lulu, and Rózsa had been strangers to me . . . strangers with interesting, dramatic, and sometimes tragic lives. But unexpectedly, in the process of writing this book, they have become real. They were real people and they were my family. In my dreams and in my darkest moment, I am there, a witness, in that little room in a Hungarian border town on New Year's Eve, 1942. I want so desperately to save Ferenc and Ili from their fates, and there is nothing I can do but weep for them. If my father were alive now, I would ask him to go there into the little room with Ili and Ferenc and witness and weep with me. I understand why he never told me he was a Jew . . . because to do so would have cracked open the lid of a box of horrors that he told himself he must protect me from.

Both my parents wanted to make a contribution to the war against the Nazis. My mother trained as a volunteer nurse's aide in the Civilian Defense Corps. Paul, though employed in a war industry occupation with Atlas Aircraft, wanted to do more.

He watched newsreel footage of the blitz, the nightly Luftwaffe bombing raids on London, a city that had recently been his home, and he imagined a precise, defensive weapon. I found a carbon copy of a five-page, densely written proposal that he sent to the

Madeleine (second row, far left) in a nursing class in New York.

War Department. In the paper he describes a projectile that is held and directed within the beam of a searchlight, as if it were inside a tube. Descriptions of photoelectric controller organs, explosive loadings, steering organs, as well as complex mathematical formulae, are included in the proposal. It must have taken a lot of time and thought. The proposal concludes:

> . . . *Further studies of the inventor in collaboration with military specialists would lead in a relatively short time to a definite project and its execution. If the Military Authorities would meet the above-mentioned requirements, the invention shall be used in the present war. . . .*

A standard form letter from the War Department acknowledges receipt but there appears to have been no further response.

In the meantime he had inquired about obtaining an officer's commission in the Army Corps of Engineers but was ineligible for an officer's rank because he was not yet a citizen of the United States.

Finally he appealed to his draft board to have his classification changed from 2B—"Registrant deferred in support of War Industry Occupation" to 1A —"Registrant available for unrestricted military service." The appeal was approved on April 11, 1944 and Paul was ordered to report for a pre-induction physical on July 13. He was ultimately rejected for service due to unspecified health reasons.

———————————

During the same period that my father was trying to become a soldier, the situation of Hungary's Jews changed drastically. Until the spring of 1944, many persuaded themselves they were relatively safe. Hungary, after all, was an ally of Germany, and the fate of men like Ferenc, in the Jewish labor battalions, was rationalized as a cost of war. Never mind that conditions in the labor battalions were far worse than those in the regular units of the Hungarian army.

This strange rationalization was supported by the fact that while the Nazi deportation of Jews was widespread in the nations bordering on Hungary, Hungarian Jews were *relatively* untouched. Also, as the tide of the war changed, the Horthy government secretly negotiated with the Allies and stalled plans for the deportation of Jews to concentration camps. But this worked for only so long. German forces finally invaded Hungary on March 19, 1944. Adolf Eichmann, the principal architect of Hitler's Final Solution, arrived in Budapest shortly afterwards. In the countryside Hungarian gendarmes rounded up 437,000 people. With the efficient collaboration of the Hungarian National Railway, they were sent to Auschwitz in the space of six weeks. The most disturbing aspect of the Hungarian scenario was the speed with which it happened. Gábor Somorjai, a Hungarian American scientist whom I interviewed in Berkeley, was a child of a middle-class Jewish family in Budapest during this time.

The whole attitude of Hungarian Jews was they were first Hungarians, and second they were Jews. When the Polish Jewish refugees came through Hungary and told us what was happening to them, we thought "Oh, that could only happen in

Poland. It could never happen in Hungary." Many of the Poles who escaped survived by moving to Israel or somewhere else in the world, but the Jews in Hungary were exterminated. They didn't escape. In fact the Hungarian Jewish leadership provided the authorities with all the documents needed to count the Jews and find them because we were a very well-organized people. We document everything. That was part of the reason for the success of the Germans and the Hungarian fascists.

Deportations of Jews in Budapest started later than in rural areas. On April 4, by order of the Hungarian prime minister, all Jews were required to wear a bright canary-yellow, six-pointed star, ten by ten centimeters, on the top left side of their clothing.

Martha Loewinger and her children in the ghetto, Debrecen, Hungary.

My grandfather, step-grandmother, and aunt complied. Little Pál told me how in mid-April, his mother was taken from a group she was with on the street . . . perhaps because of her remarkable beauty. She was brought to the "Vagrants' House," a way station for deportees. Andor was able to bribe the authorities at the Vagrants' House to ensure that his daughter would be given a secretarial job there rather than be deported. Lulu could only communicate with her family using official, pre-printed postcards.

June 27, 1944. My sweethearts. I am well. Please, if possible, send me a blanket. I don't need anything else. Everything is all right. Many kisses, from Lulu.

July 8, 1944. I have received your package. I am working here. When I have time I try to get some sunlight. Dear Father, please be calm. There is no reason for worry. Dear Mother, you must be a good girl and take good care of Father and yourself. Regarding me, be at ease. You know everything about me from Tibor. Tomorrow I will talk with him.

Lulu never spoke to the family about her job in the Vagrants' House, but after she died, my cousin Anna, Little Pál's sister, had a conversation with a woman who had been held with Lulu in the Vagrants' House. Lulu's job was to type the daily list of names of those chosen for the next train to Auschwitz. Anna said:

We never talked about her time in the ghetto. Only once when she was close to her death, she said they had to live each day as if it were their last day. They dreaded death every day. And it turned out (I just got the information a couple of months ago) that it was her job to write the list of persons who were going to be executed. It made her mentally sick in a way. We should forgive her for this.

Tens of thousands of documents, some legitimate and some forged, were used by Jews to attempt to escape roundup and deportation. Little Pál showed me a fragment, just one quadrant, of a document with Andor's picture and signature on it, and a stamp from the Swedish Embassy in Budapest. It is a genuine *Schutzpass*— a protective pass issued by the Swedish Embassy certifying that the holder was under the protection of Sweden. Andor also procured a

Schutzpass for Rózsa and Lulu and, in mid-August 1944, was able to secure the release of Lulu from the Vagrants' House. In addition to the document certifying her release, there is an authorization to obtain food ration coupons.

A fragment of Andor Weidlinger's Schutzpass, a protective pass issued by the Swedish Embassy in Budapest.

But my family's ordeal was not over. In the war, the battle for Budapest was equaled in ferocity only by Leningrad, Stalingrad, and Warsaw. The first Russian units reached Budapest on November 2, 1944. The full siege of the city began on Christmas and ended with the German and Hungarian surrender on February 13, 1945. As many civilians died as defending soldiers. Hundreds of thousands lived huddled in basements of large apartment blocks, tortured by hunger and lack of water. Those who ventured into the streets to collect melting snow were often shot indiscriminately. After Christmas, food supplies ceased almost completely. A brief respite came when 30,000 German and Hungarian cavalry horses, starving from lack of fodder, were slaughtered on December 31. Still, many children starved to death.

The Jews of Budapest occupied their special section of hell. Their torturers were the Arrow Cross, a regime of Hungarian fanatics and criminals, installed by the Nazis after Horthy announced an "armistice" with the Allies and was arrested by the Germans. Even as the Russian army was closing in on Budapest, the roving gangs of Arrow Cross men were determined to make Hungary "Jew-Free." They didn't bother with the logistics of deportation. They simply hunted and executed Jews on sight.

A Jewish ghetto, sealed off by high walls, originally imprisoned 200,000 people. The Weidlinger flat was actually just inside the ghetto, but Lulu, Rózsa, and Andor did not stay there, preferring to take their chances hiding out among the general population. If discovered in the street they would likely be shot. In the basement shelters of tenement blocks they risked being denounced. Several safe houses had been established for Jews under the protection of the Swedish Embassy, but despite their Schutzpass, it does not seem that the Weidlingers stayed in one. In any event, toward the end of the siege, the Arrow Cross no longer recognized the neutrality agreements that made such protection feasible. A preferred place of execution was on the lower quays of the Danube where men, women and children were made to strip and were shot into the river. An eyewitness account describes this.

In one of the streets leading to the Danube I saw a column of thirty to forty people, all in white. As they approached I saw men and women in shirts, undershirts and petticoats, with snow and broken glass crunching under their bare feet. Appalled, I stopped in my tracks, and when they reached me I asked one of the Arrow Cross men who they were. I shall never forget his cynical reply: "The Holy Family." I stood petrified for a long time, until the sound of submachine gun salvos from the Danube embankment made me realize that it had been these people's last journey. MEMOIR OF DEMA

Ili, addressing herself to Ferenc, who died in the Ukraine in 1943, describes her own experience during the siege of Budapest.

I remember a winter day in 1945. At that moment death passed over me. Every tenth person was shot to death. I did not know I would survive as the ninth. I did not shatter, crawling beneath the hail of bullets on Szondi Street. I still had the strength to get up on my shaking legs and walk toward the possibilities of a new life. I wanted to fight for justice, to make your dream [of a communist society] come true. If I do not succeed, I will tell you so that you will remember, so you will not let it go.

One of the places I visited in Budapest, during the filming and research for this project, was a quay on the banks of the Danube. On the spot where many executions took place, there is a modest memorial consisting of a few dozen pairs of old shoes, men's brogues, ladies' pumps, flats, boots, and even thin sandals. Perfectly realistic, scuffed, worn and frayed, they are cast in dark metal, freezing in time the fashions of 1944. One can imagine that each pair belonged to a human soul shot into the Danube. There is no protective railing at the site, as you would expect to find at any public monument in the United States, only the dark shoes, the edge of the stone embankment, and the cold waters below.

For a long time my father did not know if his family had survived. Finally in August 1945, six months after the Russian liberation, there is a short note from a Hungarian American soldier passing through Budapest. It confirms that Lulu, Rózsa, and Andor are alive. On December 31, 1945, almost a year after the Soviet liberation of Budapest, Andor writes to tell my father of the family's situation.

> *My dear Pali: When the news of the liberation came, we were in a basement between dead bodies and ruins. Our home was hit by a bomb and our stuff, that which had not been stolen, was destroyed: there were expensive carpets, almost all of the furniture, and Lulu's hard-earned trousseau. It seems almost impossible to write down or speak about what we have been through. We are mentally and economically ruined; they took everything we had. From the immediate family circle we miss: István Weidlinger, Ferenc Pándi, Ferenc Berger and Gyula, and everyone from Komárom except Ilus. Vera's husband is also missing. The packages that you wrote about haven't arrived yet, but we will be very glad to get them as we are pretty much out of everything. We have a hard time finding a living because the country was plundered before the liberation.*
>
> *My dear Pali, I know that I face you with a difficult task when I ask you to do everything humanly possible for us to emigrate from here, to go to you. For us this question is about living or not living. Today I went to the American Embassy and they told me that if my son is in the United States, we the parents and siblings don't have to get on the waiting list; the immigration approval will be given from Washington. They said that this information is correct only if my son is an American citizen—so probably you would need some connections to do this.*
>
> *If we had to get on the waiting list it would be hopeless for us, as there are already so many on that list. If you got a job*

as a professor, maybe we wouldn't have to get on the list and we could emigrate.

And now I will get down to material questions, and I'm asking you to answer honestly. Are you in such circumstances that you could provide a living for us at the beginning, until we will be able to find a job? Lulu has studied furniture design and also has worked as an assistant for a photographer. Mother learned the craft of making hats. I am not young enough to do heavy office duty, but I am able to do sketches and put ideas on paper.

36 Rákóczi Street, where the Weidlingers had lived, was bombed during the siege of Budapest.

Andor, once feared by Paul as the enforcer of strict discipline, the omniscient fixer who "scraped him out of the crap" in 1932, who spent everything he had to keep his daughter out of Auschwitz, had become his son's supplicant.

As I write about my family, I am haunted by my memory of the shoes on the banks of the Danube on that gray winter day. I feel the same grief and helplessness that I felt about Ili and Ferenc on their last night together. I have a dark thought: I imagine myself back on the embankment. I am taking off the hiking boots I always wear and adding them to the collection of metal shoes. Then I let the river take me.

17. DARKNESS AT NOON

I do not have Paul's response to Andor's letter begging for help. Apart from sending packages with food and clothing, there was not much he could do. My parents were not yet citizens and, therefore, not in a position to sponsor the immigration of the rest of the family.

Paul got a job in Washington, DC, working for the National Housing Authority, designing housing for war veterans. My parents moved to a suburban home in Arlington, Virginia. Among photographs my mother made is a large picture of a bookshelf in the living room. Books were very important to her. They *were* knowledge. Here, neatly framed, was evidence of my parents' accumulated understanding of the world in 1946. Legible titles in the picture include *American Dams and Bridges*, Einstein's *The Meaning of Relativity*, *The Plays of Henrik Ibsen*, several slim volumes of poetry, and *A Basic History of the United States*. My parents probably studied the latter in preparation for their citizenship test.

My mother also made some self-portraits in the living room. In one she poses in a man's immaculate, tailored tweed jacket with a handkerchief folded into the breast pocket. Her hair is short and severely bobbed, in the fashion of the day. Her gaze is penetrating, but she does not look happy. She wrote in her photo album: "I dislike immensely the suburban living—forgotten-wife-alone-with-the-household-problems kind of living. Michèle does badly in Arlington's public school." Further describing this period during which atom bomb tests were in the headlines, she wrote: "I remember discussions with friends on the implications of atom fission and the hypothesis of a possible disintegration of all matter as a result of a chain reaction."

I can imagine those conversations: My father and his friends were fascinated by the hypothesis of an unstoppable nuclear chain reaction and would have parsed out the topic and its ramifications in great detail. Madeleine observed: "Fluency in the new tongue of 'technological jargon' was the order of the day." Yet the horror of nuclear annihilation was too big to be directly addressed in these conversations.

During the Cold War, such psychic disassociation from the fear of nuclear holocaust became endemic. Prescriptions for sedatives and tranquilizers increased exponentially. "We are all harassed, whether we know it or not, by interior psychological pressures or by exterior bombs and fall-outs," wrote the cartoonist Robert Osborn. "One sees all kinds of people quietly coming apart, or trying to hold things together with alcohol, or behaving as though this were the Age of Beasts. . . . I don't think any amount of smiley advertising and fake togetherness can conceal how little we like to observe the sharpest relations of things."

Madeleine, deeply empathic, could not help but see the "sharpest relations of things" and be moved by them. She acutely felt the ramifications beyond the intellectual perceptions of the world that my father cultivated. But she found no resonance for her feeling in the world of postwar, post-Holocaust, scientific intelligentsia that Paul thrived in.

At the same time my father worried deeply about Andor, Rózsa, and Lulu, but he did not share his worries or even the facts of their suffering with Madeleine. What was the cost of this silence? With his

Madeleine in Arlington, Virginia, in 1946.

own internalized contempt for weakness, he could not share an anguish that filled his being, leaving no space for a loving connection with my mother. She wrote him a long letter on their wedding anniversary:

Today everything seems to be at an end between us. For months I just could not believe it. When I asked you for a separation in a moment of greater depression than usual, I was still hesitating, saying to myself "It is not possible, he will take me in his arms saying 'Stop worrying'—everything is over, it was a bad dream." If I look further back I see that we have been terribly happy. We had made wonderful plans: a little home, a little Jack and Jacqueline. . . . Somehow when the possibility of the execution of our plans was at hand we did not seem to give our hearts anymore. Maybe I was not very diplomatic; I made bad scenes over little things. . . . I always I broke my head against the wall of your passivity. Maybe with a little less intelligence and a little bit more heart, we could have been happy.

You said, "I did not do a thing to you. I did not disturb you. What do you want from me?" Don't you see that this is exactly a sign of the indifference, which I cannot accept as the basis for a life together? Do you not see that this lack of interest in each other, this lack of impulsion toward each other is just what is making life together impossible? Please let us separate right away. Because seeing you every day, always thinking, "This cannot be real," always coming home to your unfriendly face, feeling all the indifference in the intonation of your voice, your sighs—all this takes my strength away. I am almost not a human being anymore.

One day Madeleine just packed up and left for New York with Michèle. Paul sent her money and eventually he abandoned his work in Washington to return to New York to be with her. They did not separate, and Madeleine entered a life crisis. My father tried to respond but could not, on an empathic level. Survival meant constructing an "objective" scientific reality of how the world was. For Paul it meant solving the problems of structural engineering in order to ensure safety. It meant providing for his family in a material way. But he was unable to comfort my mother because he was unable to comfort himself. If feelings about the fate of the family in Hungary, about the Holocaust, about being a Jew, were allowed free rein, they might lead to their own chain reaction and terminal despair.

When my father spoke with me about the evolution of my mother's illness, he seemed in awe of his own helplessness.

> *She had this strange illness which nobody understood. In the morning before I went to work, I would have to make breakfast for her, and I would bring Michèle to school, go to work, come home at noon, make lunch for her, go back to work. In the evening I would pick up Michèle from school, make dinner for her and make dinner for Madeleine. This went on for about two years. And we went from doctor to doctor and she had all kinds of pains. This is where I first learned the expression, "psychosomatic." I was told this is a psychosomatic illness.*

My mother's face began to change. Her eyes receded into their sockets. Paul made sketches of her changing physiognomy. Gradually

 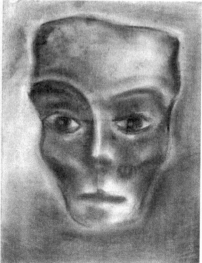

Paul's sketches of Madeleine in 1947.

her face became masklike. In her photo album Madeleine places a caption under two pictures of Michèle, aged seven: "Michèle is worried as I become ill—my eyes."

"Psychosomatic" tipped over into psychotic in the fall of 1948. My mother went alone to see the movie version of *Hamlet*, starring Laurence Olivier. The critic for *The New York Times* wrote, "Olivier portrays no cold and sexless Hamlet. He is a solid and virile young man, plainly tormented by the anguish and the horror of a double shock."

The play set off something inside Madeleine. In her mind Paul was Hamlet, and she was Ophelia, his spurned lover. My father told me:

She came home and she was utterly confused. She wasn't sure whether she was part of the movie or not. We went to bed and I held her in my arms and finally she quieted down. When I woke up she was gone. She ran out into street without her clothes and with just a coat over herself. And this is how it started. She did that several times. I remember I used to chase her in taxis. Then . . . I remember seeing this doctor and he . . . he said, "Well, she has to be brought to an institution."

At the time of our interview, my response to his account was ambivalent. I wanted to hear what he was saying, and I did not want to hear it. I confess I thought he was exaggerating the gravity of her condition for dramatic effect, and placing himself in a heroic, long-suffering light. But the fact is that when I return to the interview transcript twenty years later I have a very different reaction. What my father told me seems completely credible. I also feel this scary identification with my mother, much the way I felt about Ili and Ferenc on their last night together. I have the same deep-set eyes that she had, and growing up, I often wondered if they might be a harbinger of madness.

Now a strange thing happens. I think I may be losing my mind just like Madeleine. The back injury that I mentioned earlier in the chapter about Ili and Ferenc flares to intense pain, and I became convinced I am permanently crippled. I can hardly eat food and have suicidal thoughts. Over a period of two days, I lose the will to accomplish even the simplest of tasks. Seeking help I learn that I am not going crazy but experiencing something called *intergenerational post-traumatic stress disorder.* As a teenager I had defended myself against the fear that "I was going crazy too" by vehemently putting as much distance between myself and my mother as possible. But now, in order to write about her, I must be close to her. Gradually I am learning this is possible. I can be there with my mother in her suffering but not become her.

––––––––––

My mother's diagnosis was schizophrenia (paranoid). Her symptoms fit the profile, including "a belief that an ordinary event has special personal meaning, a false belief of superiority, hallucinations, depression, fear, and persecutory delusions."

There are several bills from psychiatrists who saw my mother in March and April of 1949. Then there is a bill from an attorney for "application for commitment of Mrs. Madeleine Weidlinger to the Institute of Living, Hartford, Conn." and finally a receipt from the Institute of Living for $729.14 to the account of Mrs. Paul Weidlinger.

There is a genetic predisposition to schizophrenia. Several key genes, when damaged, increase the risk that the disease will become manifest. This is much more likely to happen if triggered by external stress. A forty-year longitudinal study in Finland showed that protective family factors reduce the likelihood of schizophrenia by up to 86 percent.

For a long time I "convicted" my father for the crime of causing my mother's madness. But it's not a conviction that would hold up in any tribunal that I could imagine. There are too many unknown factors and, if he did drive her mad, he did not do it with intent but rather with his own fear of her despair at seeing the "sharpest relations of things," things that were too dark for open conversation.

He did the best he could. The Institute of Living was, for its time, one of the most forward-thinking places of its kind. I went to visit the buildings where it was housed. In the 1940s it was a beautiful place, more like a country club than the images conjured up by the phrase "mental institution." This was evident in the literature and some photographs of the Institute during those years. I think my father's choosing this place is a measure of how deeply he felt a responsibility toward Madeleine. He said to me:

> *It was a very fancy, beautiful place, and the fee for every day she stayed there was about what I made in a week's salary. And I was absolutely desperate. I went to see this psychiatrist, the doctor who advised me . . . and I said, "What am I going to do now? How am I going to pay this?" And he looked at me and he said, "Don't give me that bullshit! You can make all the money you want to. You are an engineer, you can work, start your own office, do whatever you want. Make the money!"*

The Institute for Living in Hartford, Connecticut.

Notwithstanding the pleasant accommodations, the treatments for schizophrenia were few. In 1949 antipsychotic drugs had not yet been developed. The Institute experimented with a wide range of physiotherapeutic "cures" including massage, steam baths, and wrapping the patient in warm, damp sheets. The most controversial treatments were insulin coma therapy and electroconvulsive (electric shock) therapy. Both were administered to my mother. In insulin coma therapy, now completely discredited, the patient was given insulin injections, which caused blood sugar levels to drop precipitously, inducing a coma. The patient was left in the comatose state for thirty to sixty minutes and then revived with a glucose injection. When the patient's psychotic symptoms were not reduced after twenty or thirty induced comas, electroconvulsive treatments were tried. Early treatments of ECT caused convulsions that were so severe that bones, including the spine, could be broken. By the time my mother was receiving ECT, muscle relaxants and anesthesia made the procedure less dangerous. Still, patients were shackled to their gurneys and a mouth guard had to be used to prevent them from biting their tongue. A side effect of ECT was memory loss during the period of treatment and sometimes for much longer.

I know almost nothing of the details of my mother's experience at the Institute. Her only mention of it is in a typed caption in one of her photo albums, accompanying a picture of Michèle and her nanny mentioned below.

In 1949 I was in the hospital for six months; the most horrible experience, for I did not want to be there. It was totally against my will. Michèle has suffered much from that separation but was kept in good shape because of the intervention of Clara, an illiterate Southern woman who was her constant companion during my absence.

Following the end of the war, during the period that my mother was becoming ill, there was a brief period in which it was possible for Hungarian citizens to travel abroad. Moscow had not fully consolidated its control over Central and Eastern Europe; Hungary's borders were not yet closed by the Iron Curtain. In early 1947 Lulu, my father's half-sister, came to visit him and Madeleine in New York. Though Lulu came on a tourist visa, Andor hoped that she might find a way to stay. At home she was being wooed by a man whose father was Ágoston Valentiny, the Hungarian Minister of Justice for a short tumultuous period after the war. Being connected with the family of such a person was risky when the winds of political favor were constantly shifting.

There is a picture of Lulu and Paul with seven-year-old Michèle nestled between them. Lulu told my father about everything that happened to the family in 1944 and 1945—her arrest and incarceration at the Vagrants' House, Andor's bribes to prevent her from being put on the train to the concentration camp, and the family's great suffering during the siege of Budapest. Since Lulu spoke only Hungarian, Paul would have had to translate for my mother. But I do not think that he did. I believe he protected her from the horrific facts, just as he did me.

Paul, Michèle, and Lulu Weidlinger,
Paul's half-sister, in New York, 1947.

One day Paul took Lulu to the top of the Empire State Building where they paid one dollar to make a "Voice-o-Graph" souvenir recording to send back to Hungary. Sixty-eight years later, I listened to this recording with Lulu's children, Little Pál and Anna. Little Pál translated for me. Paul and Lulu are laughing and joking. Paul's ears are frozen. Lulu has a touch of vertigo—she feels as if the building were swaying in the wind.

LULU
"I can't speak in English!"

PÁL
"Not true, you can swear in English!"

BOTH
"Many kisses for all."

After three months Lulu returned to her dangerous lover in Hungary. Thereafter my family was separated by the Iron Curtain. Bridging the distance between New York and Budapest became impossible politically, economically, socially, and personally.

The starkest contrast was between the lives of Paul and Ili, childhood friends who had shared everything with each other, including their daring involvement in the communist youth movement in 1932. After the war, as Paul was drawn into work focused on protecting against a perceived Soviet nuclear threat, Ili embraced the transformation of Hungary under Soviet influence and became a Communist Party secretary for a district of Budapest. Paul was intuitive and logical and often cynical. Ili was idealistic, driven and zealous. She wrote in her memoir:

> I was not Miss Porcelain any more, but a young woman who wanted to live life, the life I had won back. At the railroad station I stood in a boxcar and shoveled potatoes into the baskets that people handed to me. In the evening, completely exhausted, we noticed with laughter that we had forgotten to save any for ourselves!
>
> At one Party meeting I suddenly jumped on the stage and talked about all the horrible things that had happened to Ferenc. He was killed as the husbands of other women were killed. But now we can fight again with honor on the side of progress. We widows should get revolvers, so that we can join the fight. The crowd applauded with excitement and at the end

a sergeant came to me and gave me a gun as a present for the
nice speech. I was touched. I took it, but I will admit to you, I
realized, that I cannot kill. . . .

Ili and Paul had something in common with another Hungarian Jew, the journalist Arthur Koestler. They all embraced the ideal
of a socialist utopia as young people. Paul had met Koestler's wife,
Dorothee, in London in 1937 while he was working for Moholy-Nagy
and she was working for her husband's reprieve from execution in
a Spanish prison. Koestler had been reporting on the Spanish Civil
War for the Loyalist news agency and for the international communist organization, *Comintern*. He had been captured and sentenced
to death by Franco's forces.

Thanks to Dorothee's efforts and some strategic diplomatic
pressure from the Hungarian Embassy, the British government, and
the Vatican, Koestler was eventually released. He went on to write
his famous allegorical novel, *Darkness at Noon*. The story is about
a political prisoner who is also facing execution. But significantly
his interrogators are not fascists (as were Koestler's jailers) but communists. Without naming Russia or Stalin, *Darkness at Noon* clearly
evokes the great Stalinist purges between 1936 and 1938.

The protagonist, Rubashov, is a man who devoted his life to the
Communist Party only to be betrayed by the totalitarian system he
helped to create. At the end of the novel, Rubashov is ordered to
make a public confession. He asks his interrogator: "How can it serve
the Party that her members have to grovel in the dust before all the
world? I have pleaded guilty to having pursued a false and objectively
harmful policy. Isn't that enough for you?" The interrogator replies:
"What is presented [to the people] as Right must shine like gold; what
is presented as Wrong must be black as pitch. Your testimony at the
trial will be the last service you can do the Party." And so Rubashov
complies, confesses to crimes he did not commit, and is shot.

For Ili and my Hungarian family, *Darkness at Noon* was eerily pre-scient. In the years following the war, the Russians consolidated their control over Hungarian political affairs. The *Államvédelmi Hatóság*—the secret police—suppressed opposition through intimidation, false accusations, imprisonment, and torture. Lulu's father-in-law, Valentiny Ágoston, who had been the Minister of Justice for a brief period, was imprisoned for treason and war crimes.

Ili recalls hearing the public confession of László Rajk on the radio. She wrote: "When I heard the voice of this honorable man accusing himself, I believed him." Rajk, Hungary's Minister of the Interior, was a hero in the war and a loyal communist but had run afoul of the Stalinist elite. Though the charges of treason against him were trumped-up, he signed his confession and was shot. More purges followed as the members of the party judged a threat to the leader-ship were tried.

A close friend of Ili's was arrested and she wrote that:

> *When the security service interrogated me for three days, I could only repeat in my desperation that I had been blind, a gullible petty bourgeois, I did not realize that this man was an enemy.*

Then, as a district party secretary, Ili was required to help with the "cleansing" of undesirables.

> *I was instructed to invite the wives of those who were arrested in my district, men in leading positions. I was to convince the wives to reject and divorce their husbands. If they did not, I had to take away their party membership ID. It was a cruel task, but I did it. In a quiet voice I tried to explain that love had made them blind, that they did not notice with whom they were living.*

Ili could have been talking to herself. The pact she made with her lost lover Ferenc, to live life in service of the dream of a socialist

utopia, had made her blind to the brutality of the regime that rationalized every cruelty and injustice in the service of that dream. In
fact, she repeatedly addressed herself to Ferenc in her memoir . . .
as if reassuring him that she was keeping the faith. If she could not
cling to that faith, what was there to live for? She wrote that most
of the women she spoke with chose to stay loyal to their husbands.
She admitted that she cried with them. Soon she was fired from her
position as district secretary and sent to teach Marxist ideology at
the Party School.

Meanwhile Andor, Rósza, and Lulu started life over, scraping
together a living as best they could. Andor rewrote his résumé to
underscore his participation in the "Red Army" during the 1918 and
1919 revolutions and highlighted his proletariat credentials, having
begun his career as a bricklayer. He downplayed achievements that
implied his success and wealth as a building contractor.

My parents received their American citizenship in August 1948,
too late to help our Hungarian family come to the States. By then travel
to the West was impossible. My father sent fifty dollars in cash and a
letter every three months, which was read out loud at family gatherings.
Most of these letters started out with the phrase "Nothing much has
happened since I last wrote to you." He confined his writing to describing "normal" family life. He never mentioned Madeleine's illness.

18. THE STRENGTH
BEHIND THE BEAUTY

NEW YORK, 1949-1958

My father had heeded the advice of the indignant psychiatrist (who, incidentally, was also Hungarian) when he committed my mother to the Institute of Living. In 1949 he founded a company in order to earn enough to afford the weekly bill from the Institute. It was not Paul's first business venture. He had been part of Alfa in Bolivia and one-half of a short-lived partnership that he began in Washington, DC in 1946, before he followed my mother back to New York. The new company, known as Paul Weidlinger, Consulting Engineer, and later on as Weidlinger Associates, would become world-renowned.

The firm began with three employees in a one-room office at 101 Park Avenue. There were no computers. The tools of the trade were pencil and paper, chalk and a dusty blackboard, a slide rule, and Friden machines—electromechanical calculators that looked like a cross between a typewriter and an old-fashioned cash register.

Early clients were referred to Paul by other emigrants who belonged to the Bauhaus circle of designers and architects. Moholy-Nagy and György Kepes were working together at the new Bauhaus school in Chicago, and it was probably through them that Paul was introduced to Walter Gropius, the father of the movement that had infused his thinking about art and architecture in the 1930s. Gropius was building schools in North Africa for the United States Agency on International Development (USAID) and the campus of Baghdad University in Iraq. Paul's new company did the engineering on these projects.

Paul had trained as both an architect and an engineer and had designed several Modernist reinforced-concrete buildings in Bolivia. This was a double-edged sword when it came to his relations with architects. Some of them loved working with him because he was keenly interested in the way engineering could influence and support the aesthetics of a building. Others were not so enamored, because he could be blunt to the point of insult. If my father didn't like an architect's design, he said so, just as he had done with Villanueva when the famous Bolivian offered him the job on the Monoblock. Sometimes Paul "fired" his clients, returning their money if he didn't think their design was up to snuff. This irritated his business partners to no end. Matthys Levy, the last living partner from the early days of the firm, told me:

> Paul was a terrible PR guy. His sense of PR was, "If they don't know me, if they don't come to me, then why do I have to go after them?" So his relationship with architects at the beginning was quite difficult. Either he didn't like their work and then he sloughed them off, or he simply didn't have the patience to deal with them.

One architect who really liked working with Paul was Gordon Bunshaft, who designed several of New York City's landmark skyscrapers, with their sleek curtain-walls of glass and steel. The conversations that my father and Bunshaft had are part of company lore.

They would sit at the large marble table, which dominated Paul's small office. Bunshaft would make a pencil sketch of his design and then Paul would look at him and say, "No, no, you can't do this because then, it is not going to work!" and he would draw over Bunshaft's sketch what he proposed to do structurally. Then they would yell at each other . . . and Bunshaft would say, "But you can't take that out of my design!"

And Paul would say, "Well, I can if you don't want it to fall down!" And this would go on for hours. Matthys Levy recalled that Bunshaft and Weidlinger "got along famously . . . and the nice thing was that Bunshaft absorbed ideas from Paul."

The first building they collaborated on was the Banque Lambert in Brussels. The client had hired Bunshaft for his New York "style," but the architect realized that a glass and steel skyscraper would not fit in the heart of an eighteenth-century European city dominated by stately masonry facades. The solution that my father suggested was completely modern, yet at the same time echoed the facades with recessed windows that characterized the historical buildings. Hundreds of precast concrete crosses were fitted together to form the façade of the Banque Lambert. The radical nature of the design is that the crosses are not joined, top and bottom, at the level of each floor, but rather midway *between* floors. Moreover the columns are tapered and joined to each other by specially designed stainless steel hinges. This gives the entire building a feeling of lightness and modernity, while complementing the historical buildings that surround it.

The use of prefabricated elements became a hallmark of subsequent collaborations between Bunshaft and Weidlinger. Yale University's Beinecke Rare Book & Manuscript Library has the same cross-shaped elements as Banque Lambert; but this time the crosses are made out of steel, not concrete. The entire weight of the roof and exterior walls is supported by corner hinges that allow the structure to breathe, which prevents the cracking of translucent marble inserts in the walls that would otherwise occur due to expansion and contraction from temperature shifts.

Model of the Banque Lambert in Brussels.

*Model of Yale University's Beinecke Rare Book & Manuscript Library,
New Haven, Connecticut.*

When I paid a visit to Weidlinger Associates' New York headquarters to do research, I did so with trepidation. As a child, whenever I had visited my father's office, I felt a certain confusion. What did my father actually do there? Who was this man who was the boss of so many? I was incredulous at the deference with which everyone treated him, and as the boss's son, I was either avoided or addressed with exaggerated bonhomie.

As the company grew, it moved its headquarters seven times over seven decades, while establishing branch offices in Los Angeles, Washington, and Cambridge, England. In 2015 the firm occupied two entire floors of Trump Tower at 40 Wall Street. In the reception area, the firm's logo and name were emblazoned in large letters in gold relief against dark wood paneling. Though my surname was on the wall, I still had to go through a rigorous security check administered by a cheerful receptionist before being admitted to the inner sanctum. I passed through vast rooms filled with engineers in cubicles, intent on complex graphics on computer screens.

I spoke with several of the current partners at the company, including Ray Daddazio, the CEO, who still keeps Paul's marble table in his office. Everyone I met had been hired by my father fresh out of graduate school in the 1960s and '70s. He had been their mentor. They spoke of him as a genius and as a terror to work for.

In the company's photo archives, I pored over images of buildings under construction, buildings that Paul and his partners had worked on. The roster of the men who designed these buildings reads like a *Who's Who* of mid-twentieth-century architecture. Gordon Bunshaft's cylindrical Hirshhorn Museum sprouts like a mushroom on Washington's National Mall. There is Gyo Obata's St. Louis Abbey, looking like a modernist artichoke with its three tiers of parabolic arches. The foundations of Eero Saarinen's CBS building straddle New York's Sixth Avenue subway line, in a bold engineering solution that employs massive girders to redistribute the building's weight to keep it from crushing the subway tunnel. Known as the Black Rock Building, it was the first reinforced concrete office building in New York. There are US Embassies in Athens (Walter Gropius), Baghdad (José

Luis Sert), and Jakarta (Antonín Raymond). There are artist's sketches of a floating airport that was conceived by my father but never built, as well as pictures of monumental sculptures by Pablo Picasso, Jean Dubuffet, and Isamu Noguchi that were engineered by him.

What is the relationship between architect and structural engineer? How do they work together? Architects conceive the form. Engineers are the mediators between the idea of the form and its manifestation in concrete, glass, steel, brick, stone, and wood. Looking at the pictures in the archives, I kept wondering what my father and his associates *did* on these buildings. Are their creative fingerprints visible? How does engineering support aesthetics?

I put these questions to two engineers and an architect of HGA (Hammel, Green, and Abrahams) Architects and Engineers. They had recently completed the restoration of the façade of the Walker Art Center in Minneapolis. This famous museum was designed by Edward Larrabee Barnes and engineered by Paul Weidlinger. John Cook, the HGA architect, speculated about the conversations between Barnes and my father: Barnes probably started with a simple all-steel column-and-beam design. Paul recommended integrating concrete, given his previous success using precast concrete elements. In this case, the concrete elements are long "T" shaped girders, with the vertical stems of the Ts resting on the steel framework, and the horizontal bars forming both the ceiling and the floor above it. The result is a beautifully ribbed ceiling, and a floor that could support the weight of massive sculptures weighing several tons. Although the geometry of the plan appears very simple, from an engineering standpoint it was quite difficult. The two engineers explained it this way:

> *Paul Asp: The purity of intersections between window glass and brick means that the structure has to be offset from those. And you can do it in a way that makes it very complex and difficult to build. One of the things that I admired about the Barnes building is that the structure had a sensibility of simplicity. It is kind of like an iPod or iPhone. It looks very simple*

on the outside and it operates very simply but the engineering behind it is extremely complex.

Jan Shagalov: As engineers we get involved in the beauty and aesthetics of the building, and we try to make it work. We often say as structural engineers we provide the strength behind the beauty. And this makes us proud of the building altogether.

19. A SIGNAL FROM HEAVEN

The treasure trove in the company's photo archive has caused me to look ahead and foreshadow some of my father's professional accomplishments, but in 1952, the enterprise of Paul Weidlinger, Consulting Engineer, was just three years old and not yet famous. Nevertheless, my father was doing well enough to pay for a summer vacation in Europe. Madeleine's psychiatrist warned him that patients are rarely cured of schizophrenia and that he should be prepared to live with her illness for the rest of their shared life. But my father recalled that when she was released from the Institute of Living, "all of a sudden, miraculously, she was perfectly all right. She came back and we probably spent the happiest year of her life. It was a wonderful year." Her paranoia, her delusions, and her symptoms of acute agitation were gone.

Their summer vacation was a triumph. In London, where my father had struggled to eke out a living in 1936, staying just one step ahead of immigration authorities, he booked rooms at the five-star Park Lane Hotel, looking over Hyde Park and very close to Buckingham Palace. He, Madeleine, and Michèle did all the things that tourists do. I wonder what went through his mind when my twelve-year-old sister became fascinated with a beggar in Hyde Park drawing with colored chalk on the pavement. Seventeen years earlier, practically a beggar himself, he had been absorbed by a similar scene. "How will I feel . . . when I think back of this time?" he had written in his journal.

A trip to the top of the Eiffel Tower was the first thing my family did upon arriving in Paris. So much had changed since my parents had made the same pilgrimage as young lovers and gazed down upon the 1937 International Exposition, dominated by its foreboding monuments to German fascism and Soviet communism. Paul and Madeleine had survived the war, brought a child into the world and prospered. They posed in photos with Michèle on top of the tower. Michèle wrote in her diary:

It was very, very windy. I closed my eyes and stood very, very still, and I could feel the swaying of the tower. Looking down I felt quite dizzy and everything looked very small. The steel framework was frail and beautiful, like a spider's web.

On top of the Eiffel Tower.

She also noted "the funny (slanted) elevators that were designed by my great-grand-uncle (Dezső Korda), who received the Legion of Honor from the French government."

Judging from her diary, my sister wanted to remember everything. Each day of vacation was momentous and deserved a detailed account. Brief histories of the countries visited have been copied in pencil from an encyclopedia. My sister's own diary entries are typed. (Did she type them after getting home, or had my mother brought along her prized, portable machine?) Most of the pages are illustrated with drawings and photographs. Michèle also drew flight paths over maps she traced from an atlas. The longest flight, from New York to London, was required to make refueling stops in Gander, Nova Scotia, and Shannon, Ireland. It ran into a storm over the Atlantic. Michèle drew a picture of the cabin interior with luggage flying everywhere and some very scared-looking passengers.

Michèle's descriptions of the famous landmarks of London and Paris are written in the knowing, authoritative tone of an adult tour guide. Here is an entry from June 26, 1952.

> In the afternoon I went with Mommy and Daddy to Versailles.
> . . . The French revolution came about because of big taxes,
> which Louis XIV imposed on his people. When the people were
> about to storm the palace Marie-Antoinette, his wife, asked
> her courtier, "What do they want?" and he answered "They
> want bread, your Majesty" (meaning they had nothing to eat)
> and she answered: "Well, why don't they eat cake, if they have
> no bread!"

Michèle described the Changing of the Guard at Buckingham Palace, the gargoyles of Notre Dame, and, perhaps a little enviously, boys with toy sailboats in Paris' Luxembourg Gardens. She ate a huge bowl of ice cream in a Paris café and traded Mickey Mouse comics with Italian boys on the Riviera. Paul had to return to work in New York after a couple of weeks, but Madeleine and Michèle continued to Switzerland, where my sister was introduced to my

mother's extended family. Relatives doted on her, took her on pic-
nics, to a horse show and a fireworks display, and plied her with
chocolate and pastries. In my mother's hometown of La Chaux-de-
Fonds, Madeleine pointed out the haunts of her own childhood and
Michèle explored the narrow streets on a rented bike equipped with
the luxury of gears. A small boy, perhaps one of the cousins, rode
on the seat behind her.

My sister's diary entries, illustrated with Madeleine's photos, are
charmingly precocious. Rarely is there anything childlike about them.
The typed pages, maps, and historical summaries involved a huge
amount of work. Originally I thought the scrapbook must have been
conceived as a school project, but I have come to see it as a magical tal-
isman. Twelve-year-old Michèle was carefully collecting and editing
irrefutable documentary evidence of a happy, privileged, and normal
childhood with loving parents in a peaceful world. At the center of
this world is a perfect daughter—attentive, intelligent, hard-working
and seemingly mature beyond her years. She was what psychologists
now call a *parentified child*, a child so fearful of abandonment that
she mimics the demeanor and takes on the responsibilities of an adult
in the hope that it will hold her family together.

After almost three months, Madeleine and Michèle returned
to New York, where Paul was waiting for them at Idlewild Airport.
Michèle wrote:

*I saw him waiting for us. I saw him standing behind the rope,
and I impatiently jumped over the rope to give him a hug and a
kiss. The customs officers scolded me because it was forbidden.
Soon we were in a cab on the way home. Flossie [my sister's
Border Collie dog] welcomed me joyously.*

Perhaps, miraculously, my mother really was cured. Back in
her native land, she had been warmly received by her family. She
had renewed friendships from before the war and taken a lot of
photographs with her Leica. Some of these pictures were color trans-
parencies. When I was four or five, I was spellbound by her slide

shows. She would wait until it got dark and turn off all the lights. Then she flicked the switch on her hand-operated projector and the cooling fan purred. Taking a transparency from the top of a carefully ordered stack, she slid it into the circular slide holder and rotated it into the path of an intense white beam, causing the Eiffel Tower to appear suddenly on our living-room wall. Then she began to narrate the story of that glorious European summer before I was born.

I have been procrastinating writing about my own arrival into my family's life. I have been scrutinizing the photographs of me as a baby, willing these images to reveal the world as seen through my young eyes. I hope for memories and insights into an almost forgotten childhood.

My birth changed my father's trajectory only slightly. At thirty-nine, he had already had enough adventures to fill a lifetime. When I was born, his story becomes my story and my story becomes only a part of his. There are no clean edges for me where he ends and I begin.

Perhaps the dream that I had last night is a way in. I am servant to a beautiful princess who has a lover. Their affair must be kept secret. It is my job to help keep that secret, tend to the princess's luggage while caring for a tiny, perfectly formed little man, a homunculus dressed in the tweeds of an English lord. This tiny human is lifeless, yet not dead, not decaying. An autopsy must be performed. A band of miners, professional excavators, demand to do the job. But their tools are crude. What is needed is something more delicate and precise. Upon waking from my dream I realize I must both protect and uncover secrets. The princess is my sister. The homunculus is me.

My birth was unexpected. I was conceived shortly after my mother and Michèle returned from the European summer vacation. I was born in the early afternoon of Memorial Day, 1953. From her hospital bed, my mother could hear the sound of a marching band as veterans came down Manhattan's Second Avenue. My father said:

When you were born, it was for me a signal from heaven that everything was wonderful, and that had a great effect on my feelings about you. I was just completely crazy about you. I always had to restrain myself because I was aware that I was overdoing it. With Michèle I used to be critical; she did something wrong and I would say it was wrong. But I was very uncritical with you, and I used to run around with you and hold you. . . .

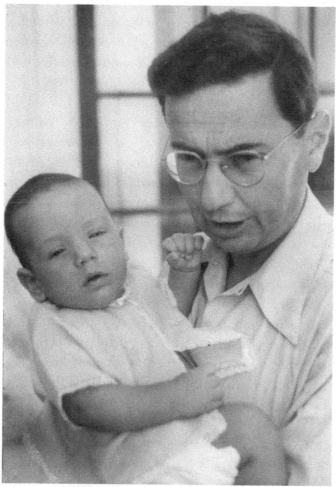

Paul Weidlinger, with his newborn son, Tom.

My earliest memories are not of my father's active physical affection but rather of lying next to him in a grey canvas hammock as he read the newspaper. As the hammock swayed the world tilted gently, and sunlight filtered through pine boughs swaying in the breeze coming off Higgins Pond. We were at our summerhouse in Wellfleet, Massachusetts, on Cape Cod. I was with my father but also separated from him by his absorption in his newspaper. It's just the same scene as he recalled, being separated from his father, with his paper, as a boy.

One person who remembered me as a toddler was my sister's friend Susanna Deiss. She and Michèle used to haul me along the sandy back roads to the ocean beach in my red Flyer Wagon. Susanna recalled that "Your mother just kind of handed you over to Michèle a huge amount of the time." One day I called Michèle "Mommy," and this made my mother extremely angry with my sister. Susanna recalled:

> Michèle seemed very intimidated by your mother. You know, not being able to please your mother, who would be very short with her. She would be reduced to tears by things your mother would say . . . and I thought your mother was totally unreasonable. But I remember Michèle feeling rather guilty, and I was constantly telling her that she was right to rebel and right not to submit. Sometimes I would spend the night over there and felt I had to tiptoe around 'cause your mother was more rigid than what I was used to.

Mostly I remember being alone. I caught frogs and stroked their cool, warty skin, letting them go when they wet my hands. I remember being fascinated by and a little scared of dragonflies with iridescent wings, which settled on the bulrushes at the edge of the pond. I played for hours at the water's edge with a toy boat, a plastic sand bucket, and a shovel.

When I was five or six, I was given my first real boat, a tiny flat-bottomed skiff with a double-bladed paddle. I started to fish. I used wire mesh to encircle and trap minnows for bait. Minnows were good for pickerel, the long thin barracudas of the freshwater world.

Freshwater mussels, dug out of the shallows and pried open, were good for sunfish and yellow perch.

One year we arrived at the beginning of summer to discover the skiff had been vandalized. Somebody had blasted a hole through the bottom with a shotgun. My mother set about repairing it, making a patch from a scrap of marine plywood obtained from Nickerson's lumber yard, carefully bolting and caulking the patch and repainting the whole boat blue and white. I knew that my mother loved me. I was the focus of her life. The violence against my little boat also seemed to confirm for me her view that the world was a dangerous and hostile place, a place that I needed to be protected from as I grew older and begged, fruitlessly, to visit other children in their homes.

We saw my father only on weekends when he came up from the city. He spent most of his time in the hammock with his paper, but I do recall being with him on the ocean beach and his showing me how to make sandcastles. We made a slurry of sand and water in a bucket and then let it drip from our hands to form sand stalagmites, crazy spires that became the towers of castles. My father also shaped life-sized human figures in the sand, quite perfectly formed. When I think of them now, they remind me of the homunculus in my dream, lifelike yet not living. This leads me to think of the way my father related to me. I was his little man, his homunculus.

When he judged me old enough to grasp the story of my name-sake, he told me about Evariste Galois. (My full name is Thomas Evariste Weidlinger.) I was five or six when I learned that Galois was a famous French mathematician who died a tragic death at the age of twenty in 1832. (Galois laid the foundations for two major branches of abstract algebra, known as Galois theory and group theory.) Like my father, Galois was a teenage firebrand arrested for anti-monarchist activities (against the French king, Louis-Philippe), but he did not die for his political convictions. He was killed in a pistol duel over a woman. He was a poor shot and knew his chances of survival were not good, but he fought anyway. To my father there was a romantic poignancy to this. But I was confused. On the one hand, it was flattering to be named after a genius. On the other, being associated with a man who died a pointless death did not seem to augur well.

I have always felt that my father loved me but he did not see me. He loved what I represented to him, a signal from heaven. I would speak to him, telling him of the fish I had caught or the things I had seen on the far side of the pond, but I was pretty sure he was not listening. He asked no questions, but told me he loved to listen to the sound of my voice, prattling on. He loved me, he provided for me and cared for me in the ways he knew how, but he neither heard nor saw me.

Michèle, although she was thirteen years older than me, did see and listen to me. When I was seven and she was midway through college, I have a vivid memory of an adventure. She breezed into our place on the Cape, back from a college semester abroad in Paris. I suspected she lived in a world of mysterious international intrigue. She is the princess in my dream. Yet when she peeled off her traveling dress and put on her faded jeans and tickled me until I cried uncle, she was still my sister. She'd cocked a forefinger to my head and whispered in a desperado voice, "Talk to me, pardner, or you're a goner! Tell all." I told her about a mysterious creek that let out of the pond near our summer house. With my skiff I had patrolled the shore but had never ventured up the creek. It lay there, darkly silent and beckoning. Michèle held up a hand to silence me and said, "You and me, pardner, we're headed downriver."

The next morning we packed sandwiches and went. At the edge of the lake, we had to force the skiff through a bed of reeds to get into the main channel. Then, abruptly, we were in a forest tunnel. It was spooky, and Michèle imitated the screeches of baboons and exotic jungle birds. She made me admit that I saw crocodiles in the bulrushes and hippos lurking beneath the lilies. Like our father, she had a creative imagination, and I was completely seduced by the stories she told. I was so happy, so grateful to have her all to myself for one long summer day.

The next day our whole family went swimming at the ocean beach. Michèle struck out for deep water. She was a strong swimmer and no one noticed until she was just a speck in the water, still heading away from the shore. We called to her but she could not hear us. Then we lost sight of her. There was no lifeguard. We knew there were riptides. It seemed a very long time before we saw her again, heading back to us. Strangely, none of us said a word when she came out of the water, spread her towel on the sand, and lay down to work on her suntan, loosening the back strap of her bikini.

Michèle and Tom Weidlinger in Wellfleet, summer 1959.

The adult world that my parents belonged to on Cape Cod seems entirely separate from my childhood memories, yet it is also a part of this narrative. It was thanks to Marcel Breuer, the Hungarian architect, that my father bought four acres of land and built his house on Higgins Pond in Wellfleet. Breuer was part of the circle of Bauhaus émigrés around Walter Gropius, who discovered a little piece of paradise on Cape Cod and there erected their summer homes. Our summer place was built the year I was born. It was like a tree house . . . or a ship in the forest.

I loved this house fiercely. I loved how the late afternoon sunlight cast the shadows of pines on its white interior walls. I loved hearing the distant sound of surf when the wind was blowing onshore. I loved early mornings, waking up in a silence so deep I could hear the blood pulsing in my ears. I loved the wet prints my feet made on the wooden ramp after I went swimming in the pond. I loved that somehow, despite all the inexplicable tensions between the members of my family, I felt completely safe in this house. Throughout my life, it is a place I return to in my dreams.

In their book, *Cape Modern*, architectural historians Peter McMahon and Christine Cipriani write: "The house is a clear structural diagram, a small glimpse into the thought process of one of the twentieth century's great engineers." The design is elegant in its simplicity, a rectangular box built on a slope with its southern end floating in space amongst the trees, supported by slender stilts. The south and west walls of the living room are floor-to-ceiling sliding glass panels that create the most delicate and permeable boundary between inside and outside. The house is honest in its use of simple materials, adhering to Bauhaus principles.

Paul, casting himself as an iconoclast, loved to tell the story of its design.

When I began to work on it, there were a lot of famous architects in that neighborhood and they offered all kinds of suggestions. I totally ignored them. Then Le Corbusier came to New York and I spent some time with him and he told me that

I did everything wrong. And then when the house was built, one of the architecture magazines featured it, and there was a list of the names of the foremost architects in the world whose advice I totally ignored.

The Weidlinger House in Wellfleet, Massachusetts.

Wellfleet in the 1950s was a charmed place, a serendipitous artists' colony for European émigrés as well as notable authors, scientists,
and artists. Gropius, Breuer, György Kepes, and Weidlinger were
joined by Saul Bellow, Philip Roth, Edmund Wilson, Dwight Mac-
Donald, Mary McCarthy, and Arthur Schlesinger, Jr. Kepes' daughter,
Julie, was another friend of Michèle's who also remembers towing me
around in my wagon. She recalled:

*Many of us had funny accents and came from other countries.
But it was a wonderful, idyllic kind of situation. Everybody
was so close and we all played together. The parents had cock-
tail parties and went swimming together. There was the group
that went to the beach and everyone was naked. There was the
group that worked all the time. . . .*

What Julie, my sister and I didn't know was that our families—
the Weidlingers, the Breuers, the Kepes, the Chermayeffs—had a
secret in common. Julie said:

*The kids never knew many of us were Jewish. But there was
this undercurrent of knowing and not knowing. Of nudging
and prodding.*
*I would tease my mom. The fridge was always full of food,
and I would say "Mom, what's the problem? You have to stock
up for the pogrom?" And she would say, "Oh no, don't be silly.
We are not Jewish. Don't talk like that!" It was something you
didn't joke about, even though I thought it was hilariously
funny. But I seriously wanted to know: "Who am I? Where did
I come from? Why these secrets . . . why is this angst present?"*

I asked Julie: "How is it possible that you did not discover, defini-
tively, that you were Jewish until the age of forty?"

*I think it is a form of denial that many of us children of sur-
vivors have . . . that we didn't want to push our parents back*

into that pain if they weren't willing to go there . . . and one can say, and I guess people do, that it was too horrific to remember, or the guilt was too enormous to bear, or they were protecting us. I think all those things are true.

20. THE SLEEP OF REASON

My most vivid recollections are from the Cape, but I do recall our apartment, not far from the United Nations building in New York. One winter I went through a period of night terrors. I was terrified of skeletons under my bed. My father would take me in his arms and pace back and forth in my bedroom, singing the lullabies that his German nanny had sung to him as a child. He also sang an old English folk song that he had heard on one of my mother's Burl Ives albums:

> *When I was a bachelor I lived all alone*
> *I worked at the weaver's trade*
> *And the only, only thing that I did that was wrong*
> *Was to woo a fair young maid.*

> *One night she knelt close by my side*
> *When I was fast asleep*
> *She threw her arms around my neck*
> *And then began to weep.*

She wept, she cried, she tore her hair
Ah, me, what could I do?
So all night long, I held her in my arms
Just to keep her from the foggy, foggy dew.

Again I am a bachelor, I live with my son
We work at the weaver's trade
And every single time that I look into his eyes
He reminds me of that fair young maid.

Did my father feel he had been wrong to woo my mother who had borne him a son? Would she leave him? Would he abandon her in her anguish? In retrospect the song seems like a premonition.

My mother's schizophrenia had not been cured but was in remission in the years after my birth. But when I started going to school, sometimes a schoolmate's parents would collect me along with their child after classes because my mother had "taken ill." Or arrangements would be made for our maid to take care of me until my father got home. My mother would be gone for weeks for stays at various hospitals.

There were periods when she was fine, when she took good care of me, when I keenly felt her love. Then she would be gone again. The hardest times were when she was home but sliding into madness. She was scary, sometimes hearing voices, seeing things that weren't there. She was physically large and also large in her gestures; she had a way of completely dominating the space she occupied. There was this feeling of pent-up emotion. Safety (or the illusion of safety) lay in being able to predict and defuse a violent outburst.

I have been dredging for specific memories with trepidation. The following one hit me viscerally, I began to sweat and my breathing became constricted. Suddenly I was seven years old. It was lunchtime, and somehow I was not at school but sitting in the kitchen of our New York apartment. My mother was very angry for some small oversight in the way I was dressed, or perhaps I had not combed my hair. Beyond this she was angered by the way a sales clerk at D'Agostino's grocery store had spoken to her. She believed that all the store personnel were watching her, waiting for her to make some misstep for which she would be reported to a nameless authority. It was important to my mother that I side with her against the grocery store people. Could I not see what they were trying to do to her?

I was afraid of what she would do to me if I did not validate her madness. She slammed plates of food on the table and began eating. She made loud smacking noises with her lips and chewed noisily . . . like an animal. (I learned later that this a manifestation of tardive dyskinesia, a side effect of early antipsychotic medications.) The person who had been my mother just a few hours earlier was gone, replaced by an angry animal. I was scared. Somehow I managed to retreat to my room, where I had a set of wooden blocks. I started to build a tower with the blocks, as tall as possible. This calmed me.

As an adult I want to soothe this frightened child who is suddenly there again, inside of me. I feel great sorrow and compassion for him. In my mind I sit down on the floor across from him. The tower of blocks is between us. With his permission he lets me add a block to the tower. Then he adds another. We are very careful, very quiet and very gentle in our actions.

My parents kept all the letters that I wrote to them. I did not keep their letters but my mother made carbon copies of some of hers and I have these now. The earliest letter I can find that I wrote to my mother is from November 1962, during one of her stays in a hospital. I am nine.

Dear Mom: Thank you for the ski hat and the muffler or whatever you call it. I am sorry you cannot be with us on Thanksgiving. I hope you get out soon. Cheetah [my cat] is home again and meowing as ever. My report card is coming next week. We have a gallon of fresh cider from the country. Love Tom.

My mother wrote back to me from the hospital with praise for a good report card which my father had sent to her.

Dearest Tom: It makes me happy to know that you are doing well at school and that you are a good boy. I feel much better today, and your letter and Dad's arrived to cheer me up. Every morning and evening I look at the blue [origami] bird you sent me, and it is like you were sending me a kiss. Every morning also I think, "Maybe today I can go home." But the doctors are very cautious and slow. Many kisses from Mammy.

———————

Weeks later I came home from school to find both of my parents sitting on their bed. The fact that they were sitting was odd. My father never sat. He always lay back with his newspaper. My mother was weeping, but instead of comforting her, my father just sat frozen. That evening they explained to me that they were getting divorced but that they each loved me very much.

Because my mother frequently had to go to the hospital and my father had to work at the office, it was explained to me that I would be sent to boarding school. I was told I would really like this school. It was on a farm in the Adirondacks. There were horses to ride and there was skiing.

I remember boarding school as a time of loneliness and awkwardness. I did not make friends easily, as I had had little practice. I was very tall for my age, not good at sports, and generally didn't fit in. Yet, according to the letters I wrote to my parents, I loved boarding school. The letters are filled with vivid details of my accomplishments and claims of friendships with my roommates. I did catch my young self in one outright lie. I wrote: "This year I am trying out for the soccer team and I will probably be accepted." I was undoubtedly the worst soccer player in the school but persisted in trying until I broke my leg in a spectacularly uncoordinated move.

Also, there are many requests and acknowledgments of things that my father sent to me: a chemistry set, a kit to build model airplanes from delicate balsa wood, a new pair of ski boots with buckles (not laces, like the old ones had.) Then I started receiving "care packages" from my father's new wife, Solveig, whom he married as soon as the divorce with Madeleine was finalized. Solveig made good brownies.

My father kept my report cards, and they show that I got good grades. My house-parents sent glowing reports of my good behavior. The evidence suggested that I was a model child and student. It is all eerily reminiscent of my sister's European diary. We both worked so hard to be good children. To be otherwise risked threatening whatever connection we had left with our parents. I often asked my father to visit me at school. I wrote: "You are working so hard at the office, surely a short vacation in the Adirondacks would do you some good." I also wrote to my mother but did not ask her to visit. Being embarrassed by her unpredictably bizarre behavior in front of my schoolmates was not something I wanted to risk.

Yet I had no power to keep her away, and she was the one who usually showed up at parents' weekends. She brought her camera. In all the pictures of me—on horseback, sitting on a rail fence, in typing class—I look sullen and self-conscious. The pictures (rather than the brave words in my letters) seem a more accurate representation of how I remember feeling at the time.

My mother was an avid supporter of my cultural education, and during school vacations when she was not in hospital, she took me to many of New York's museums. I was awed by the brontosaurus at the Museum of Natural History and disturbed by Picasso's contortions of the human body at the Museum of Modern Art, but there is one image that deeply resonated for reasons my ten-year-old self would have been hard pressed to articulate. This was an etching by Francisco Goya, entitled *The Sleep of Reason Produces Monsters, 1799*. It shows a man asleep at a table as sinister dark-winged beasts swarm around him.

When I was a child, my mother and father often appealed to my "sense of reason" when I disagreed or argued with them. When I was wrong, I was not being "reasonable or rational." In Goya's picture the sleeping man was the personification of this quality of reasonableness which I rejected, for intuitively I felt that what was called "reason" or "rational" discourse in our family was a kind of lulling sleep which simply ignored, or even denied, the existence of the frightening monsters produced by my mother's madness. I wanted to sound the alarm. Unreasonably, I wanted to wake the sleeper before he was devoured by the demons that were descending upon him.

The Sleep of Reason Produces Monsters,
by Francisco Goya (1799).

The divorce agreement between my parents stated that "The Wife shall have the custody, care and control of the Son during his minority. . . ." subject to Father's visitation rights. When I was alone with my mother between the ages of ten and fifteen, there were often monsters in the room. In the house on Cape Cod (which my mother received in the divorce), I was often scared of her. She would fly into unpredictable rages, and I would hide behind the woodpile underneath the house or climb up into the sheltering boughs of a pine tree. The safest refuge was to go out on the lake in my skiff for hours and fish. Then at twilight my mother would stand on the shore and call out to me, telling me to come home to dinner. I remember a nightmare in which her voice was like a fishing line, and I was hooked, being reeled in toward a whirlpool of madness.

During the school year when I was thirteen and old enough to take the bus by myself from school in upstate New York to the city, I went AWOL over Thanksgiving vacation. I hid out in a schoolmate's Greenwich Village apartment rather than go home to my mother.

My most vivid recollection, the point at which I could assert to my father that my mother really *was crazy*, not just "difficult" or "eccentric," was when she came to pick me up at school at the beginning of summer vacation. (I learned later that she had stopped taking her anti-psychotic medications months earlier.) I was fifteen at the end of sophomore year, having skipped a grade. After graduation ceremonies she made a scene, loudly accusing my house master of being a homosexual in front of students, faculty, and parents. Then, on our drive back to the Cape, she dangerously swerved off the highway, skidding to a stop on the gravel shoulder. When I asked her why she had done this she looked at me with absolute incredulity. "Did you not see the man who was aiming his gun at us from a passing car?"

That evening my mother tried to climb into my narrow bunk bed with me. Terrified, I pushed her away. I lay awake until I could hear her snoring in the adjacent room. Then I put a few things in my school rucksack and crept out of the house, walking in darkness the two miles to the state highway. I then hitchhiked to New York City and rang the doorbell of my father's apartment.

When I told Paul what had happened he gave me money to go to Portland, Oregon, where Michèle was living and where I could attend a kind of urban summer camp organized by Quakers.

I have letters between myself and my mother during those summer months, and also letters from my sister to my father during the same period. What is extraordinary about them is their universal politeness and "reasonableness." My mother is frankly mystified at why I left her so abruptly. I explained to her in great detail everything that I was doing and experiencing at the Quaker camp, emphasizing what a positive experience it was for me. She missed me and thought it would be much better for my "development" if I returned to her on the Cape; but she begrudgingly allowed me to spend two months with the Quakers and my sister in Oregon.

Afraid to be alone with her again, I wrote to her: ". . . if you still love me or Michèle and are expecting either of us to come to Wellfleet, it is imperative that you visit a psychiatrist and prove to me, Michèle, and Daddy that you are in a normal mental state. We love you very much and are thinking of you. Love, Tom."

She replied: "I can only say that this smacks of arrogance and it sounds like an ultimatum. If you are not here by the third of August, as decided, I shall take legal steps necessary to reestablish my right to your custody. . . ."

How could my father, who was a "reasonable" and "rational" man, give custody of me to my mother who, on many occasions, had shown herself to be unreasonable and irrational, a danger to herself and others, and in need of psychiatric hospitalization? Surely it had something to do with this dangerous sleepiness that I felt was expressed in Goya's picture. When I approached this topic in my interview with him in 1996, I did so with rage, but with a rage crouched behind a tone of "reasonable" interrogation, which I had become quite adept at in my work as a documentary filmmaker.

PAUL
And she got a lawyer, and I remember I was so upset about it I didn't even want to have a lawyer. . . . She told me everything that she wanted, and I just agreed to everything. You know, she insisted that you live with her and . . . I realized that you were very important for her.

TOM
What do you mean?

PAUL
When . . . you know, the fact that she was taking care of you was very important for her.

TOM
What was your perception of me at the time and how I was relating to her?

PAUL
I . . . again I . . . you know . . . my perception was that everything was okay because I . . . I couldn't . . . I wouldn't have accepted it if it was. . . I couldn't live with it if it wasn't.

TOM
I see.

I had no choice but to go back to the Cape as my mother had demanded. She had reported me to the police in Portland as missing from home. My sister came with me and tried to effect a reconciliation, but neither she nor my father seemed able to perceive the monsters in the room, to acknowledge my mother's madness. To be sure, it was only intermittently manifest and concealed behind a strong set of well-reasoned values about right and wrong and what was appropriate for the upbringing of her son.

Back at boarding school, I continued with the careful and reasonable tone of my letters, hoping that detailed descriptions of my life and accomplishments would keep my mother from too drastic an exercise of her legal authority. She responded with long, typed letters filled with beautifully reasoned opinions and loving advice, which I ignored. I avoided seeing her as much as possible. Sometimes she would call me late at night on the communal phone in my house, waking up my house-parents and other students. "You bitch," I would say over the phone. "Stop bothering us." Though the words "Love, Tom" are written at the bottom of all my letters to my mother, I both feared and hated her. Hatred seemed to only way to resist being reeled in toward the whirlpool of madness, which I believed could drown me.

Here is the conclusion of my conversation with my father in 1996.

PAUL

I lived under the illusion that everything was fine with . . . that she was taking care of you and everything.

TOM

I remember going through periods when I was extremely angry at both of you.

PAUL

Yeah. Oh sure.

TOM

And . . . I just wonder if you remember that. . . .

PAUL

Oh, yes.

TOM

. . . and . . . what your . . . if you understood why, you know, what was going on there.

PAUL

Oh yes, I fully understood it. I just didn't want to accept it. I mean I saw it. I understood it. But I didn't believe it. Or I didn't want to believe it. And you know, you fool yourself. I . . . I had a . . . you know, I always had the feeling about you that you were a completely self-sufficient, reliable person and I said everything's going to be okay because . . . Tom knows how to deal with everything.

TOM
It's a little naïve, isn't it?

PAUL
Of course it is naïve, yeah, it is. But one stops being rational when you are faced with unsolvable issues.

I confess that it is with some satisfaction that I heard my father actually admitting to the fact that he was not always rational.

21. THE COLD WAR

The disintegration of my parents' marriage paralleled the escalation of the Cold War and Paul's increasing involvement in nuclear deterrence. When I was little, he used to tell me that he was a three-star general in the US Air Force. I was dubious. If this were true, where was his uniform? Smiling, he would tell me that he was so important that he didn't need one. I found out that in a manner of speaking, this was true. A Noncombatant Certificate of Identity was issued to Paul Weidlinger by the Air Force, giving him the rank of "general" and stipulating that he was entitled to "the same treatment and . . . privileges as an individual of corresponding rank." Paul loved to tell how, on a remote base in Arizona, he had outranked a visiting colonel who was forced to surrender his VIP quarters to him.

What was Paul doing for the Air Force as a "general?" He was rather vague about this, but it had something to do with protecting us from the Russians. When I was nine, he explained to me the military doctrine of *détente* based on "mutual assured destruction" which he referred to by its acronym, MAD. This was disturbing to me. My child's logic went like this: My mother's name was Madeleine. Friends sometimes called her Maddo, and she often signed her letters and notes "Mad." I worried that my mother was crazy mad. MAD meant mutual assured destruction and this meant that all of us were pre-destined to go mad and be destroyed. I never actually shared this fear with my parents. I would not even have been able to put it into words.

Paul explained to me that the theory of mutual assured destruction made three assumptions about a nuclear stand-off between two super-powers. 1) The enemies want to destroy each other. 2) Each has enough nuclear weapons to destroy the other side. 3) Either side, if attacked for any reason by the other, will retaliate with maximum force. The result would be an unstoppable escalation of hostilities, resulting in the total destruction of each side. Since neither side would rationally choose this, this resulted in a tense but stable global peace, called *détente*.

The earliest evidence I have of my father's defense work is three photographs I found among his papers. In 1957 they would have been classified as top secret. They show different views of a plastic model airplane emerging from an odd-shaped cardboard box. Interestingly, at my father's request, the pictures were shot and developed by my mother.

Paul and his young partner, Matthys Levy, had designed a shelter, a kind of underground parking garage, to protect a B-58 bomber from the blast wave of a thermonuclear bomb. In my mind I replay slow motion footage of early atom bomb tests in which solid structures—trees, vehicles and entire buildings—eerily lift, splinter, float, and tumble in a blast wave. Paul and Matthys calculated that, while the blast wave would sweep away and incinerate all above-ground "soft"

Paul and Matthys Levy's B-58 bomber shelter.

structures within a certain radius of ground zero, it was possible to protect an aircraft inside a concrete bunker so that it could then emerge, take to the air and deliver a retaliatory blow.

The man who first kindled my father's fascination with calculating the effect of nuclear blast waves was Albert Wohlstetter, a friend who had worked with him on postwar veterans' housing. By the early 1950s, Wohlstetter had become a defense analyst. He invited my father to a conference that posed the question: "How can structures be designed to survive a nuclear shockwave?" At the conference, the most prominent structural engineers in the country declared that it was impossible to design for the extreme impact of thermonuclear blasts. My father thought this was nonsense. Just because it hadn't been done before didn't mean it couldn't be done.

To embrace this challenge, my father sought help from a mathematician, Mario Salvadori, who had worked on the Manhattan Project, which produced the atom bombs dropped on Hiroshima and Nagasaki.

Salvadori wrote in his own memoir:

> We started working on whether a structure of a building could be built nearer to ground zero [the point where a bomb could fall] than what had been established so far. After a few months' work, we had designed a structure that could be built fifty times nearer to ground zero than the specialists had believed possible. Paul presented our paper to a large group of experts in the dynamics of structures. When he concluded the talk with our figure of "fifty times nearer to ground zero," the amazed audience remained silent for a few seconds and then exploded into prolonged applause.

Salvadori asked Paul: "What are we going to do with this success?"

> "We are going to ask for money from the National Science Foundation or the Pentagon," he said, "and refine our calculations . . . and then we are going to get more money."

Salvadori became one of my father's principal partners, staying with the firm for thirty-five years, but after his initial collaboration he did not work on defense contracts. He could not bring himself to rationalize the horrific destruction of Hiroshima and Nagasaki, and he could not subscribe to the prevailing Cold War policy of deterrence based on the theory of mutual assured destruction.

My father *did* believe in détente based on MAD, and his extensive work on hardening structures to withstand nuclear blasts rested on this belief. More specifically, his work was rooted in the reasoning that in order to deter the Soviet Union from starting a nuclear war, the United States had to show credible evidence of its ability to retaliate on a massive scale. This reasoning became codified in the military doctrine of "second-strike capability," which was principally authored by Wohlstetter. The issue was not how many weapons we had in our nuclear arsenal, but how many we would have left to retaliate with. Therefore, it was essential to protect bombers and missiles in structures that could survive a surprise attack.

But before Paul could reap the full benefit of his demonstration with Salvadori and begin to design silos for missiles with nuclear warheads, he needed top-secret security clearance. At a time when Senator Joseph McCarthy's House Un-American Activities Committee believed that communist subversives had infiltrated every American institution, it was astonishing that FBI agents didn't uncover Paul's role in the 1932 Red Student affair in Hungary. The story of his security vetting was told to me by Nanci Buscemi, an engineer who worked with him in later years.

They interviewed him. They said, "We're shocked that you would apply for clearance when you have family behind the Iron Curtain." But they needed him and he knew it. There was a room full of one hundred and twenty men and they questioned him. Someone asked him, "Well, what would you do if somebody threatened your family to get secrets from you?" He told them, "I would commit suicide."

This was the ideal solution from a security standpoint. I think Paul also really meant it. As teenagers he and Ili concluded that suicide was morally acceptable—even heroic under certain circumstances. My father's answer earned him his top-secret security clearance, which opened the way for some twenty-five years of defense contracts.

Within the logical framework of the doctrine of second-strike capability, the work done by Weidlinger Associates' new Applied Sciences Division made sense. In the late 1950s, missile guidance systems were pretty inaccurate, and it was estimated that most missiles would miss their targets by miles, yet their shockwaves would still cause damage over a very large area. Weidlinger showed that at relatively little expense, concrete abutments, bunkers, and hardened missile silos could protect weapons against this shockwave, provided they were not too close to ground zero. But the solution was temporary. As guidance systems improved and missiles were expected to hit closer to their targets, more and more robust and expensive measures for protection would be needed.

The doctrine of second-strike capability demanded that these measures be taken. But how far could one go? Nanci Buscemi, who worked with Paul on the design of missile silos, posed this question.

I started thinking maybe I shouldn't be doing this . . . designing protection for [nuclear] weapons. Once I saw how much pressure was going to be on our structure [from a nuclear blast] I realized that there wouldn't be any people left. So what are we doing here? What's the point? Paul was there in my office and he just wrote one word in big letters on my blackboard: "DÉTENTE". That was it.

My father didn't wait for Nanci's response. He just left the room.

In the United States, the heroes of the nuclear age were people like my father. In an imagined World War III, G.I. Joe would be replaced by the brilliant defense intellectual—scientists, systems analysts, and practitioners of game theory. Extrapolating from the experience of World War II, these defense intellectuals believed that Stalin and his successors would, like Hitler, aim for world domination. This fear was supported by Stalin's brutal purges and early Soviet testing of nuclear weapons. It was made visceral for Jews who had survived the Holocaust, my father among them.

The place where defense intellectuals congregated, worked, and challenged each other's hypotheses about modern warfare was the RAND (an acronym for Research ANd Development) Corporation, a think tank created by the Air Force. In an article titled "The War of Wits," the journalist John MacDonald, writing in *Fortune,* described RAND as "a kind of secular monastery—worldly in rubbing shoulders with the physical and social sciences, industry, and the military . . . yet monastic in its security isolation." In *Life* magazine's lavish photo essay, entitled "A Valuable Batch of Brains," nerds are heroes and RAND is their playground. The *Los Angeles Times* exalted RAND "as the treasure of the new era, the abstract jewels of men's minds, the unleashed thoughts, the soaring, science-spurred image upon which the future floats. . . ."

General Paul Weidlinger was identified on his Air Force ID card as "Research Analyst, The RAND Corporation." It didn't hurt that he was a Hungarian. The physicists Edward Teller, Eugene Wigner, and Leó Szilárd, and the mathematician John von Neumann were all Hungarians who had worked on the Manhattan Project building the atom bomb. There was a certain mystique about Hungarians. In the RAND canteen, a joke circulated, "The aliens have landed and they are among us. They are called Hungarians."

Paul loved that he had won admission to the inner sanctum of American defense intellectuals. He said to me:

> *They had all these geniuses around there and . . . the modern computer was invented by John von Neumann. The first time somebody told me about computers it was von Neumann.*

Von Neumann had demonstrated that a computer could have a simple, fixed structure, yet be able to execute any kind of computation without the need for hardware modification. By the early 1950s, computers based on von Neumann architecture began to be used for limited commercial and military application. The Cold War fueled and coincided with their development.

Up to this point, the calculating tools in my father's office were slide rules and electromechanical Friden calculators. But the calculations required to determine the effects of nuclear blasts were so complex they could only be done by a computer. Contracts with the Air Force and the Defense Nuclear Agency propelled Weidlinger Associates into the computer age.

When I was eight years old, I remember my father taking me into a magical room full of consoles with blinking lights, banks of cabinets with spinning reels of tape, and white-coated technicians. Everything seemed choreographed to the exciting, staccato click and whirr of punch card readers. It was August in New York and very hot outside . . . but inside this inner sanctum, housing the room-sized IBM 1620 mainframe, it was cold, kept so by the powerful air conditioners needed to counteract the heat generated by the machine's hundreds of vacuum tubes. I was in awe. My father's authoritative air and the respect with which the men in the computer room spoke to him made it clear that this was his show; he was their fearless leader. This could have been a scene in Korda's film, *Things to Come,* in which engineers build a new world.

Computers did the calculations, but it was humans who came up with models and hypotheses that were being tested. Paul had an uncanny, intuitive sense about what would work. Ray Daddazio said:

> *The extreme loading [impact of a shockwave] on a structure was well beyond what engineers had ever been trained to design for. . . . So how did we know what to do? Paul came up with something in the ballpark from his first guess. I remember one of the analysts from the Applied Science Group came running into his office, saying, "Paul! Paul! We just got . . . we just*

got the analysis back, and your design is going to work!" Paul had this back-of-the-envelope drawing in pencil for the head works of a missile silo on his desk, and he said, "I knew that my silo was gonna work, but now I know that your program is gonna work!"

The young men and women Paul hired out of grad school to work with him on these problems both respected and feared him. Here is what they said:

He was a bit of a father figure. He was always the boss. That was clear, and don't screw it up. And if you did, you're going to get yelled at.

I was always scared of him. He was very intimidating.

He was mean sometimes, if you made mistakes or asked something silly that didn't make sense. Sometimes he would make fun of people.

There are legendary stories of people quitting on their first day here because of something he said to them.

There was rarely a subject you could touch on that he didn't seem to know a lot more about than you did! You could never one-up him.

You didn't want to cross your dad.

Why did they put up with him? He had one of the most brilliant minds in the field, and they knew they could learn from him. Everyone I interviewed made a career at Weidlinger Associates, and many of them, if not retired, are now in senior management positions. A younger generation of engineers who came to work for the firm in the 1980s reverentially referred to my father as "The Wizard" because of his startling ability to see the heart of an intransigent structural problem and solve it with the single deft stroke of an equation on a chalkboard.

My father was not modest about being smart. He claimed he had an IQ of 154. Matthys Levy recalls that when he was struggling through a particularly thorny mathematical problem, Paul would often chide him, saying, "I learned how to do that in Hungarian elementary school."

In 1958 the Air Force estimated that the Russians were far ahead of us in nuclear weapons production, creating a dangerous "missile gap." According to Air Force intelligence, the Soviets had 700 to 1,000 intercontinental ballistic missiles, or four to five times more than the United States. Panic ensued. Many people took seriously the possibility, even the likelihood, of an all-out Soviet nuclear attack on the United States. US missile development and production became a top priority, and civil defense films were made to educate Americans about what to do in the case of a nuclear attack. They are heartbreakingly naïve. They advised teachers and parents to train children to "duck and cover" if they saw a bright flash in the sky. The films suggested that a few weeks' supply of canned foods in your fallout shelter could get you through a nuclear war.

Between 1952 and 1957, hundreds of thousands volunteered for the civilian Ground Observer Corps, organized to scan the skies for enemy bombers. Posters, leaflets, and radio announcements exhorted citizens to "Wake up! Sign up! Look up!"

Many flocked to apocalyptic religion. In the summer of 1957, evangelist Billy Graham mobilized two million people in the streets, lecture halls, and pavilions of New York to worship Jesus Christ. Graham warned of the "End of Time." "I have the feeling that something is about to happen, some great thing above all that we ask or think, when we shall have to pay with our blood for following Christ."

I think of Ili, my father's childhood friend, on the other side of the Iron Curtain. She lived in a place where fear was also virulent and people who dared to speak their truth were persecuted. Her defense, her *religion,* was Stalinist communism . . . so, Paul's bosom friend became his "enemy."

What must this have been like for my mother? She was aware at times that she was ill, that she saw things that weren't there and imagined threats to herself and her family that were not real. But she also lived in a society pervaded by fear, which often bordered on the irrational. Both Paul and Madeleine had been socialists, if not communist sympathizers, in their youth. Perhaps they were being secretly targeted by McCarthy's spies? Might this explain the hostile and furtive behavior of individuals that Madeleine imagined when she came into contact with people in public places? If you know you are crazy but are also living in a crazy world, how do you distinguish between individual and collective insanity? To make matters worse, what animated my father, his fascination with the physics of nuclear war, was not something that he could talk about with my mother. Could he too be part of the conspiracy against her? Madeleine, Maddo, Mad . . . Mutual Assured Destruction.

A major turning point in the Cold War came in 1961. Satellite imagery produced a stunning revelation: the feared missile gap was a fiction. The Soviet Union had only four operational intercontinental ballistic missiles (ICBMs), instead of the 700 to 1,000 that had been estimated by the Air Force three years earlier. My father, the RAND Corporation, the Air Force, and the entire US defense establishment had been working feverishly and spending millions of dollars to respond to a threat that did not exist. One of the pillars of the doctrine of mutual assured destruction was not there. It was not true that "each side had enough nuclear weapons to destroy the other." The Soviet Union had next to nothing.

I interviewed Daniel Ellsberg, who had been a young analyst at RAND in the late 1950s and early '60s. When Ellsberg joined RAND, he declined to accept a very generous pension plan requiring small contributions from his monthly paycheck. He told me, "I did not think I would live to enjoy the RAND retirement program." He believed nuclear annihilation was more than likely.

Ellsberg's perspective changed with the revelation that the Soviets had only four ICBMs.

I am sorry to say it, but your father made no contribution to the security of the United States, nor did anyone at RAND, including myself. And it was worse than that, because we carried on this belief in an imminent Soviet surprise attack. RAND was crucial in killing the idea of a test ban on warheads, which would have prevented the ICBM buildup on both sides. Then, when Khrushchev was replaced by Brezhnev in 1964, he gave the Soviet military what they wanted, which was what the US had by then—several thousand warheads. So RAND contributed to keeping the arms race going when there was no race. In the 1950s we could have focused on averting a Soviet ICBM force by restraining our own buildup, but both sides ended up with thousands of warheads. What we now know about nuclear winter is that a couple hundred of those would destroy life on Earth. The RAND contribution was disastrous. Looking back on it, I see myself as having been a member of a cult, an apocalyptic cult.

From the 1960s through the mid-1980s, the Applied Science Division of Weidlinger Associates continued to work on ever more robust missile silos to defend against the increasing accuracy of missile guidance systems. Paul's protégé and closest collaborator on this work during the latter years was Eve Hinman. She recalls:

Paul proposed to the Air Force that he could design a missile silo that was much stronger than anything else in existence. He loved making these big claims. He said, "It could be in the crater." Being in the crater was a big deal . . . something crazy. So they hired him, and he came up with this interesting shape, like a capsule rounded on both sides, so it could bury itself in the earth and protect itself in that way.

Paul had a whole entourage of engineers go with him to
San Bernardino, California, for this meeting with the Air Force
where he was barraged with questions. "Why did you do this?"
"How come you're doing that?" It was very aggressive question-
ing, and Paul relished every minute. Up to that point I hadn't
really seen him in action. He was amazing. When they wanted
to put a seven-foot by three-foot doorway into the missile silo
so you could go in and inspect it, Paul said, "Why is that? So
that the general with his big hat can pass through the opening?"
[laughing] He had a comeback for everything. He loved that
confrontation, he just loved it.

When I was a very small child my father played a game with me
called "Where shall I jump?" He would encase me in his arms and
pretend that his forefinger was an impatient, talking flea. "Where shall
I jump?" asked the flea, and I would point to a place on my body. But as
soon as the flea landed, it asked the question again . . . and again and
again . . . faster and faster. I could not keep up. I was very ticklish and
the "flea" would torment me until I cried uncle. Even though I always
lost, I wanted to play the game because I got my father's attention.

As a teenager I had qualms about the defense work Paul was
doing, although I only had a vague idea of it. When I tried to engage
him in a moral debate about the nuclear arms race, our conversation
felt like a game of "Where shall I jump?" There was no way I could stay
ahead of him . . . no way to pin him down. With my father there was
no "right" or "wrong." Everything was relative, depending on how you
looked at it. My father kept changing the frame and the perspective of
our conversation. In the end my head was spinning. I felt like an idiot.

Lorraine Whitman, a woman much more articulate than my
teenage self, had similar qualms and perceptions. She was a senior
research engineer in the Applied Science Group working on how to
hunt and kill the Soviet Typhoon-class nuclear submarine.

Your father was very sophisticated, very subtle, and could come
up with fifteen ways to get around whatever your argument

was. His arguments were probably based on a kernel of truth, but he would stray from that kernel in order to best you. He enjoyed playing games. I could have brought up the conflicts I was feeling, but I didn't feel that he was the kind of person I could bare my soul to.

Playing games, postulating alternate scenarios, was also the approach of Herman Kahn, a nuclear war strategist at RAND, and one of my father's closest friends. Paul told me:

He was the brightest person I ever met and had a great influence on me. He had a hundred times the knowledge and education in physics than I had, but I had interesting ideas. He was willing to listen to them and take them seriously.

Kahn came to our apartment in New York when I was eight years old. I worried that he would break our furniture. He weighed about three hundred pounds, and there was no way that one of our delicate, modern Danish, three-legged chairs could support his bulk. He sat on the couch. He spoke very fast, like a standup comic. In a *Life* magazine article, under the heading, "I am one of the ten most famous obscure Americans," he said:

I am big, fat, and lousy Jewish, and they take it. They take it because they know I'm worried about the country. They take a lot of crap from me that they wouldn't take from anyone else.

In a *New Yorker* review of *The Worlds of Herman Kahn,* Louis Menand sums up the man:

He was a marathon Spielmeister, whose preferred format was the twelve-hour lecture, split into three parts over two days, with no text but with plenty of charts and slides. He was a jocular, gregarious giant who chattered on about fallout shelters, megaton bombs, and the incineration of millions. Observers

were charmed or repelled, sometimes charmed and *repelled.*
Reporters referred to him as "a roly-poly, second-strike Santa
Claus" and "a thermonuclear Zero Mostel." He is supposed to
have had the highest IQ on record.

In 1960 Kahn published his controversial book, *On Thermo-nuclear War,* which described how a nuclear war might be started, waged, ended, and (possibly) survived by some remnant of the American population. In my father's copy of Kahn's book, the author wrote:

Dear Paul: This is a report that will not be lightly revised. You
can read it safely. However, if you have any suggestions, send
them. I hope to have a new printing soon. Herman.

The book is not a report, but rather a series of speculations about thermonuclear war, including a doomsday machine.

Assume that for, say, $10 billion we could build a device whose
only function is to destroy all human life. If, say, five nuclear
bombs exploded over the United States, the device would be
triggered and the earth destroyed. Barring . . . coding errors,
(it) would seem to be the "ideal deterrent."

Kahn only posed the idea of a doomsday machine (he did not advocate it), but the idea was adopted in Stanley Kubrick's film *Dr. Strangelove,* which ends with the annihilation of the planet. Thereafter, Kahn was sometimes referred to as "the real Dr. Strangelove" in the media.

What does it say about Paul that he called Herman Kahn his close friend? What did they have in common? Certainly they were both phenomenally intelligent. Each gleefully twitted the military establishment. Paul loved his verbal skirmishes with Air Force brass when defending his latest silo model. Kahn peppered his talks to the same audience with morbid jokes and enjoyed posing hypothetical questions that made people squeamish, like, "How much collateral damage, how many millions of Soviet and European civilians, would we be willing to kill in order to preserve a remnant of American society?"

Both my father and Kahn possessed a flea-like evasiveness when it came to being pinned down on *moral* questions about right or wrong action. Kahn's unsanctioned biographer, Sharon Ghamari-Tabrizi, writes:

> *Kahn would start to demonstrate something, veer off onto another topic, qualify this second idea, then flip it over and contradict what he had just written, immediately taking off on another idea, leaving behind a trail of unfinished thoughts. The strongest impression I had was that here was a kind of nuclear Scheherazade. The narrative frame for* One Thousand and One Nights *is that every evening Scheherazade tells a story to the King, who plans to execute her the next morning. To forestall her death, she tells such intricate tales, stories within stories, that the resolution of each plot is perpetually suspended in yet another digression. Something close to that kind of anxious deferral was in Kahn's book.*

I was scared of Herman Kahn as a child and would have good reason to be scared of him as an adult. His voice was among the loudest against a test-ban treaty that could have averted the arms race. Daniel Ellsberg told me that if he, my father, and their colleagues at RAND belonged to an apocalyptic cult, then Kahn was their guru.

In their world, moral questions were dumb questions. Answers, if they existed, could only lie along a game theorist's probability curve. The war planner's job is to attribute to the enemy the darkest possible motives and choices and plan for them. Even the most tentative belief that one's opponent might act out of concern for the good of humankind and the planet is judged to be hopelessly naïve.

For men like my father, survival depended on a grid of rational thought within which solutions were postulated to the most fearful scenarios. To be sure this survivalist's stance was rooted in the shared memory of the Holocaust. But when is fear rational and when is it irrational? By 1961, when satellite imagery had shown the feared missile gap to be a fiction, there was a moment in history, an opportunity to end the arms race. Unfortunately, Weidlinger Associates' Applied Sciences Group and our national psyche and treasure were deeply invested in the theory of mutual assured destruction. But this was a theory and a belief not based in fact but in assumption. It was a belief in hell.

When I was a teenager, Bob Dylan's famous anti-war anthem "Masters of War" seemed to be about men like my father and Herman Kahn: "Like Judas of old you lie and deceive. A world war can be won, you want me to believe."

In my boarding-school dorm room, I played the song over and over on the little portable turntable Paul had sent me. Another part of me was dimly aware that money made from defense contracts paid for my tuition at the Quaker boarding school I had chosen for my last two years of high school. The teachers were pacifists, and we routinely protested against escalation of the nuclear arms race and the Vietnam War. For this another stanza of Dylan's song served well: "I think you will find when your death takes its toll, All the money you made will never buy back your soul."

22. MICHÈLE AND JULIEN

M y father feared for the people he loved: for myself and for my sister. We felt the weight of his fear in our growing-up years, a weight heavier than a simple and natural concern for our well-being. When I was a teenager in boarding school I wrote:

> *Dear Dad: Each time you call me, I believe that you are half expecting me to admit that I have become a heroin addict, acquired a case of syphilis, been thrown out into the streets without food or shelter, plus innumerable other hardships. . . . Even more absurd is your statement that I "sometimes need a home." Why do I need a home now, after I have been without one all my life? A home is not an apartment or a house, it is a set of relationships that never existed within our family.*

At some point I changed . . . from being the good child who tried to reassure my father in every way possible to the angry teenager who wanted to wound him.

Unlike me, Michèle never expressed (at least in writing) anger or disappointment with our father. Instead, in the letters and postcards

Paul kept, amid vivid descriptions of her adventures and insights into art, literature, and poetry, there is a persistent yearning for approval. There are also many apologies for "scenes," things said for which my sister felt guilty. One scrawled note reads: "Dear Dad: Now that you know what a monster I am, had you better not let me go?"

My father teased her and called her a flibbertigibbet but also pleaded with Michèle for her approval. During her college years at Sarah Lawrence, he sent her mock "surveys" with multiple-choice questions about her feelings toward him. Here is one example:

Dear Sir or Madam,

You have been selected as the only subject of an international survey on Michèle-Father relations. Please answer the following questions by putting an "x" in the appropriate box:

1. Daddy, don't bother me, go to hell. ☐ Yes. ☐ No.

2. I love you. ☐ Yes. ☐ No.
(If answer is "no" do not explain.)

3. I need: ☐ Money. ☐ You.

4. I am happy. ☐ Yes. ☐ No.

5. I enjoy getting letters from Daddy. ☐ Yes. ☐ No.

If the above form is returned within 5 days, as a token of our appreciation a small, useless present will be sent by return mail.

Signature: _____

Michèle invariably checked all the right boxes, but the question-naires kept coming. Then there was another layer to their relationship, which my sister's friend Susanna Deiss observed:

Paul was always too flirtatious with Michèle. I felt this was emotionally disturbing for her. He was a man, after all, and she was a young woman. Even if there is never any inappro-priate physical contact, courting your daughter isn't a good thing. She needed to separate from her family, particularly her father, and move out into the world looking for someone who wasn't like him.

Away from Paul, Michèle thrived in college. She spent her junior year in Paris, studying at the Sorbonne and soaking up the sights and sounds of the Latin Quarter where she lived. She visited 20 rue Oudinot, where our father had lived in 1938, and imagined walking in his footsteps. She wrote to our Hungarian family: "I wish I could paint, to express the feeling this beautiful city inspires in me." She told them about her interests in the theatre, history, and psychology and her dream to become a kind of itinerant teacher, traveling the world after she graduated from college.

When she did graduate she went to the Pacific Northwest, a part of the United States she had never experienced. She imagined "the West" to be an excitingly rough and uncivilized place and was surprised to find that Coca-Cola vending machines could be found there. At twenty-three she applied for a job as a French professor at a small Quaker college outside Portland, Oregon. Our father, recently divorced from Madeleine, let her go reluctantly. She wrote:

Dear, dear, dearest Daddy: You were very afraid to let me go, and I felt your anxiety and it pains me. There is not the slight-est thing to worry about. I know exactly what I am doing, and for once it is in the most relaxed and unreservedly happy way possible. I feel saner now than I have ever felt and certainly more at peace than you or Mom have been for a long time.

While Michèle was en route to Oregon, my mother had another psychotic break and was hospitalized. Since there was no one else to look after her, Paul stepped in to manage her affairs despite the fact that they were divorced. Michèle got the news while staying at a YMCA residence in Portland.

Poor, poor Daddy: you are now all alone to take care of every-thing, and I do want to help if there is anything I can do. Therefore since George Fox College told me that they would know definitely about my job on Thursday, I have decided to wait until then. That way, if you and the psychiatrist want me to come back, hopefully you'll let me know before then.

The need to be of use to my father conflicted with the trajectory of her own life. Fortunately she got the teaching job. A few weeks into her first semester she proclaimed, "I am a natural-born teacher!"

I love teaching French and finding time to explore its litera-ture and reread books that suddenly have so much meaning to me. I love telling about France, New York, and traveling. I love arguing with my Catholic roommate. I love pick-ing fruit, vegetables, and nuts and helping the head of the Literature Department with her chickens while discussing Villon and Daudet. I love walking to my first class as the sun rises. I love hearing about the Oregon Trail, timbering, and Indians from several town characters I've befriended. I love our cats and can watch them for hours stalking flut-tering autumn leaves.

Oregon was a place to begin a new life among people who seemed less conflicted than the family we grew up in. Religion attracted Michèle, and she engaged in earnest theological debates with Quak-ers, Seventh-day Adventists, and Catholics. Her students loved her. She discussed underground movies and the "death of God" with them and became involved in teach-ins on the Vietnam War and an

Michèle in her classroom at George Fox College in Newberg, Oregon, and as Joan of Arc.

ecumenical gathering of priests and swamis. She played Joan of Arc in a community theater production.

Michèle made two close friends. Florence Angelelo was a professor in the English Department, "a hip Seventh-day Adventist, who is married to an Italian truck driver and knows more about Chaucer than a great many scholars. She is part Indian and is the most refreshing, open, and spunky person I have met in a long time."

One day Paul telephoned Michèle, and Florence answered. My sister was not home, and they had a long conversation. Paul was acutely worried about Michèle, despite her bubbling, enthusiastic descriptions of her life. He told Florence that he had received a letter from Michèle in which her handwriting had changed. Was this a sign that his daughter slipping away from him? A few days later Florence wrote our father an astonishingly blunt letter.

> *Your daughter loves you very much. She also loves her mother very much. There has been constant conflict within her where loyalties are concerned. One way to solve the problem is to put as much space between herself and her parents as possible. That is what she is doing. She has to learn that you are not*

*omnipotent. You may as well face it; your divorce, the years
prior to your divorce, have all been hard for her. . . . Michèle
is, perhaps for the first time in her life, beginning to relax. A
lot of her little nervous habits are leaving. Don't question her
way of life here. You wouldn't understand it, but it is a good
way of life.*

Joyce LeBaron was Michèle's other close friend. "She is so wise at
heart," wrote Michèle to Paul.

*We made a little covenant on the eve of her marriage to see
each other regularly, to learn songs and study writers that are
coming into our angle of vision. The latest is Rabindranath
Tagore. We composed music to one of his poems and recorded
it with the sound of running water in the background.*

Joyce shared with me her impressions of my sister. She spoke
haltingly at first. At times there were tears in her eyes.

*She was charismatic, beautiful, searching, yearning, con-
flicted, a wonderful friend. . . . We were soul sisters. For years,
for decades, I had dreams of her.*

Joyce recalled that men were attracted to Michèle, but that she
would "slide out of relationships. Several really nice men were interested in her, but I don't think she ever saw herself in a long-term
relationship."

Then she became pregnant. In June of 1966 she had a brief affair
with Paul Golightly, a medical student who was visiting Portland
from the East Coast. Then in July, Michèle and our father went to
Hungary to visit family there. If Michèle realized she was pregnant,
she revealed it to no one. My cousin Pál remembered my sister's physical beauty. His sister, Anna, recalled Michèle's sensitivity to the faces
of people on the streets of Budapest, seeing in their expressions sad-
ness and resignation to life under communist rule.

After Hungary Michèle went to Paris to stay in the apartment of a college friend, Joelle Schroeder, who was away at the time. Even though abortion was illegal and dangerous in both France and the United States, she considered whether or not to have her child. Michèle wrote to Joelle:

I have had unsatisfactory relationships with men . . . and have the conviction that there are far better ways to live than within a marriage. I have never seen myself as a wife . . . a mother, yes, but not a wife.

She had made her decision. Michèle told my father when she was two and a half months pregnant that she was carrying a child and she intended to keep it. He thought this would be a disaster. He wrote to Joelle begging her to persuade Michèle to get an abortion. Joelle responded:

Dear Paul: I am in full agreement with her decision. I will try to let you know what difficulties she encounters. I fear they will be mostly material, as finding a good job in France is not easy. You should not worry too much, Paul. At this point there is nothing you can do. Try to accept what you reject emotionally. Love, Joelle

It is significant that Michèle did not tell the father of her child that she was pregnant until very late in her term. Her own father was still the principal man in her life. She wrote to him:

Your phone call Monday really shook me up. This is the first time in my life that I have heard you plead with me, that you appear utterly convinced that my decision is a wrong one. . . . You allude to deep-seated psychological difficulties of which I am unaware and which are better left unclarified. I need to understand more. What questions can I ask myself that would give me an inkling of what you mean when you say "you feel these things with every fiber of your body"? How can you be so certain of "irrevocable destruction"?

Daddy, I am *a woman now. I am in control of my destiny. In your letter, you mention several times what I have the potential of becoming. Some of that potential has been realized. Can I not build on this, knowing that involving another human being who will be dependent on me is of immeasurable importance? But of what use are such demonstrations if you know I am "deceiving myself"? It gives me a spooky feeling that no matter what I could evoke to diminish your fear, it would have no effect on your conviction.*

When I first read these letters from Michèle to my father, I was angry with him—that he would think so little of her capacity to live her life. What right did he have to tell her to get an abortion? Then another way of understanding his warning of "irrevocable destruction" dawned on me. He was like Cassandra who, given the gift of prophecy, was cursed never to be believed. Paul was hypervigilant to the signs of incipient mental illness in the way that only a person who has loved and lived with someone who develops schizophrenia can be. Knowing there was a genetic predisposition, Paul's deepest fear was that my sister and I would go crazy like our mother.

Michèle was much more mercurial and high-strung than I was, but nobody could see anything crazy in her behavior. However, Paul's fear, heightened by his past experience, caused him to interpret Michèle's personality quirks as signs of impending disintegration.

Paul could not tell my sister that she should get an abortion because he feared she would go insane. To do so could crush Michèle's already embattled sense of self and, perhaps, become a self-fulfilling prophecy. How could he tell anyone this? It would make *him* sound crazy. No one else who knew Michèle at the time saw her the way he did.

My nephew, Julien-Luc Golightly, was born in March 1967 in Paris. Michèle's choice took courage at a time when having a child out of wedlock was considered a moral disgrace. Susanna Deiss came from Rome to visit her. She gave Michèle her own platinum engagement band to wear to ward off public condemnation, but this did not prevent the nuns at the Catholic hospital where Michèle went to give birth from saying cruel things.

My mother, who had been kept in the dark, was informed at the last moment. She flew to France to be present at the arrival of her grandson. In the photographs she took of Michèle and Julien in the maternity ward my sister looks luminously happy. All the angst of her pregnancy seems to have melted away. Julien was a beautiful and healthy baby. His arrival gave my sister and my mother a new lease on life.

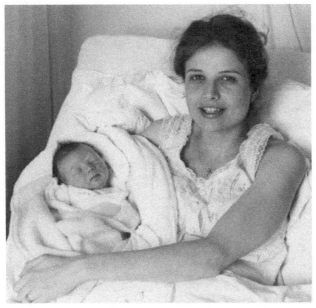

Michèle and her son, Julien.

Madeleine invited them to spend the summer on Cape Cod, and Michèle accepted. My mother's photographs of her daughter and grandson that summer of 1967 convey a feeling of deep joy and contentment.

One year later on a school break, I went to visit Michèle and Julien in Portland. She had settled into the life of being a single mother. While I was there she wrote to Paul:

Over these months of solitude, I've accumulated a lot of thoughts that are waiting to be shared. With Tom I seem to be able to share them so easily. I feel confident with him because he respects me. We're close enough in age to share a lot of the same language and worldview. We love each other, but not with the emotional hang-ups between parent and child. . . . "Noodle" has somewhat taken to Uncle Tom, though he prefers my babysitter's hoodlum boyfriend, but that's another story.

I loved being Michèle's confidant. She had put some distance between herself and our mother, who was all too willing to take charge of her grandson and arrange for his "proper" upbringing. For the first time we talked about Madeleine's schizophrenia. Michèle called it a whirlpool, and we both realized that many times we had been sucked into accepting the premise of an evil world that our mother insisted upon. Strangely, it was a happy moment for both of us because we each sensed the possibility of ultimately breaking free from it.

I went back East to school. Another year passed . . . and the thing that my father feared most began to be manifest to two of Michèle's friends. I learned from Joyce LeBaron, when I spoke with her in 2013, that Michèle had started having visions.

One of her visions was that she was Mary, Julien was Jesus, I was Elizabeth, and Swithin, my son, was John the Baptist. Her behavior became more erratic. She felt misunderstood, no longer at home in the world.

Susanna Deiss, who was living in San Francisco at the time, drove with her husband, a psychiatrist, to visit Michèle in Portland.

We knocked on the door. She opened the door and invited us in. She had been playing "tiger" on the floor with Julien and roaring. Afterwards my husband said, "She is psychotic." I said, "She is not psychotic, she was just playing with her child." He

said, "No, you are wrong. There is something really the matter."
On a euphoric high, my sister wrote to my father:

*Life is more beautiful than I could have dreamed. I have a
beautiful lover. It's my first affair, and I feel like an adolescent
and a mature woman at the same time. It's really a gas. This is
the first real vacation I've ever had. Julien is grooving on it too.*

My sister had fallen in love with a man named Harvey. Harvey
had hepatitis, most likely from a needle, and Michèle and Julien had
to get preventative gamma globulin shots. Then Harvey left to serve
a jail sentence for "ridiculous trumped-up charges."

In June 1970, I graduated from high school and married my high
school sweetheart. Paul wanted me to go to Harvard, where he was an
adjunct professor, but I vowed to get as far away from my parents as
possible. Dian and I went to live with Michèle and Julien in Portland
and enrolled in a state college. Michèle had come East for our wedding and seemed happier than I had ever seen her. She said that my
marriage to Dian was an encouragement for her to find a husband
and a father for Julien.

Michèle's sudden conversion to the idea of matrimony seemed
desperate. Julien was three years old. His father was black. Michèle
came to believe that as a mixed-race child, Julien would face prejudice. She now believed that this was what my father was warning
against when he said she should get an abortion. She blamed herself
for not listening to him and feared that, without a father to guide him,
Julien would lose his way.

When Dian and I arrived in Portland, we were just kids, fresh out
of high school. Being around Michèle and Julien was confusing and
somehow scary, but I could not have said exactly why. Awkwardly, I
tried to talk with my sister, but our conversations always seemed to
be left unfinished, usually interrupted by some small need of Julien's.
Only in retrospect am I able to give a context to what happened.

One by one Michèle cut herself off from her closest friends—Florence, Joyce, and others who might have helped her. She trusted no

one. Then one morning she told me that she and Julien were leaving for New York on an afternoon flight. She said she was going to look for a job and proper schooling for Julien because Portland had become "intolerable." It was the last time I saw her and Julien alive.

In 2014, when I tracked down Julien's father, Paul Golightly, he agreed for me to come to Atlanta and interview him. When I was fifteen, Paul Golightly was my friend. He did his medical residency at a hospital in New York City, and I often visited him and his wife, staying over at their apartment on the Upper West Side. He was a gentle man, and he treated me like an adult.

Now, in his house in Atlanta, Paul sat quietly turning the pages of a photo album I made for him with pictures of Michèle and Julien. Overcome with emotion, he did not trust himself to speak. Then gradually the words started to flow. He said that when Michèle finally told him he was going to be a father, she asked only that he give Julien his name, though he was ready and willing to do much more. He would have married my sister except that, by that time, he was married to another woman. They stayed friends and he had even come to Portland to visit one Christmas when Julien was two.

Although Paul Golightly spent time with Michèle and Julien the day before they died, he had no premonition of tragedy. In our conversation, we tried to piece together what had happened . . . as if knowing the exact chronology and facts would make a difference.

I do know that Michèle stayed briefly with my father in New York, but was unable to leave Julien in order to look for a job. Matthys Levy remembers my sister "behaving abominably" at a dinner with the family. "She was so angry at your father, it was unbelievable. She just didn't understand why your father and mother separated. She wasn't able to deal with that."

A week after Michèle left Portland, I spoke with her on the telephone. She told me that she was coming home. New York had been a dead end. It confirmed her feeling that the mistakes she had made were "irrevocable," giving voice to the same fatalistic words that my father had used. She hung up halfway through a sentence. I called my father at his office and told him to go home. Michèle needed him, but by the time he got home, Michèle and Julien had left. My father called Paul Golightly to see if she was with him, but he did not know where she was. Then Michèle called my father and told him she was going to kill Julien and herself. He was frantic. He did not know where his daughter was. The next morning the police found them in a motel room near Kennedy Airport. They were dead from an overdose of sleeping pills. When my father gave me the news on the phone, his voice was so small and tired I could hardly make out the words. He asked for Dian and me to come to New York as soon as possible. I told him "yes" and even thanked him for letting me know. I felt completely numb.

My father also called Paul Golightly, who told me:

I remember shock. And then he asked me if I could go identify the bodies. I said I would. I guess it was too emotional for your dad to do it himself. After that I went over to his house. It was the first time I met him.

I was afraid, not of death, but for my family and myself. Overnight, the facts of Michèle's suicide and Julien's death became clear, and we felt the full and terrible weight of this knowledge. I was afraid we would not survive. I was afraid that my father would age and die in unspoken remorse. I was afraid that I would follow the same path as Michèle.

When Dian and I got to New York, everyone was being very controlled. We sat together in the living room and had drinks. We said nothing. There was no script, no social map for how to act in such a situation. The silence was terrifying. Later my father came into my room and said that he needed my help more than he ever had. He wept in my presence for the first time in my life, crying convulsively. He asked for my forgiveness and blamed himself for Michèle and Julien's deaths.

The next morning we went to the funeral home. Michèle and

Julien lay together in a single coffin.

I have never told anyone that Julien was murdered. I don't think Michèle intended it that way. I believe in her mind she was protecting him. When asked, I say, "Julien died also."

At the time I could not forgive my father. I believed he was right to blame himself for their deaths, that his huge fear for the fate of his daughter, his grandson, and me had created a self-fulfilling prophecy. Paul Golightly said:

I can remember walking down the street to the morgue. I thought that this was such a profound tragedy that no single evil could produce something of this magnitude. It had to be two evils that would come together and magnify themselves exponentially.

Two evils: madness and fear. In our fear of madness, we were unable to face it with love and compassion. At the time I didn't understand that it wasn't my father who drove my sister crazy. I did not understand that madness, though not preordained, was written into our DNA. I did not know what this journey through my family's history would reveal. I did not know that forgiveness would come. I was only seventeen years old.

23. ON THE ROAD

CROSS COUNTRY, 2014–2016

M y mother died six years later while staying at a YWCA residency in Boston. She was partly shielded from grief over my sister's death by her mental illness. She persisted in believing that both Michèle and Julien had been murdered by minions of the same unnamed but malign force that had relentlessly persecuted her for three decades. When the attorneys and investigators she met with politely declined to pursue her imagined persecutor, she judged them to be in league against her.

For my father, it felt like everything ended with Michèle and Julian's death. His colleagues in the office described him as a broken man. They observed that for months he wore heavily tinted dark glasses, and he developed a nervous tic, a slight, involuntary sideways jerking of the head.

Over time he returned to life. He was already eight years into his second marriage. His wife, Solveig, was everything that my mother was not: quiet, dependable, guileless, and completely sane. My half-sister, Pauline, was six, and my half-brother, Jonathan, was three.

Paul had a whole new family that depended on him, that gave him a reason to go on living. Almost every evening, when he was not away on business, he sat with Pauline and Jonathan and narrated and drew pictures for *The Never-Ending Story*—a whimsical ongoing graphic novel of their life as it unfolded.

———————————

At the office he hired young women at a time when very few female engineers were admitted into the fraternity of defense intellectuals. Nanci Buscemi and Eve Hinman were surrogates for the daughter my father had lost. Paul often took them to parties, dinners, and on business trips to Europe where their presence was not strictly necessary. While they worked for Weidlinger Associates, the firm paid for their tuition at Columbia University to complete their doctoral studies. Paul flirted a lot, but it does not seem that he crossed the line. Eve told me that he liked to ask her into his office at the end of the workday. She would just sit next to him while he wrote pages and pages of differential equations on yellow legal pads—equations that just flowed from his mind, having nothing to do with the projects they were working on. Eve said, "It was like he was working out his life story through mathematics. It healed him and helped him understand who he was. It seemed to be his medicine."

———————————

The year Michèle and Julien died was also the year that the Walker Art Center was completed. I think of photographs of other buildings under construction that I saw in the Weidlinger Associates archives. They span four decades and are scattered all over the United States and the world. The pictures were a revelation to me, as I had known very little about what my father did for a living while I was growing up. I went on a pilgrimage to visit and film some of the structures that are his legacy. I hoped that by standing in front of them, I might understand something viscerally about his creative energy. Perhaps I would also learn something about myself by making more accessible the archetypal father that I carry within.

The earliest building of Paul's that I visited was George Nakashima's studio in New Hope, Pennsylvania. I found myself in a world completely removed from the urban environments I had associated with his work. A woodland hamlet informed by a Japanese aesthetic is the site of the Nakashima family compound. Nakashima, one of the bright lights in the American Crafts movement, was an architect turned furniture maker. He famously proclaimed: "Furniture is architecture on another scale." This idea resonated with the Bauhaus ethos that brought together architects, craftsmen, and artists in a movement dedicated to simplicity and beauty in everyday life.

I grew up with Nakashima chairs around our dining room table and imagined my father being so inspired by their perfection that he sought out the genius that had made them. Nakashima needed a structural engineer for a roof that would span a forty-foot by forty-foot studio without interior columns or load-bearing walls. Paul proposed a *conoid* (having the properties of a cone), thin-shell concrete roof that was arched on one end and had corrugations—like undulating waves, at the other. The shapes (both the arch and the corrugations) gave the roof its tensile strength over its large span.

Mira Nakashima, who inherited her father's furniture business, told me:

> *This studio was a major experiment. I don't think anyone had designed anything like it. A similar kind of shell had been poured in Princeton a month before ours and it collapsed; so Dad was very apprehensive.*

Paul's conoid roof did not collapse. When I walked into the studio, I had a feeling of expansiveness and light, of being both inside and outside at the same time. All around were flowering trees, carefully pruned and nurtured, and inside was the work of the master—exquisitely simple, elegant furniture.

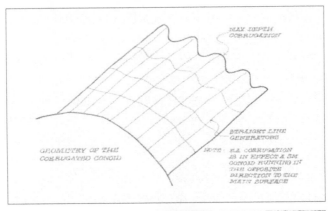

Conoid roof drawing and Nakashima studio under construction.

Nakashima studio interior in 2015.

Nakashima's roof was a precursor of the firm's dramatic use of thin-shell concrete (as well as a variety of other materials) for very large-span structures. Weidlinger Associates' Georgia Dome, a sports stadium in Atlanta, was the largest cable-supported dome in the world when it was completed in 1992. With a roof covering 8.6 acres, it seats 74,000 people.

Paul's success with his shell roof for Nakashima may be why he received an urgent call in early 1961 from the architect Marcel Breuer. Something had gone horribly wrong with the church that Breuer had designed for the community of Benedictine Monks in Collegeville, Minnesota.

Breuer knew my father socially. It was he who had persuaded Paul to build a summer home on Cape Cod, but he had never consulted with him on an engineering matter. Breuer's design of the St. John's Abbey Church called for a zigzag, folded-plate, concrete roof covering a very large span. But almost as soon as the wooden forms had been removed, cracks began to appear in the concrete. It seemed possible that the roof could fail.

Paul and Matthys Levy studied the original blueprints and realized that the engineer on the job had not provided sufficient reinforcement. Levy recalls: "We came up with a scheme of post-tensioning—applying cables that pushed the thing up from the bottom, at the center, to keep it from falling."

Bob Gatje, an engineer working in Breuer's office, told me, "The near failure of the abbey folded plates was a terrible affair—kept completely confidential within the office and at the abbey. . . . But your dad and Matt had saved the day, and they became our favorite engineers." They were chosen to engineer Breuer's second church for the Catholic parish of Norton Shores, Michigan.

I visited and filmed both churches. I drove first to St. John's across flat Minnesota farm country in pouring rain. The structure, revealed through sheets of water pushed aside by my wipers, looked like no church I had ever seen, but rather like an extraterrestrial monolith fronted with a trapezoid belfry on insect legs. Both ancient and modern at the same time, Breuer's work is described as *Brutalist*. The term Brutalist does not derive straight from the word "brutal," but originates from the French *béton brut*, or "raw concrete." Nevertheless it did look brutal. My first thought on seeing it was, "Perhaps Paul and Matt would have done better to ignore the architect's plea for help and let this concrete monstrosity implode."

Then I went inside, and it was a revelation. The world fell away. The vast church echoed with the intonations of vespers. Light filtered through stained glass that did not represent biblical scenes, but was composed of abstract shapes concentrating all the colors of the rainbow. I felt as if I was not so much in a specific church as in a vast capsule that levitated above the wet farmland, the little Midwestern town that marked its location on the map, and the banal trivia of everyday life. Can architecture evoke a spiritual experience? Here, in Breuer's church, rescued by my father and Matthys, it did for me.

The second Breuer church that Paul and Matthys worked on was St. Francis de Sales in Norton Shores, Michigan. It is also brutalist concrete, but its exterior is less intimidating. It is a three-dimensional trapezoid that appears, from certain angles, to be launching into flight. Its walls peel outwards as if morphing into wings. They are hyperbolic parabolas, saddle shapes that follow a convex curve along one axis and a concave curve along the other. I was curious about how such a radical structure, so unlike what churches usually look like, came to be accepted by a small Midwestern parish in the 1960s. I interviewed Mary Ann Howe, one of the parishioners who had been a young mother at the time when the architect came to present his idea to the congregation:

> And then there was a model that was going to be shown. Marcel Breuer himself came and, as a parish, we walked in procession around the property with the cross in front, the altar boys, Father, and then the model. We prayed for the completion of

*the project. We were overwhelmed with the amount of money.
At that point in our lives a million dollars seemed like a tre-
mendous amount. But we paid for the church. And I will tell
you something. It was a wonderful investment. More than we
thought. Father used to talk about sacred space and that's why
churches are built so tall. We have that in abundance.*

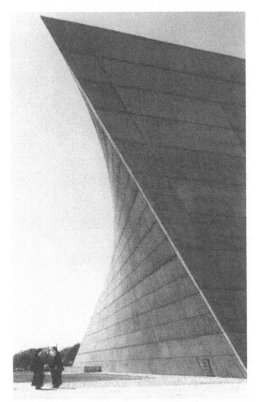

St. Francis de Sales Church in Norton Shores, Michigan.

Paul and Matthys were fortunate to have found a creative collaborator in Breuer. At the same time that they worked on St. Francis
de Sales, they did the structural engineering for Breuer's Whitney
Museum in New York. I stood across the street from this landmark,
guarding a slender tripod supporting my camera as it recorded a time-
lapse sequence. The compression of time, resulting in the swirling

frenetic movement of New York City traffic and pedestrians, gave the building itself a magisterial stillness and solidity.

––––––––––

In St. Louis I sat down with an ancient monk who had been present at the genesis of the idea for another church, the Church of the St. Louis Abbey, designed by Gyo Obata and engineered by Paul and Matthys. With benign incredulity, Father Timothy Horner said to me:

> *Almost the best feature of it was that neither the architect nor we knew what we were doing, and so we really had to sit down and think out just what we wanted because we had never planned a church before. . . .*

Paul would have absolutely loved this. Father Timothy continued:

> *Gyo Obata produced two models. One was a frilly concrete roof with glass walls. It was decent. It was airy and perfectly safe. It was rather dull. The second model was rather ugly. It looked sort of like an artichoke but it was alive in a way that the other was not.*

The alive and radical approach that Father Timothy and the architect favored was almost rejected by the abbey's prior, but Obata requested the opinion of Pier Luigi Nervi, the world-renowned Italian designer of concrete shell structures. Nervi gave his blessing, and the project went forward. When it was completed, *Architectural Forum* waxed rhapsodic, calling it "the most elaborate example yet on the North American continent of a circular building in a convoluted shell form. Its three circling, pyramidal tiers of arches, which front the radiating vaults and a belfry, look like some artfully folded and stacked-up white napkin."

The structure was built in an unorthodox way, by shooting a dry mix of concrete though a high-pressure hose onto wooden forms

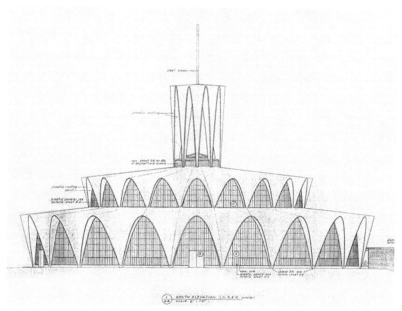

Elevation blueprint for the Saint Louis Abbey Church.

Construction of the Saint Louis Abbey Church.

shaped as parabolic arches. Then the concrete was smoothed by hand to a uniform thickness. Paul and Matthys came up with the idea of building it in sections. There are twenty massive arches in the first tier of the circular church, but only five adjacent sections were poured at one time. Once the concrete set, the forms could be reused and repositioned with a crane, leapfrogging around the circle. Key to the success of the project was the extraordinary cooperation between client, architect, engineer, and contractor.

What did I learn about my father from visiting these three churches? He embraced the playful, the idiosyncratic, daring, and extravagant visions of architects who wanted to do things that no one had ever done before, and he made these visions manifest. He created the strength behind the beauty. This hits me viscerally as I animate a series of pristine color photographs that show the entire construction, step by step, of the Saint Louis Abbey Church. The handcrafted wooden forms used half a million board feet of lumber. There were 210 separate concrete pours. The photographs show it all—from the circular foundation to the building of the massive curved forms, from the spraying and smoothing of the gunite concrete, to the lowering of the steeple with a crane . . . one senses that everything is being done this way for the first time. Father Horner confirmed this:

> It's really a handmade church. The forms were made by hand, the concrete was shot on by hand, it was smoothed by hand . . . with a great plank. . . . I mean literally they did this (he gestures smoothing). It was then polished by hand, painted by hand, and on the inside all the plaster was finished by a chap doing it with a bathroom sponge.

In Minneapolis I visited the Walker Art Center. Having described my conversation with the architect and engineers who restored its façade as a way of illustrating the basic relationship between architect and engineer, I wanted to see how it *felt* to be inside the museum.

There is a paradox inherent in the concept of a good museum. It must be both *there* and *not there*. Painting and sculpture must be seen in space, not framed and constrained in overbearing or ostentatious rooms. The architect Edward Larrabee Barnes wrote:

> *We want the visitor to remember paintings in space, sculpture against sky, and a sense of continuous flow. It is flow more than form that has concerned us. The sequence of spaces must be seductive. There must be a subtle sense of going somewhere, like a river.*

Barnes and Weidlinger achieved flow in the way the museum's galleries spiral around a central core. This was not easy to engineer. Paul Asp explains:

> *The complexity of having these pinwheel levels of galleries is unlike a typical building where one floor interconnects everything. . . . Instead you have one level and then a quarter level above it, you have a disconnected floor, yet all of these floors have to be connected together to resist wind and earthquake forces. So it is very difficult to achieve the lateral stability of each of those independent floors.*

I experienced the flow of the building as I slowly ascended the spiral, climbing up a few broad steps from one gallery to another. Moving through the Walker, I thought of my father's idea of the joy of space. "In architecture we experience relationships in space. This experience is both active and passive at the same time: We move through the space and experience its effect upon us."

It was a blustery fall day in Chicago when I set up my time-lapse camera in Daley Plaza. Cumulus clouds were scudding over the tops of skyscrapers, and their glass, steel and stone facades were alive with flowing shadows. At the center of the plaza is a monumental steel sculpture known simply as "the Chicago Picasso." Paul did the engineering. Though it weighs 162 tons and is five stories high, it feels light. Though my viewfinder, the clouds racing overhead created the illusion of a great bird in flight. No one is sure what the sculpture is

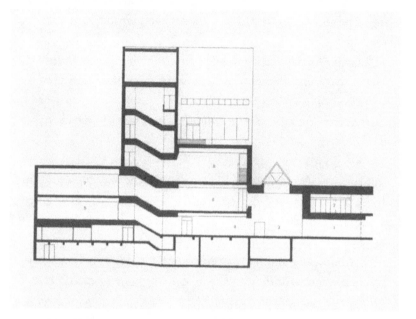

Walker Art Center staircase elevations and gallery interior.

supposed to represent. The project's sponsors said it was the head of a woman. To others it is an angel. Picasso himself remained mute on the topic.

The morning that I filmed, several small children discovered the sculpture. I watched as they clambered up the steep incline of the base upon which two great "wings" are supported. Then they slid down and climbed up and slid down, over and over.

Much public art in US cities is calm and stoic, depicting historical figures in heroic poses. But in the 1960s, as modernism flourished in public architecture, sculptures were commissioned to complement the buildings.

During the time Paul was working on Chicago's Picasso, he kept a light cardboard model of the sculpture on the big marble table in his office. A colleague remembers him blowing hard, as if blowing out the candles on a birthday cake, to see how this might deflect the "wings." When he ran out of breath, he brought in an electric fan and aimed it at the model. This is hardly a scientific approach to wind-stress testing, but is seems to have given him enough information to design a model in steel that successfully stood up to rigorous blasts in a wind tunnel. Paul never met Picasso, but he was very proud of his contribution, calculating the thickness of the steel and the bracing to ensure that the sculpture would withstand the fiercest storms of the Windy City.

I reached Detroit at the end of a long day of driving. The Detroit Civic Center Plaza on the banks of the Detroit River felt forlorn, almost empty of people, save a few pedestrians crossing quickly in the evening light, a lone skateboarder, and a homeless man. Above a vast basin lined with concentric cobbles hovers a huge silver donut that looks like a flying saucer with small holes in its sides resembling portholes. The donut, twenty-six feet in diameter, is supported by two tubular splayed legs that jut down and out at forty-five-degree angles. The portholes house water nozzles. Commissioned as part of an inner-city rejuvenation project, the Horace E. Dodge Fountain and a nearby twisted pylon were designed by the sculptor Isamu Noguchi. Paul Weidlinger was one of the engineers he consulted. Noguchi

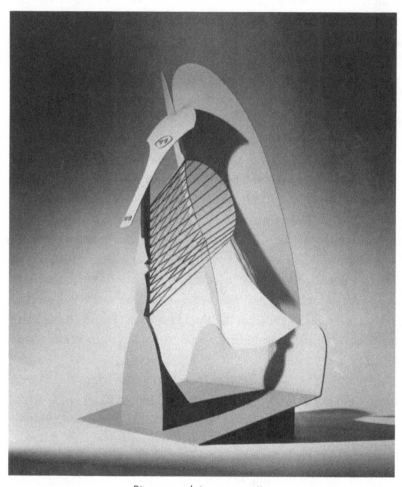

Picasso sculpture maquette.

said he did not want make a typical fountain, but rather a fountain "which represents our times and our relationship to outer space." Dramatically promoting his design to the city's Fountain Selection Committee, he said:

> *This great fountain, projected as the most magnificent in modern times, rises from the plateau of primal space. It is an engine for water, plainly associating the spectacle to its sources of energy—the engine—so closely a part of Detroit. It recalls and commemorates the dream that has produced the automobile, the airplane, and now the rocket. . . . The fountain will be an engineering feat in metals.*

Indeed it was. According to the artist's biographer, Noguchi kept changing his mind about the design, and these changes did not always please the engineers. But I know that my father loved Noguchi. He often spoke of him fondly. He told me he had first heard about him in a *Life* magazine article about Noguchi's room full of sculptures in New York's Museum of Modern Art.

> *At least a dozen top US critics and museum heads believe that the puzzling objects shown left and right . . . are first-rate art. [Noguchi] patters happily about in his bare feet, cutting up marble slabs to fashion even more statues like these. . . .*

Never mind the slightly condescending tone of the author. My father was simply delighted by the idea of Noguchi working in his bare feet. Paul was probably introduced to Noguchi through Gordon Bunshaft. All three worked on Yale's Beinecke Rare Book Library. Bunshaft had explosive quarrels with Noguchi, whom he had asked to design a garden space for the building. These arguments sound like the ones that Paul and Bunshaft had over the design of Banque Lambert. Paul recognized Noguchi as a kindred spirit, an independent thinker, who had dedicated his life to the "sculpturing of space," which is how Paul saw architecture at its best. If you replace the word "sculpture" with "architecture" in Noguchi's credo below, he could be speaking Paul's mind.

> *The essence of sculpture for me is the perception of space, the continuum of our existence. . . . Since our experiences of space are, however, limited to momentary segments of time, growth must be the core of existence. Growth can only be new, for awareness is the ever-changing adjustment of the human psyche to chaos.*

This last phrase makes me think of how Paul sought refuge from his inner chaos by the contemplative writing of long differential equations, as a way of ordering and sculpting space—defining reality. His protégée Nanci Buscemi struggled to come up with a metaphor, a way of explaining to me the ecstasy that elegant mathematical solutions can bring:

> *You know, you're trying to solve an equation and you take it so far to get an exact solution and . . . it's just. . . . It can blow your mind. It's like being at a Grateful Dead concert. It's more than that.*

I drove over the Delaware River from Camden, New Jersey, to Philadelphia on the Ben Franklin Bridge. Rush-hour traffic veered right around a park-like circle on the Philadelphia side and, for just a moment, I caught a glimpse of a jagged steel lightning bolt grounded to the earth by an enormous key. On top of the lightning bolt, ten stories high, was a shining kite. This was Noguchi's *Bolt of Lightning . . . Memorial to Ben Franklin,* a reference to Franklin's famous electrical experiment in a lightning storm, with a key at the end of a kite string. Noguchi said, "The kite is an expression of America. It is nothing, but it trapped the energy [of lightning]. It has contact with the deepest forces of nature, but is also linked to the ground—an expression of intelligence and practicality. . . ."

My father said, "The sculpture is mad. I would not have done it for anyone I didn't like a lot." Noguchi's biographer, Hayden Herrera, describes how they worked on it:

> *As Noguchi kept revising his monument, it grew from sixty to one hundred feet. The revised height was made possible by the engineering genius of Paul Weidlinger. . . . Weidlinger took Noguchi's model, measured it, entered the coordinates into a computer, and then generated drawings. He analyzed how the asymmetrical monument could withstand the force of gravity and discovered that the shape Noguchi had planned made it nearly impossible to engineer. . . . At one point Weidlinger decreased the degree of the lightning bolt's "zigzag," which made the sculpture taller. Noguchi trusted Weidlinger . . . but he was not happy with the less pronounced angularity of the bolt, and he went back to his original plan. When the engineering studies were finished and Noguchi saw how the kite structure would look, he told Weidlinger, "I'd like to tilt it." Weidlinger agreed.*

Noguchi had an impish quality about him. So did Paul. There is a photograph of the two of them huddled down, nestling together within the steel latticework of the lightning bolt during its fabrication. They look like co-conspirators and are clearly enjoying themselves. Images of the erection of the sculpture itself reveal its scale as tiny men in hard hats wrestle to guide and bolt together gargantuan prefabricated segments, lowered from a crane. In the final photograph in the sequence the sculpture is completed and Noguchi himself is kicking up his heels in the foreground in a kind of elfin victory dance.

My father loved antiestablishment revolutionaries, nonconformists, iconoclasts, and all sorts of free spirits. He respected the artists he rendered his services to above all others—more than architects and certainly more than the high-ranking military men and State Department officials who ordered bomb-proof structures.

The artist Paul was closest to was the French painter and sculptor Jean Dubuffet, with whom he shared a lively correspondence.

Paul Weidlinger and Isamu Noguchi inspect the fabrication of Bolt of Lightning . . . Memorial to Ben Franklin.

The artist, Isamu Noguchi, dances in front of his Bolt of Lightning.

Dubuffet, arguably one of the most important French artists of the second half of the twentieth century, sent a telegram to Paul on the occasion of his birthday in December 1972. It reads, "The holy man takes off his cap to extend blessings and bows deeply." In his telegram Dubuffet is referencing an old photograph of himself wearing an "oriental cap" which Paul had unearthed somewhere and sent to the artist after adding his own modification to the image—an angel's halo above the artist's head.

Twenty-three kilometers southwest of Paris, in the village of Périgny-sur-Yerres, there is a place that is a legacy to the whimsy of Jean Dubuffet. It is a predominantly white environment of jagged walls and undulating terrain shaped from sprayed gunite concrete and painted with thick black lines enclosing organic cell-like shapes. It is a place where the artist intended to "evoke not strictly a landscape, but a mental and schematic representation of a landscape." At the center of the site is a building that looks like a gigantic melting iceberg, with no corners or straight edges. What is it for? One can give no clear answer, and any attempt to decode the artists' own statements only serves to deepen the mystery. Dubuffet said, "I built the Villa Falbala expressly to house the *Cabinet logologique*," with its double doors painted with two abstract figures that Dubuffet named *Le Paladin* and *La Paladine*. One is tempted to say it is an icon, an intimate shrine, the holy man's holy of holies, but Dubuffet would have tolerated no such categorization. About the *Cabinet logologique*, all he said was that it was his "philosophical exercise room."

As an artist, Dubuffet challenges us to do philosophical exercise—to question our perception of reality:

> *We must realize that things we take for real . . . and which appear strongly as such, are nothing more than an arbitrary interpretation of things that might as well be substituted by another. The distinction we make between real and imaginary is unfounded. The interpretation of reality that seems true, irrefutable, is only an invention of the mind, or let's say, an antique invention, collectively adopted, that our mind believes. . . .*

The Villa Falbala in Périgny-sur-Yerres, France, with its creator, Jean Dubuffet, in the right foreground.

It is not impossible to imagine, for the interpretation of the world, other decipherments . . . than those which, so far, have our full trust.

Dubuffet's refusal to be pinned down to the accepted descriptions of reality infuses his art and reminds me of the "Where shall I jump?" flea game with which my father used to torment me as a child. Yet here there is no torment, only a creative defiance that encourages us to take nothing for granted. I think this appealed deeply to my father, who repeatedly thought outside the box when challenged by a vision for a roof, a sculpture that seemed to defy gravity, or a bunker that could survive the force of a nuclear explosion. My father identified with Dubuffet's kaleidoscopic perspective of the world.

Paul's first meeting with Dubuffet was in Paris in October 1969. The artist had asked him if he would do the structural engineering for the Villa Falbala. In the following weeks photographs of a maquette and then the maquette itself were sent to New York, and Paul presented the artist with a maximum estimate of $30,000 for the cost of the engineering, including precious computer time on the IBM 1620. My father wrote that the job was outside the "frame" of the work normally done by the firm but "because I am very interested in your work, we are ready to do the calculations at cost" [actual time and expenses].

Dubuffet responded, "I remain frightened by the enormity of the sums which have been enumerated for the cost of this study." Paul then proposed to do the work for free. He understood that the Villa Falbala was for Dubuffet, at the age of seventy, an entirely personal work. There was no client, no intention to sell it to anyone, and therefore no money for the project, save what the artist paid out of his own pocket.

For twelve months during 1969 and 1970 there are over 200 pages of correspondence between Paul, Dubuffet, and assorted technical advisers regarding design, engineering, and construction. The original shape of Villa Falbala was created by Dubuffet using a hot wire to slice into and sculpt a block of polystyrene (Styrofoam). The next step was to build a special tool—a pantograph—that could scale up the small model to a larger maquette that could be sliced into sections. Precise measurements of these slices would provide spatial coordinates that could be input into the computer, which could then produce the structural requirements for the actual building. But the material used for the maquette was so light and friable it proved impossible to slice it into sections. An alternative method proved successful and over several weeks a design evolved. Dubuffet imagined a building that is simply a large fiberglass shell, but it became quickly apparent that reinforcing was needed. Paul came up with an idea to use steel tubing that could be bent to match the contours of the iceberg's irregular walls. The tubing, interspersed and connected with wire mesh, would be sandwiched between layers of rigid polyurethane foam on the outside and plaster on the inside. But the computer showed that even this design was insufficient to withstand the force of winds and the weight of snow on the roof. The final solution was to replace the tubing with trusses (fabricated with tubing of a lesser diameter) having internal triangular bracing. Of course each truss was uniquely shaped, following the organic contours of the maquette.

There were numerous misunderstandings and setbacks with contractors. Dubuffet hired a project manager whom he then fired

The steel skeleton of the Villa Falbala.

and later rehired. In his letters to my father, the artist seems increasingly beside himself with frustration and at one point begs Paul to come to France to take over the supervision of the project. My father could not leave New York for an extended time, but he responded to each of Dubuffet's panicked pleas with sound advice and recommended a competent project manager and contractor to fabricate the metal skeleton.

Dubuffet trusted Paul completely and followed his advice. A year after they started working together, the artist wrote to Paul: "You have been wonderfully generous with me. But I have a feeling I am abusing this. I can see that this construction has cost you a great deal of time and effort, and I would like to compensate you for at least one part of it." The following month Dubuffet sent Paul one of his paintings, *Le Train des Vacants*. After receiving it Paul wrote: "It is a great joy to see it when I come home. Somehow I feel that your choice was wonderful . . . there's something very personal in my response to the painting, which I was not aware of before."

Even as Villa Falbala began to take shape on the ground, Paul began work on the engineering for Dubuffet's *Les Quatre Arbres* (The Four Trees), a monumental sculpture commissioned by David Rockefeller for the Chase Manhattan Bank Plaza in New York. I filmed it the same day I did the time-lapse shot of the Whitney. After a few minutes, a building security guard chased me off. I wish I'd had in my pocket the letter that Rockefeller wrote to my father after the sculpture's dedication in 1972:

"*. . . though its magnificence is M. Dubuffet's, its strength is an ingenious Weidlinger backbone. The quite extraordinary substructure you devised will assure that our trees stand firm for all seasons. This taxing assignment was executed with consummate skill. Mrs. Rockefeller and I are deeply grateful for your thoroughness and dedication going far beyond the principal task at hand. With best wishes. . . .*

The Four Trees in the Chase Manhattan Bank Plaza in New York.

In my father's world, artists were kings and saints with halos. His love of artists contained within it a nostalgic yearning for a road not taken, a life in which his creative genius was not constrained by practical applications.

Paul continued to go to his office until his death in 1999. In his final ten years, he was less and less involved with clients. He was drawn instead toward problems of pure mathematics, proofs, and paradoxes, which he gleefully proclaimed "had no practical purpose whatsoever."

———————————

By far the strangest place I visited in search of my father's practical and structural legacy was a large fenced-in enclosure in the rangeland north of Cheyenne, Wyoming. Site P5 is the location of a nuclear missile silo.

For my father and the young engineers and programmers working for him in the 1970s, a silo that would protect a missile from a Soviet first strike was a kind of Holy Grail. They sought this with the enthusiasm and righteousness of crusaders, using computers to test mathematical models of structures that had never been built or even imagined before.

Site P5 and forty-nine other silos north of Cheyenne once housed LGM-118 Peacekeeper (MX) missiles, the most destructive weapon ever produced, capable of delivering ten independently targeted thermonuclear warheads. The missiles are gone, decommissioned in response to the SALT II Treaty, but their silos are still there. I found the GPS coordinates of Site P5 on the Internet, and my smart phone helped me navigate to it. Because I knew from Google Earth images that the site was surrounded by a very high fence, I brought an aerial drone that could fly over the fence and take video, looking directly down upon the silo headworks. Though I was a little anxious about "trespassing" on US government property, I was completely alone in the landscape surrounding the silo. I fired up the drone, piloted it over the chain-link fence, and hovered it over the silo, shooting downwards.

The view was disappointingly unimpressive. I steered the drone back but, before it cleared the fence, it hit a light post and crashed irretrievably inside the silo enclosure. I considered calling Warren Air Force Base in Cheyenne and asking if I could retrieve my drone, but thought better of it. Fortunately, I was able to get good shots of the silo by simply shooting video through the chain-link fence.

I had expected to find awesome evidence of my father's engineering genius. Matthys Levy had told me about a design for a silo protected by dashpots, dense concrete slabs resting on hydraulic springs that would compress in response to a blast, thereby dissipating some of its force. There was nothing like that here, just a concrete slab in the ground.

Why?

Deeper research revealed that the fifty silos had not, in fact, been engineered by Weidlinger Associates. In the 1970s Congress approved funding for production of fifty MX missiles, but money was not budgeted for the elaborate silos to house them. By the time the missiles were ready to be deployed, Cold War tensions were beginning to ease, and the cost of nuclear weapons was less justifiable. What I found in Wyoming was the Air Force's cost-saving solution: the missiles were housed in outdated and repurposed Minuteman silos. The one I filmed and forty-nine others like it were completely vulnerable to Soviet attack.

The silos that Paul, Eve, Nanci, and others engineered were never built. They were just one part of an elaborate, theoretical shell game that spanned thirty years. In one scenario, missiles would be randomly shuttled along an underground railroad between alternate launch sites. In another, the silos would be invisible from the air, covered by a layer of soil that the missiles would burst through when launched. A third solution was Weidlinger's, super-hardened silos that could conceivably withstand a close hit. None of these solutions was ever deployed.

At the end of my travels, I came back to the place where the idea for this project had its genesis, the house my father built the year that I was born in Wellfleet. I had been given a one-month residency in the house by the Cape Cod Modern House Trust, and it is where I will bring this book to a close.

24. HOME

My father put me back into his Last Will and Testament along with my half-brother and half-sister. My portion of the inheritance, which came to me in 2015, after the death of my stepmother, gave me the space and time to write this narrative. *The Restless Hungarian* started out being about a man whose life was mostly outside the framework of father and husband. He was a witty, brilliant, fiercely independent, and courageous man who made his way in the world as a creative genius and captain of industry. But in the end, I could not avoid my own experience of the father who was haunted by fears, both real and imagined, who was less than stellar and very different from the public persona he created.

Before Paul's death, I had not known the story of my Hungarian family and their suffering during the Holocaust. Initially Andor, Rózsa, Lulu, Ili, and Ferenc were just fascinating characters in a sort of "novel" I was writing. Then, without warning, they became *my people*, assimilated into my psyche.

The day my ancestors become more than just names on a family tree was when my cousin Pál and I visited the wild forest that is the Kozma Street Jewish Cemetery on the outskirts of Budapest. Pál brought along his eight-year-old son, Támas (Tom), who is named after me. He is called "Little Tom," just as Pál was known as "Little Pál" to distinguish him from my father. We brought gardening shears, a hoe, a stiff brush, and a broom to clear off the graves. I have already mentioned that my father's Aunt Paula rests here, watched over by the fierce Turul bird on her headstone. In a dense thicket beneath a layer of light snow and leaves, we found my great-grandparents, Sámuel and Eleónora Weidlinger, and then the grave of my grandmother, Júlia, who died in 1918, when Paul was just four. It looked unremarkable until Little Tom felt a slab beneath a thick layer of leaves and soil. Excited, the three of us cleared earth from the slab. A beautiful bas-relief Tree of Life was revealed. Amid its branches was the Jewish six-pointed star of Abraham. I cannot explain why, but I was filled with deep gratitude. Somehow, through the branches of that carved stone tree, I felt connected and rooted in my family. I was happy that Little Pál and Little Tom were there with me.

As for my closer family, never before had I felt so intensely the sorrow and grief over my mother's madness, my sister's suicide, and the death of my nephew, Julien. Years of therapy have alleviated the pain and guilt and made life possible, but never had I allowed myself to be so close to them, to feel their pain as if it were my own.

With me in my father's house, as I write this last chapter, is my wife, Sharon, who has stood by me these past months when the going got rough, when it became increasingly difficult to separate an objective and compassionate narrative from the narrative I have carried inside myself my entire life.

The house has been beautifully restored. A derelict hulk, once slated for demolition, has been reborn. Deeply respectful of the original design, the Trust has gone to extraordinary lengths to restore the sense of a permeable boundary between inside and outside. Immense, triple-glazed glass panels in sliding steel frames, custom fabricated and transported from Austria, replace the rusted and broken panels from sixty-four years ago. The space that once was the cursed repository of memories of scary times with my mother is, again, filled with light and warmth.

As an angry teenager, I wrote to my father that "a home is not a house or an apartment but a set of relationships between people . . . relationships that never existed in our family." Now, before even realizing it, we have created "home" here. For one glorious, privileged month, we swim naked in the pond, walk to the ocean, cook for each other, and make love in my parents' old bedroom. Two dear friends, Seth and Carolynn, whom we call "chosen family," come to stay with us for a long weekend, and we talk of our lives, the good times and the bad. We laugh and we weep together. I read to them the chapters of my boyhood here . . . and we can all see clearly and embrace the boy who once lived in this house, caught frogs and went fishing, built drip sandcastles with his father, and hid behind the woodpile when his mother was angry.

Often we are in silent awe of the beauty of this place. I am reminded how my father, as a young man, wrestled with and defied the strict edicts of logical positivism to come up with his own idea of "the joy of space," a joy which he made physically manifest in this house, floating on its slender stilts in a forest overlooking a pond. That brilliant and idealistic young man is here among us, as is the young woman who was my mother, who wrote the most beautiful love letters, who loved to cook sumptuous meals for her friends, and who played "Greensleeves" on a guitar which, when she was not playing it, hung like a promise on the white eastern wall of the living room.

I cringe at fake happy endings, and God save me from doing anything like that. Yet I believe there is a point, a purpose, in descending into the depths of the past and befriending the sorrowful souls who still dwell there in our hearts. Like Ili who, as a little girl, arranged photographs of the living and the dead on her bedspread and peered into the waters of the fountain of her imagination to animate their lives, I have done this with Andor, Rózsa, Lulu, Ili, Ferenc, Paul, Madeleine, Michèle, and younger versions of myself, hoping not only to make them completely real in my heart, but perhaps reaching though the veil of time and space, to let them know that they are truly seen, honored, and loved. I say to them, "Look, dear family. I am well. I am alive. And I embrace you."

PHOTO CREDITS

Pages 11, 14, 35, 100, 161, 167—Courtesy of Pál Valentiny

Page 20—*Az 50 éves Vállalkozók lapja: jubileumi album, 1879-1929* (50 Years of Entrepreneurs' Paper: Jubilee Album, 1879-1929) Budapest, 1930

Pages 22, 23, 24, 29, 38, 46, 48 (bottom), 49, 57, 61, 63, 71, 80, 82, 97, 104, 105, 109, 111, 112, 115, 117, 126, 127, 130, 134, 141, 142, 143, 145, 146, 153, 156, 163, 175, 177, 182, 195, 199, 203, 205, 220, 243—Personal collection of the author

Page 48 (top)—Photo by Endre Merenyi, © Peter Lengyel

Pages 75, 76—Courtesy of Hattula Moholy-Nagy

Page 85 (bottom)—© F.L.C. / ADAGP, Paris / Artist Rights Society (ARS), New York 2018

Page 88—NPG Ax134274, vintage bromide print, 1954, National Portrait Gallery, London

Page 119—Bolivian National Railways Atlas

Page 124—Courtesy Museo Tambo Quirquincho, La Paz, Bolivia

Page 149—Courtesy of Ágnes Kálmán

Page 165—United States Holocaust Memorial Museum, United States Holocaust Memorial Museum, courtesy of Hannah & Nissan Lowinger

Page 171—BTM Kiscelli Múzeum Fényképgyűjtemény / Kiscelli Museum Photography Archive

Pages 180, 252 (bottom)—Photographs by author

Page 190 (top)—Banque Lambert - © Ezra Stoller/Esto

Page 213—Public Domain

Page 239—1966 L'Ami Yearbook, George Fox University Archives, Newberg, Oregon

Page 252—Courtesy of Mira Nakashima

Page 255—HB-30662-Z, HB-30662-K - Chicago History Museum, Hedrich-Blessing Collection

Page 257 (top)—Hellmuth, Obata and Kassabaum, Inc., St. Louis Priory

Page 257 (bottom)—Father Paul Kidner, O.S.B., St. Louis Priory

Page 260—Courtesy Walker Art Center Archives.

Page 262—© 2018 Estate of Pablo Picasso / Artist Rights Society (ARS), New York / Photo courtesy of Thornton Tomasetti

Pages 190, 266 (top), 270—Courtesy of Thornton Tomasetti

Page 266 (bottom)—Photograph by Gary McKinnis © 1984 / Courtesy of the Association for Public Art

Page 268—© 2018 Artist Rights Society (ARS), New York / ADAGP, Paris

Page 272—© 2018 Artist Rights Society (ARS), New York / ADAGP, Paris / Photo by Arthur Lavine

INDEX

INDEX

ACKNOWLEDGMENTS

I am indebted to the many people, on three continents, whom I interviewed for the book and film. Others gave me good counsel and encouragement over the five years it took to bring *The Restless Hungarian* into the world.

I am thankful to the MacDowell Colony for awarding me an artist's residency, during which I wrote the first draft. Jane Brox, my editor, helped me to make the transition from "thinking like a filmmaker" to "thinking like an author." Agnes Miklos-Illes, my Hungarian and German translator, stuck by me for the long haul, going through the process of deciphering and translating my father and mother's handwriting.

In Hungary, my cousin Pál Valentiny introduced me to a world I had not been aware of. Learning the secret of my father's Jewish identity from Pál was a key impetus for this book. Photographs and documents pertaining to the history of our family that Pál carefully gathered and preserved were an invaluable resource. Both Pál and his sister, Anna Valentiny, told me stories of the terrible suffering of our family during the Holocaust. Pál's son, Andor Valentiny, did research for me in Hungarian archives.

Six people whose parents were my father's college classmates described the exile of their parents. Barred from Hungarian universities by an anti-Semitic law, they completed their studies abroad and later emigrated to Bolivia to escape the Holocaust. Thank you: Gabriella Bartos, Anna Erdős, Anna Perczel, Ágnes Sebestyén, András Szurdi, and Katalin Talyigás. Thanks also to Anna Erdős, for excerpts from the unpublished memoir *Our Life in Bolivia,* by her father, Imre.

The Hungarian historian Maria Kovács recounted how Hitler's "Final Solution" played out in her country. The journalist Kati Marton shared her insights with me into the diaspora of Hungarian intellectuals—artists, writers, and scientists—to which Paul Weidlinger belonged. Professor Gabor Somorjai explained what it was like to be a Jewish child during the terrible autumn of 1944.

Veronika Major-Kathi's consummate skill as a translator enabled me to conduct real-time bilingual interviews in Hungary.

In Bolivia, my researcher, Etelka Debreczeni, spent weeks in advance of my arrival following up leads on people who were Paul's friends and employers between 1939 and 1944. Mañuel Iturralde Jahnsen welcomed me warmly and made a gift to me of architectural drawings that my father had worked on in 1941. Alfonso Barrero Villanueva, grandson of Bolivia's most famous architect in the 1930s, spoke about his grandfather's relationship with Paul. Gastón Gallardo, Carlos Diego Mesa Gisbert, and Janet Barriga Arteaga, all historians of architecture, described the creative milieu in which Paul Weidlinger designed his first modernist urban buildings. Pedro Callisaya Hinojosa, senior archivist of the University of San Andrés in La Paz, where Paul Weidlinger taught, made it his business to track down every document containing the name of Pablo Weidlinger, including original drawings and blueprints for a university campus designed by Paul and Pista Haász.

Julia Vargas arranged for me to visit a dam that our fathers had built near Cochabamba. Verónica Bartos de Chamón introduced me to Márta Suchy, whose life was saved by my mother, after her own mother, Cini Szenes, died of typhoid fever when Márta was a newborn infant.

In the United States, Matthys Levy, one of the five original partners of Weidlinger Associates, described the nature of his collaboration with Paul and with architects including Gordon Bunshaft, Marcel Breuer, and Gyo Obata.

Nanci Buscemi, Eve Hinman, Todd Rittenhouse, and Alva Solomon, who had been young engineers hired by Paul, recounted their experiences working for him on the design of ICBM missile silos at the height of the Cold War, and Joan Wohlstetter recalled how her father wooed my father to work for the RAND Corporation.

Other colleagues at Weidlinger Associates, including Raymond Daddazio, Ronald Check, Helen Goddard, Robert Smilowitz, Lorraine Whitman, and Joseph Wright, helped me understand what it was like to have Paul Weidlinger as a boss—an experience they portrayed as both exhilarating and terrifying.

Two people helped me understand the Cold War culture of the 1950s and '60s: Daniel Ellsberg, a young defense analyst at the RAND Corporation during the period my father consulted there, and Sharon Ghamari-Tabrizi, a Cold War historian who wrote a biography of Herman Kahn, the man who came to be known as the real-life Dr. Strangelove.

I would like to thank Hattula Moholy-Nagy for generously allowing me to use images produced by her father. Dubuffet Foundation facilitated my visit to film the Villa Falbala. The Cape Cod Modern House Trust gave me a two-month writing residency in the house my father designed the year I was born.

My sister's life, which ended tragically in 1970, was beautifully recaptured by her friends Susanna Deiss, Paul Golightly, Juliet Kepes, and Joyce LeBaron.

My half-sister and half-brother, Pauline Panza and Jonathan Weidlinger, shared their impressions of our father in the last decades of his life.

Thank you to Beacon Reader crowd-funding platform and the eighty-six generous people who matched Beacon's $25,000 production grant to *The Restless Hungarian*.

Thank you to my meticulous copy editor, Victoria Elliott, and the folks at SparkPress, especially publisher Brooke Warner, editorial director Lauren Wise, and publicist Crystal Patriarche, for helping shepherd this book into the world.

Finally, my gratitude to good friends Frank Rubenfeld and Dick Stein, who encouraged me along the way, and to my wife, Sharon Armstrong, who holds me in her heart.

ABOUT THE AUTHOR

Tom Weidlinger is an independent filmmaker who has been writing, directing, and producing documentary films for thirty-five years. Many have won festival awards, and twenty-five have aired nationally on public television. His work is principally concerned with themes of social justice, and deals with a wide range of topics, from the dilemmas of humanitarian aid in the Congo to the struggles of high school students with learning differences. After a lifetime of city dwelling and global travel, Tom now lives in the rural foothills of the Sierra Mountains in California. He and his wife, Sharon, live in a straw-bale house on twenty acres of land covered with oak and manzanita forest. When Tom is not writing or working on a film in his editing room, he volunteers at a community center, helping teenagers find their voice through filmmaking. He loves to snowshoe and hike in the mountains with Sharon, and takes special pleasure in close observation of the natural world outside his front door.

SELECTED TITLES FROM SPARKPRESS

SparkPress is an independent boutique publisher delivering high-quality, entertaining, and engaging content that enhances readers' lives, with a special focus on female-driven work. Visit us at www.gosparkpress.com

Mission Afghanistan, Elie Cohen, translation by Jessica Levine, $16.95, 9781943006656. Decades after evading conscription as a young man, Franco-British doctor Elie Paul Cohen is offered a deal by the French Army: he can settle his accounts by becoming a military doctor and serving at Camp Bastion in Afghanistan.

Engineering a Life, Krishan Bedi, $16.95, 9781943006434. A memoir of Krishan Bedi's experiences as a young Indian man in the South in the 1960s, this is a story of one man's perseverance and determination to create the life he'd always dreamed for himself and his family, despite his options seeming anything but limitless.

The House that Made Me: Writers Reflect on the Places and People That Defined Them, edited by Grant Jarrett. $17, 978-1-940716-31-2. In this candid, evocative collection of essays, a diverse group of acclaimed authors reflect on the diverse homes, neighborhoods, and experiences that helped shape them—using Google Earth software to revisit the location in the process.

A Story That Matters: A Gratifying Approach to Writing About Your Life, Gina Carroll, $16.95, 9-781-943006-12-0. With each chapter focusing on stories from the seminal periods of a lifetime—motherhood, childhood, relationships, work, and spirit—*A Story That Matters* provides the tools and motivation to craft and complete the stories of your life.

ABOUT SPARKPRESS

SparkPress is an independent, hybrid imprint focused on merging the best of the traditional publishing model with new and innovative strategies. We deliver high-quality, entertaining, and engaging content that enhances readers' lives. We are proud to bring to market a list of *New York Times* best-selling, award-winning, and debut authors who represent a wide array of genres, as well as our established, industry-wide reputation for creative, results-driven success in working with authors. SparkPress, a BookSparks imprint, is a division of SparkPoint Studio LLC.

Learn more at GoSparkPress.com

CPSIA information can be obtained
at www.ICGtesting.com
Printed in the USA
BVHW07s0731171018
530365BV00002B/8/P

2 370000 61106